Racing for Innocence

Racing for Innocence

Whiteness, Gender, and the Backlash
Against Affirmative Action

Jennifer L. Pierce

STANFORD UNIVERSITY PRESS
Stanford, California

Stanford University Press
Stanford, California

Printed in the United States of America on acid-free, archival-quality paper

Library of Congress Cataloging-in-Publication Data

Pierce, Jennifer L., 1958- author.
    Racing for innocence : whiteness, gender, and the backlash against affirmative action / Jennifer L. Pierce.
        pages cm
    Includes bibliographical references and index.
    ISBN 978-0-8047-7878-7 (cloth : alk. paper)—ISBN 978-0-8047-7879-4 (pbk. : alk. paper)
    1. Affirmative action programs—United States—Public opinion. 2. Whites—United States—Attitudes. 3. Lawyers—United States—Attitudes. 4. Women lawyers—United States—Attitudes. 5. Racism—United States. 6. Mass media and public opinion—United States. 7. Whites—Race identity—United States. 8. Collective memory—United States. 9. Public opinion—United States. 10. United States—Race relations. I. Title.
    HF5549.5.A34P54 2012
    331.13'30973—dc23
                                                                            2012014467

Designed by Bruce Lundquist

Typeset by Newgen in 10.5/14 Bembo

For Gabriella

Contents

Acknowledgments   ix

Introduction: Telling Stories About Race in an Era of
Colorblindness   1

1 Innocence and Injury: The Politics of Cultural Memory
in Print News Media   19

2 Filming Racial Progress: The Transformation of
White Male Innocence   42

3 Racing for Innocence: Stories of Disavowal and Exclusion   64

4 Stand by Your Man: Women Lawyers and Affirmative Action   84

5 Small Talk: A Short Story   118
      Commentary: Ambivalent Racism   131

Conclusion: Still Racing for Innocence   137

Appendix A: Reflections on Methodology   153

Appendix B: Hollywood Films   167

Notes   169

Bibliography   205

Index   227

Acknowledgments

This book has been a long time in coming, and I am fortunate to have so many friends and colleagues who have encouraged me over the years to see it to fruition. At the University of Minnesota, I received institutional support for this project with two Graduate School Grant-in-Aid Awards, as well as a President's Multicultural Research Award. The first grant was designed for research assistant support to help me research ten years of newspaper coverage on the affirmative action debate. Nalo Johnson, then a graduate student and now a Ph.D. in American Studies, met with me weekly to report on her latest findings. I still have ten enormous accordion folders filled with these articles, letters to the editor, and editorials, as well as every new journal article and book chapter she could find on the topic. The other grant supported Wendy Leo Moore, then a graduate student and now a professor of sociology at Texas A&M, as my research assistant to review over sixty Hollywood films that dealt with racial topics. Working together, Wendy and I also wrote an article focusing on some of these films for *Qualitative Sociology Review* titled, "Still Killing Mockingbirds: Race and Innocence and the White Messiah Lawyer in Hollywood Films," that was published in 2007. Thanks to Nalo's and Wendy's assistance, I have far more material than I needed to write the first two chapters of this book.

I have many friends and colleagues at the University of Minnesota who have read and commented on draft chapters. In presenting my work-in-progress at a brown-bag lunch colloquium years ago in the Department of American Studies, my colleagues and graduate students over the years took my project seriously and encouraged me to improve it in many ways. In particular, I would like to acknowledge the contributions of Hokulani Aikau, Pamela Butler, Karla Erickson, Rod Ferguson, Ryan Murphy, Riv-Ellen Prell, and Dave Roediger to my thinking. Dave has not only been immensely supportive of my scholarship, but also a good friend. Ryan also deserves special thanks: As a research assistant, he not only helped me complete my bibliography, but also provided editorial comments and suggestions for every chapter. The SABLE seminar including Anne Carter, Anna Clark, Lisa Disch, Kirsten Fischer, Jeani O'Brien, and Gabriella Tsurutani provided important feedback on an early draft of Chapter 4. In addition, Lisa and Jeani, who have supported my scholarly writing since I first arrived at the University of Minnesota in 1993, took the time to read and comment on several other chapters in this book. The two of them have been my good friends for many years, as well as excellent critics of my work. I am also grateful to my more recent colleagues, Awa Abdi, Susan Craddock, Teresa Gowan, Lisa S. Park, and Rachel Schurman, for their insightful comments on the book's first two chapters.

Some of the ideas and ethnographic material from Chapter 3 come from an article I published in 2003 titled, "'Racing For Innocence': Whiteness, Corporate Culture, and the Backlash Against Affirmative Action," in *Qualitative Sociology*. Robert Zussman, who was the journal editor at the time, deserves special thanks for his encouragement and advice, as do the external reviewers for the article. I have also benefited from presenting this chapter at national conferences and other venues. Very early in my research, I was invited to participate in a panel on affirmative action at the American Studies Association in Detroit, where I first presented my ethnographic research on "racing for innocence." I would also like to thank Woody Doane and Eduardo Bonilla-Silva, who chose to include my research in a session presented at the American Sociology Association meetings in Washington, D.C., as well as Christine Williams who, on very short notice, generously agreed to read and write detailed comments for the introduction to this book. In addition, I have benefited from presenting my research from different chapters in the Sociology Department at University of California at Berkeley. Michael Burawoy, then department chair, invited me to give a presentation in the Department's 2002–2003 colloquia series; and Raka Ray asked me to participate in the Frontiers of Qualitative Research Conference in the fall of 2006.

I also received a Rockefeller Bellagio Center Residential Writing Fellowship in April and May of 2006. Having the luxury of writing each day in my study in the chateau at Bellagio looking out over Lake Como in northern Italy was an enormous privilege. I am grateful to the Rockefeller Foundation for giving me the time and space to write, and especially to Pilar Palacio, the director, who is not only incredibly smart, but also gracious and kind. I benefited, too, from exchanges at the Center with Sandra Aamodt, Thomas Bisson, Jane

Burbank, Fred Cooper, Cyrus Casells, Toi Dericotte, Dedra Gentner, Russell Gordon, Helen Roberts, and David and Kathryn Ringrose.

Writing fiction is a new endeavor for me. The University of Minnesota granted me a semester leave in the fall of 2010 to write the short story for this book. The many teachers I have taken classes from for the past several years at the Loft Literary Center in Minneapolis were generous with their comments and, at times, inspirational. As teachers, Eric Vrooman, Amanda Coplin, and Robert Voedisch were especially helpful in teaching me how to think and write about complex characters. I would also like to thank Lisa Disch, Karla Erickson, Teresa Gowan, Colleen Hennen, Peter Hennen, Jeani O'Brien, Ryan Murphy, Lisa S. Park, Eli Sagan, Rachel Schurman, Gabriella Tsurutani, and Carol Wichers for their readings and encouragement along the way.

I was also fortunate to be invited to participate in a workshop organized by Donna Gabaccia and Mary Jo Maynes on Gender History Across Epistemologies, at the University of Minnesota in April 2010, where I presented my short story and an early draft of the conclusion to this book. I am especially grateful for the thoughtful questions and encouragement provided by workshop participants, including Anna Clark, Christine Benninghaus, Nancy Green, Helena Pohlandt-McCormick, Lorelle Semley, Liz Stanley, Dominique Tobel, Barbara Welke, and Elizabeth Williams. In addition, I would like to thank the History Department's Workshop on Comparative History on Women, Gender, and Sexuality. In this workshop, participants read and commented on "Small Talk," as well as my notes on methodology that now form one of the appendices to this volume. Carol Chomsky, Mary Jo Maynes, Helena Pohlandt-McCormick, Kevin Murphy, and Elizabeth Williams asked smart questions that encouraged me to think through the differences between writing ethnography and fiction.

Working with Kate Wahl at Stanford University Press has been a dream. She pursued this project via e-mail long before the first time we actually met in person to talk about the book, and she has enthusiastically supported me throughout the process in my attempts to pursue experimental forms along with ethnographic research. The external reviewers for this manuscript were immensely constructive and thoughtful in their comments. I am grateful to all of them, but want to highlight two in particular: sociologists Susan Chase and Patricia Yancey-Martin. Susan, who chose to be named in her review, provided detailed, line-by-line comments for every chapter in the book as well as general comments for the entire manuscript. Pat, who later "came out" to me as one of the anonymous reviewers for the manuscript, has long been an advocate of my scholarship. She always asks hard questions, but also reminds me that if I look closely enough at my ethnographic work, I will find the answers. In addition, I would like to thank Carolyn Haley for copyediting, Jay Harward for shepherding the book through the copyediting process, and Alex Urquhart for completing the index.

I would also like to thank the many lawyers who took time away from their hectic work lives to talk with me about their profession. Trial attorneys are alternately celebrated or vilified in American popular culture. What outsiders to the field often don't understand are the constraints of this profession. The unpredictability of litigators' schedules lends an element of craziness to their professional and personal lives that seems inhumane, especially for those who have other life or family commitments. Although that aspect of work is not the central focus of this book, please know how much I appreciated your gift of time.

Finally, this book would not have been written without my partner of over ten years, Gabriella Tsurutani. She always believed this book would happen. Of course, this is also a woman who thinks riding her bike 100 miles *on gravel* is fun! Walking along the Mississippi River, with our corgi Anna, Gabriella has often reminded me of the importance of having time to play to complement work. With love, this book is for you.

Racing for Innocence

Introduction

Telling Stories About Race in an Era of Colorblindness

In 1989 on my first day as an ethnographer and a paralegal in BC's Legal Department, I spent two-and-a-half hours in Human Resources filling out the required paperwork, getting my picture taken for my photo identification badge, and reading the company's literature on affirmative action.[1] As part of my induction, the personnel director ushered me into an empty office and turned on a VCR for my "required" viewing of a twenty-minute video on the company's affirmative action program.[2] After she left the room, I sat in the semidarkened room watching the opening scene: a factory floor filled with the smiling faces of African American men and women operating heavy machinery as a white man in a wheelchair answered phones. In the background, a soft, cheerful female voice said, "At BC, we value diversity *and* excellence." The up-beat video continued by promoting the "great success" of the company's affirmative action program, showing more footage of more smiling faces of white women, Latinos, Asian Americans, and African Americans in what looked to be a variety of clerical and factory jobs.

The narrator proceeded to describe the beginning of the company's affirmative action program fifteen years earlier. In her description of BC's program, she failed to mention what I would soon learn from others—a federal court had ordered the corporation to create an affirmative action program in response to a lawsuit filed against the company in the early 1970s for race and sex discrimination. The court's ruling was based on a finding of a documented pattern of differential treatment in the workplace. Both the video I watched and the affirmative action program were part of the corporation's effort to re-dress the very inequities their practices had created. When the video concluded, I went back to the personnel director's office to fill out more paperwork. I asked one of her assistants, "Isn't it true that courts don't mandate programs unless there's been a finding of 'egregious discrimination'?" I was taken aback when the white woman, who had been quite pleasant, began a verbal tirade against the company's affirmative action program and blamed it for the com-pany's efforts, in her words, to "hire lots of unqualified minorities."[3]

Over the following nine months, I discovered that this white woman's com-ments were only one element of a broader undercurrent of hostility directed against affirmative action in this workplace. My field notes from that time are filled with negative comments about the alleged effects of the program. In the Legal Department, some of the white lawyers complained about "those un-qualified clerks in the file room" who, as I observed, "just happened to be black or Latino." In fact, the adjective "unqualified" popped up time and time again in casual conversations as a code word for racial or ethnic minority identities. Job candidates with unremarkable previous job histories were "unqualified" when they were African American, but could use a "boost up" when they were white men. Jokes about affirmative action abounded. "It's our quota system for lazy people," quipped one attorney. For the most part, these kinds of jokes were told by one white professional to another in less public settings, like someone's office.

By the late 1980s, BC had improved the representation of racial and eth-nic minorities as well as white women in the lower echelons of the corporate hierarchy in sales, clerical, and factory work. However, the corporation had been less successful in meeting goals and timetables for managerial positions at higher levels. In the litigation section of the Legal Department where I con-ducted my fieldwork, three attorneys were African American and forty were white or of European American ancestry. Of these forty-three, nine attorneys were women: eight white and one African American. None of the lawyers were Latino, Asian American, or Native American. These small numbers did not suggest a rapid demographic transformation of the department. Why such strong feelings against affirmative action? Most puzzling of all, the lawyers and supervisors who were most critical of the program were *not* the working-class white male victims depicted by media of the 1980s and 1990s who claimed to have lost jobs, educational opportunities, or promotions to "unqualified mi-norities."[4] The employees who complained to me were highly educated, white professionals, mostly men and sometimes women, who had job tenure, good salaries, and who reported *no* lost opportunities because of affirmative action. Why was this remedial social policy such a threat to them?

When I initially began this study in 1989, a backlash against affirmative action was already under way across the United States. The backlash took place in an economic context dominated by neoliberal reforms: Federal assistance programs in welfare and education were dismantled under Presidents Reagan and Bush, while tax cuts for corporations and predatory lending deepened the divide between rich and poor. The backlash reached its zenith in the mid-1990s when the majority of California voters endorsed Proposition 209, an initiative designed to eliminate consideration of race and gender in public education and employment. These political and economic shifts, as well as my discovery that little empirical research had been conducted on people who work in organizations with affirmative action programs, compelled me to reenter the field in 1999. In light of the political and economic changes, a California corporation seemed to provide a timely window into American understandings of race and gender inequality in our post-civil-rights era.

While this book focuses on how professionals in one particular workplace understood affirmative action, it also makes broader claims about how cultural memory about work, family, race, gender, and power operated in the United States in the late 1980s and the 1990s. In doing so, it makes important connections between personal forms of remembering and dominant cultural narratives surrounding the debate about affirmative action. More specifically, it tells a story about what elite white men who work as attorneys "remember" about race and gender at work. As I found in my research, though most of these men refrained from making overtly racist remarks and deny accountability for racism, many recalled a time when they could work in predominantly white and male segregated spaces, earn robust salaries, and have a little fun at work by telling off-color jokes. Their stories of benevolence are bolstered by a Hollywood film genre that I call "white racial progress." These movies tell stories about virtuous, elite white men who ultimately become saviors of people of color, while white working-class men are cast as villainous racists. At the same time, these elite white men also draw from accounts in the print news media that emphasize the victimization of white men under affirmative action. These media accounts not only highlight white men's "innocence" of racism and the "injuries" inflicted on them by affirmative action, but also tell stories about people of color as "unqualified" and, hence, "undeserving." As *Racing for Innocence* shows, this broader cultural memory becomes the means through which these elite white men practice modern racism. At the same time that these men claimed to be innocent of racism, they resisted fully incorporating people of color and white women into their daily workplace lives. In doing so, they participated—wittingly or not—in the backlash against affirmative action.

What Is Affirmative Action?

As a number of scholars have argued, there is a lot of confusion about precisely what constitutes affirmative action policy.[5] In part, this is because there are many different kinds of affirmative action, and in part because the news media has not attended carefully to these distinctions. To avoid confusion, below I define three different kinds of affirmative action in employment as a means of clarifying these differences, as well as the kind of program that existed in the workplace I studied.

As sociologist Barbara Reskin reports in her study, *The Realities of Affirmative Action*, the vast majority of affirmative action programs in the United States are either voluntary or the result of federal contract compliance. In the first case, employers choose to use affirmative action guidelines in the recruitment, retention, and promotion of white women, people of color, and the disabled.[6] For example, in efforts to diversify their labor force, many large corporations have adopted affirmative action guidelines to help them broaden their pool of potential job applicants as well as their considerations in retention and promotion; they are *not compelled* by the federal government to do so. In the case of federal contract compliance, where the employer is either a federal governmental agency or is under a federal contract in excess of $50,000, organizations are required to practice what Faye Crosby and Diana Crosby term the "classical definition of affirmative action." This definition, which was created as part of President Lyndon Johnson's Great Society programs, and more specifically through his 1965 Executive Order 11246, maintains that

> [A]ffirmative action occurs whenever people go out of their way (take positive action) to increase the likelihood of true equality for individuals of differing categories. Whenever an organization expends energy to make sure that women and men, people of color and White people, or disabled and fully abled people have the same chances as each other to be hired, retained, or promoted, then the organization has a policy of affirmative in employment.[7]

In the case of federal contract compliance, organizations with more than fifty employees must also have a written plan that documents how closely the utilization of certain categories of people (e.g., disabled people) matches the availability of qualified people in that category. When utilization falls short of availability (i.e., a corporation employs few disabled people in clerical positions when in fact there is a large pool of disabled people who are qualified for such jobs in the region), the organization must articulate its plan for improved performance. The Office of Federal Contract Compliance is the federal agency that enforces this policy. In such cases, it requires that contractors make a "good faith effort" in meeting goals for improved utilization. Significantly, failure to meet goals is *not* in itself punishable. For instance, if contractors can demonstrate that they made a good-faith effort to recruit disabled individuals, but were still unable increase their numbers in hiring, they will not be penalized. In other words, simply making a good-faith effort to increase the likelihood of equal opportunity for people of all categories is central to the practice of affirmative action.

In contrast to the popular perception that equates affirmative action with quotas, quotas are, in fact, *not* permissible under the law. This ruling was first made in 1978 in the United States Supreme Court *The Regents of the University of California vs. Bakke* decision, which found quotas unconstitutional both federally and in the state of California.[8] The only time that the Supreme Court has ruled that courts can order hiring and promotion quotas is as a remedy for "egregious discrimination." In other words, in lawsuits where the court makes a finding of egregious discrimination for race, gender, and/or disability, the court can order the employer to create an affirmative action plan with specific goals, timetables, and quotas. The actual number of workplaces with court-ordered affirmative action program in the United States is very small. The workplace organization I studied was subject to one of those unusual federally mandated programs. The opportunity to study an anomalous case is part of what inspired this book.

Cultural Memory and Personal Memory

Amid widespread student and faculty protest, the Regents of the University of California voted fourteen to ten to strike down affirmative action in university admissions in July 1995. In doing so, they adopted a policy "ensuring equal treatment of admissions" that barred the consideration of race, sex, religion, or national origin as criterion for entrance to the university.[9] The following year, 55 percent of California voters endorsed Proposition 209, the California Civil Rights Initiative, the first initiative of its kind in the United States to ban race and gender preferences in public education, employment, and contracting.[10] Emboldened by California's success, critics of affirmative action programs organized across the nation to create ballot initiatives, legislative proposals, and legal challenges in states such as Texas, Washington, Florida, Nebraska, and Michigan.[11]

Editorials and newspaper articles attended to this issue with dramatic flair: "Let Affirmative Action Die" declared the headline of an editorial in *The New York Times;* "Affirmative Action Showdown" another headline proclaimed.[12] In news stories in the *San Francisco Chronicle,* affirmative action opponents celebrated these events as the end of unfair "race-based preferences." At the same time, national surveys and opinion polls reported that the majority of white middle-class Americans considered affirmative action to be unfair because it relied on "racial preferences."[13] Drawing on meritocratic understandings of success, these Americans argued that individuals should be judged by their talents and accomplishments and not by the color of their skin. In doing so, they endorsed an ideal of colorblindness and told a story about living in a post-civil-rights era in which that ideal has largely been achieved.

Yet, in these white Americans' daily practices, it is clear that race did matter, and that it mattered to them. Studies demonstrate that the same Americans pressing for "colorblindness" chose to live in predominantly white neighborhoods, married spouses of their own racial and ethnic background, worked in racially segregated occupations, and, if given the opportunity, hired white employees rather than African Americans or Latinos.[14] The gap between their ideal of a race-neutral world and their day-to-day practices uncovers a fault line in American culture when it came to matters of race. Most middle-class Americans proclaim the virtues of a colorblind society at the same time that they do many things demonstrating a high degree of self-consciousness about race in their daily lives. How is it that recipients of white privilege come to deny the role they play in reproducing racial inequality?

Racing for Innocence addresses this question by focusing on cultural forms of memory in the late 1980s and throughout the 1990s in the United States. What does it mean for a culture to remember? In response to this question, communications scholar Marita Sturken argues that "collective remembering of a specific culture can often appear similar to the memory of an individual—it provides cultural identity and gives a sense of the importance of the past."[15] Moreover, cultural memory, like personal memory, is not always accurate. Just as individuals may forget or misremember details and events, groups' collective remembering does not always correspond to actual historical events. For example, as Chapter 1 shows in highlighting the injuries that affirmative action inflicts on white men, the print news media does not mention the fact that only a very small number of claims about "reverse discrimination" could actually be documented. Part of this is because the process of cultural memory is bound up in political struggles about meaning; some groups may have more power than others to disseminate their version of events. As I show, despite the conventions of "fair and balanced reporting," most news stories about affirmative action tended to ignore the reality of racial and gendered forms of discrimination and to reproduce accounts of "angry white men" who had been "harmed" by affirmative action.

While memory helps to define a culture, it is also the means through which its divisions and conflicts become apparent. For instance, affirmative action may be understood by some as unfair because it relies on race-based preferences, while others see it as a remedy for contemporary and past forms of discrimination. As this example suggests, the process of cultural memory always involves interaction among individuals in the creation of meaning. But, as I show, some stories gain prominence, others are muffled, and still others are silenced altogether. Hence, memory is "a field of cultural negotiation through which different stories vie for a place in history."[16]

Racing for Innocence examines how both cultural memory *and* personal memory operated in the United States during the backlash against affirmative action. Cultural memory is produced through various means, including the news media, Hollywood films, fiction, political discourse, and activism. *Racing for Innocence* begins by looking at how cultural memories were produced by the news media in local and national newspapers through a trope I term "white male innocence and injury" and through Hollywood films in the genre of "white racial progress." While the media trope emphasizes white men's innocence of racism and the injuries that affirmative action inflicts upon them, cinematic narratives highlight the transformation of elite white men from racial innocents who through struggle and hardship ultimately become anti-racist advocates for people of color. After focusing on these dominant cultural themes in the first two chapters, I turn to personal narratives from upper-middle-class professionals who work in BC's Legal Department.[17] I first interviewed these attorneys in 1989 and then again ten years later in 1998 and 1999. Chapter 3 focuses on men and Chapter 4 on women. In these chapters, my intent is to understand how cultural memories about the affirmative action debate informed personal understandings and perceptions about race and gender inequality. Finally, Chapter 5 provides a fictional account—a short story—as a means of apprehending the complexity of personhood that lies behind conflicts about racism in an era when many Americans profess "colorblindness."

Colorblindness, Whiteness, and White Racism

A number of sociologists, historians, and communication studies scholars have described our post-civil-rights era as one in which visible forms of racism, such as jobs or neighborhoods advertised for "whites only," have disappeared, while stealth practices, such as predatory lending in the housing, education, and consumer credit markets, real estate steering, and more subtle forms of discrimination in employment, have taken their place. At the same time, a "new racial politics" has emerged that has incorporated the language of the civil rights movement and "repackaged itself as 'colorblind.'"[18] Sociologist Howard Winant, for example, describes these new politics as a "neoconservative white racial project." In his view, such a project, "seeks to preserve white advantage through the denial of racial difference."[19]

Other scholars, such as Roopali Mukherjee, locate these racial politics within the economic discourse of neoliberalism, one that celebrates the free market and individuals who are personally responsible for their choices. Neoliberalism is a set of dominant economic practices that emerged in the 1970s that include the dismantling of social welfare programs, deregulation, and the privatization of public services.[20] The underlying assumption of these practices is that a market unfettered by state intervention—Adam Smith's "free market"—will produce the greatest social good. As an ideology, neoliberalism reasserts a liberal individualism that is understood through the language of choice or, more specifically, consumer choice. Though neoliberalism and neoconservatism share many elements, especially in their emphasis on individualism and unconstrained choice, neoconservatives underscore the morality of social roles, such as women's traditional role as helpmates to their husbands and in assumptions about who is truly deserving of charity. Despite these differences, as I argue in the book, both neoliberalism and neoconservatism play important roles in supplying language and rhetoric in the debate about affirmative action in the time period addressed. More specifically, they provide the language of "choice" and "personal responsibility" as well as moral assessments of people of color as "undeserving" that all become central to anti-affirmative action rhetoric. While scholars of colorblindness have done important research in documenting and mapping the contours of this discourse in our post-civil-rights era, there has been less attention paid to how white Americans, particularly professional elites, come to deny the role they play in reproducing racial inequality.[21] How is whiteness, as a structural privilege and a systematic blind spot to the fact of privilege, constituted and reconstituted in daily life?[22] As historian George Lipsitz eloquently reminds us in answering such questions, "The problem with white people is not our whiteness, but our possessive investment in it. Created by politics, culture, and consciousness, our possessiveness in whiteness can be altered by those same processes, but only if we face the hard facts open and honestly and admit that whiteness is a matter of interests as well as attitudes, that it has more to do with property than with pigment."[23] This book contributes to an understanding of our possessive investment in whiteness by looking at everyday practices through which it is created, sustained, and reproduced among legal professionals. Borrowing a phrase from Randall Kingsley, an African American attorney whom I interviewed, I term such practices "racing for innocence." More specifically, this term describes the white men I interviewed who disavow accountability for racist practices and, at the same, practice racially exclusionary behavior.

As I argue, racing for innocence is a historically specific discursive practice that draws from a broader American discourse: that of liberal individualism. In the United States, the language of liberal individualism enshrines the rights and efforts of individuals and defines social life as the sum total of conscious and deliberate individual activities. This language serves to recast long-standing, systematic racist practices, such as discrimination against African Americans and other people of color in employment and housing, into seemingly individual, isolated incidents of personal prejudice. "Collective exercise of power that relentlessly channels rewards, resources, and opportunities from one group to another will not appear 'racist' from this perspective because they rarely announce their intention to discriminate against others."[24] As my ethnographic research demonstrates, liberal individualism not only contributes to white lawyers' understanding of success and failure in their professional world, but also enables them to overlook how their practices maintain and reproduce whiteness as a structure of inequality.

While there have been excellent historical studies on whiteness as well as ethnographic studies that focus on the development of white supremacist discourses and white racial identities, little attention has been paid to how whiteness operates among elites. In fact, working-class whites are overrepresented in sociological studies of racial prejudice.[25] Among historians who study the 1970s and 1980s, working-class whites are often blamed for the resurgence of the New Right and backlash politics. Thomas Sugrue's *The Origins of the Urban*

Crisis, Lisa McGirr's *Suburban Warriors*, and Thomas Frank's *What's the Matter with Kansas?* all contend that the Republican Party wooed these formerly Democratic voters through appeals to racially divisive issues, such as housing, crime, and school desegregation.[26] By contrast, *Racing for Innocence* shows how whiteness takes on new meaning in this time period, through neoliberal forms of economic redistribution and dispossession, by focusing on elites who benefit most from that very dispossession.[27] Thus, elite professionals, and specifically lawyers, are the ethnographic focus of this study.

As a profession, attorneys have considerable power and influence in the United States. Lawyers predominate in Congress and in state legislatures, and lawyers in large corporate firms and lawyers who work as lobbyists represent "the interests of big business before Congress, federal courts and regulatory agencies."[28] Historically, lawyers have also played a central role in constructing laws and social policy aimed at maintaining white supremacy: the Jim Crow laws in the South, anti-miscegenation legislation in the nineteenth and twentieth centuries, and the legal and de facto segregation of housing, education, and employment before the Civil Rights Act of 1964.[29] This is not to say that attorneys as a group have accepted these laws; indeed, many civil rights lawyers have fought against them. Rather, my point is that lawyers are elites with enormous political clout in this country. Collectively, their perceptions and actions have far greater consequences than do those of workers in other occupations; thus, they are worthy of sustained critical attention.

The Intersection of Race and Gender

As it elucidates race, this book also necessarily attends to the varied understandings of gender in the affirmative action debate. For example, gender not only infuses news media tropes such as "white male innocence and injury," but also appears in the small number of newspaper articles attending to women and this policy. In fact, as I show, the news media typically discussed affirmative action as if it were solely concerned with race, despite the fact that this policy was also designed to protect white women from discrimination (see Chapter 1). Of course, this doesn't mean that white women were not engaged with or unaffected by these debates. One of my central arguments is that assumptions about gender are always implicated within seemingly racial debates about affirmative action. As I show in Chapter 4, neoconservative groups such as the Independent Women's Forum (IWF) joined forces with affirmative action opponents, arguing that the policy was "injurious" to their husbands and sons. In their view, the doors of economic opportunity were wide open to women and the "glass ceiling" was a myth. Women who didn't work hard enough or long enough had only themselves to blame if they weren't successful. The IWF called for women to stand by their men and oppose affirmative action. At the same time, feminist groups such as the National Organization for Women also worked to support affirmative action policy.

While these debates and their rhetoric informed the personal narratives of the white women attorneys interviewed, the women also told, for the most part, a very different story about their workplace lives than did their male counterparts—one that highlighted opportunities but also pointed to the exclusionary practices of the "good-old-boy" network. The women's most common complaint lay in their difficulty in getting additional family leaves from work and their mostly male colleagues' perception that women were less committed to professional obligations than men were. The one black woman professional in this workplace told yet another story, providing insight into how racism and sexism operated together to the disadvantage of women of color. As Chapter 4 shows, the exclusionary and derisive practices women attorneys faced (many of whom eventually left the Legal Department) reproduced whiteness as well as masculinity as structures of inequality in this workplace.[30] In other words, those practices sustained a professional workplace that was predominantly white and male.

Chapter 5, my short story "Small Talk," continues to examine the intersections of race and gender by focusing on Robin Healy, an African American trial attorney, who is having dinner with two white men following an interview at their law firm. While this fictional account explores interracial and cross-gender dynamics, it also illuminates the thoughts and feelings behind the discomfort provoked by such interactions. In my commentary following the story, I develop the concept of "ambivalent racism" to make sense of what *might* lie behind the silence and discomfort that I found in the white male attorneys' personal narratives in Chapter 3. As I argue, this ambivalent racism is intended to conceptualize the feelings, thoughts, and practices of an individual who is simultaneously racist and not racist. Put another way, an individual's racist talk, feelings, and actions may exist simultaneously with other talk, thoughts, and behavior that may be construed as not racist. This not only provides some insight into why many of the white male lawyers I interviewed might deny racism as they practiced exclusionary behavior—their ambivalent racism makes it

difficult for them to fully elaborate their position—but also points to problems
with sociological theories that do not fully embrace contradiction and ambivalence within their theoretical frameworks.

Methods

In researching this book, I drew upon three different methods—participant
observation and interviews, discourse analysis of print news media and Hollywood films, and short fiction—as a means of apprehending different epistemological perspectives on the affirmative action debate in the 1980s and 1990s.
Each method yields distinct perspectives on affirmative action, white male innocence, and racial and gendered forms of inequality in the United States.
Together they provide a multi-layered historical account of the backlash against
affirmative action.

The methodological strategies I used in conducting my research acquired
their roots over twenty years ago, when I worked as a litigation paralegal and
covert ethnographer in the in-house legal department of a large corporation in
the San Francisco Bay Area that I have given the pseudonym "BC."[31] Evidence
for my research was collected through three means: nine months of fieldwork
as a participant observer in the corporation's Legal Department; informal interviews and formal in-depth interviews with lawyers; and an analysis of corporate documents, such as records about the affirmative action program and
attorney résumés. Over the past forty years, BC has been and continues to be
one of the largest and most successful businesses in northern California. Positions within its corporate hierarchy range from entry-level factory, sales, and
clerical work to jobs at higher levels requiring college and professional degrees,
such as an MBA or a law degree. BC's Legal Department housed over 150
lawyers, and in this regard its size was comparable to many of the Bay Area's
large law firms. What made this workplace unique was its federally mandated
affirmative action program, which was created in the early 1970s in response to
a discrimination lawsuit.

In the next phase of my ethnographic work in the late 1990s, I attempted
to contact the forty-three lawyers who had worked in the litigation section of
BC's Legal Department in 1989. I conducted work-history interviews with
thirty-three of the original forty-three. The turnover rates for both African
Americans and white women were higher compared to those of white men:
100 percent, 75 percent, and 60 percent, respectively. Of the three African
American lawyers who had worked there in 1989, all three had left the firm.

Table I.1   Interviews with lawyers who stayed or left (N = 43)

	White women	White men	Black women	Black men
Original number	8	32	1	2
Stayed	2	13	0	0
Left	6	19	1	2
Interviewed	7	23	1	2
Unable to interview	1	9	0	0

I eventually located these individuals and interviewed them (see Table I.1.). Of the eight white women who had been there, six had left. I interviewed the two who remained in the Legal Department as well as five of the six who had resigned. Of the thirty-two white men, thirteen were still employed there. Nine of the thirteen agreed to be interviewed, and I located and interviewed fourteen of the nineteen who had departed for other positions. Among the ten people I was unable to interview, one had retired and moved away from the area, several others claimed to be too busy, and another canceled interview after interview. I was unable to locate six individuals who had moved on to other jobs.

Interviews drew from a general guideline and followed the same format, but were open-ended enough to allow flexibility. Some of the questions I included were: What has your professional trajectory been since I last interviewed you in 1989? How would you characterize your current practice? Why did you stay in (or leave) BC's Legal Department? How would you characterize BC's policies for women and minorities? Throughout, I changed names of individuals and the workplace organization to protect confidentiality.

Typically, I transcribed the interviews immediately afterward. In editing the stories to make them fit into the book, I often worried about how much would be cut out, because I wanted to tell the story as fully as it had been told to me. However, it was simply not possible to include everyone's full personal narrative in one book. Consequently, in some chapters, I use lengthy quotes from one work history, particularly when I am writing about attorneys outside the dominant groups, and in others, I do not. I also present quoted material with my prompts or queries so that readers can understand specifically what the speaker was responding to in their narrative. In addition, when editing interviews, I tried to be faithful to language, but I also found some of my narrators repeated phrases such as "you know" or utterances such as "um" in every other sentence. When this seemed to distract from content, I deleted the excessive use of qualifiers. In this respect, the work life histories that appear in

these pages are not transparent, unmediated accounts, but translations. In reading and editing these personal narratives, much like Ruth Behar who wrote in
Translated Women, "I have tried to make clear that what I am reading is a story,
or set of stories, that have been told to me, so that I, in turn, can tell them again,
transforming myself from a listener to a storyteller."[32]

Editing aside, I consider my interviews to be joint productions between
the analyst (the researcher) and the narrator (the person who tells their work
history). The knowledge produced through such an encounter is always influenced by the relationship between analyst and narrator.[33] As I discussed in my
first book, *Gender Trials: Emotional Lives in Contemporary Law Firms*, my position
as a white woman, a UC Berkeley graduate student, and a former paralegal
not only influenced my relationships with paralegals and attorneys, but also
evoked particular kinds of stories about their workplace lives.[34] For instance,
paralegals were often much more forthcoming in my first set of interviews than
male attorneys were. This may have reflected our shared occupational status,
since I had worked as a paralegal for many years. In Appendix A: Reflections
on Methodology, I revisit this issue, focusing on my second set of interviews.
Significantly, I not only conducted these interviews at a different historical moment than my first interviews, but also my own professional status had changed.
Instead of being a graduate student, I was a tenured professor. As I discuss in
more detail in Appendix A, I often found that white women and people of
color were more forthcoming in their interviews than white men were.

As in most professional legal settings, the numbers of African Americans and
white women in the BC's Legal Department were quite small. In 1989, racial/
ethnic minorities represented 5 percent of attorneys, and women represented
18 percent. Given the considerable racial and ethnic diversity of the San Francisco Bay Area, these numbers are surprising. They are nonetheless similar to
those found in national studies of the legal profession. According to an American Bar Association Study published in 2004, "African Americans are the best
represented minority group among lawyers (3.9 percent), followed by Hispanics (3.3 percent)." Moreover, in large corporate law firms nationally, racial/
ethnic minority representation among partners remains less than 4.0 percent
in all but the very largest law firms.[35] By contrast, women began to enter the
legal profession in increasing numbers after 1975. Barriers to law school admissions declined after the enactment of Title IX of the Education Amendments
of 1972, which prohibited discrimination in graduate programs receiving federal funds. In 1972, women comprised only 2.2 percent of the legal profession, and by 1991 they constituted 20.0 percent.[36] Of course, this percentage is

still far below women's numbers in law schools across the nation at that time (40.0 percent).[37]

With such small numbers, I cannot generalize about the experiences of all white women or people of color who work as litigators. Rather, my intent is to critically analyze the evidence relative to my questions about how cultural memory about racial and gender inequality helps provide meaning to the stories these litigators told about their professional lives and about affirmative action. Moreover, in relying upon what Michael Burawoy calls "the extended case method," my objective is to extend and reconstruct existing theory about how whiteness as a discursive practice operates in this particular organizational context as well as in broader cultural narratives in print news media and Hollywood films.[38] In Burawoy's view, "anomalous cases" such as BC's Legal Department, are excellent sites for reconstructing social theory; they are more likely than representative cases to challenge or contradict existing theoretical frameworks. Consequently, my purpose throughout is at once interpretive and theoretical.

Because this project focuses on cultural memory in addition to fieldwork and interviews, I also conducted a discourse analysis of print news media and Hollywood films during the backlash against affirmative action. These forms of collective remembering are particularly relevant to my study for a number of reasons. As scholars have long recognized, the media is a powerful institution that influences how debates about social policy are likely to be understood by the general public.[39] Thus, in bringing the issue to national attention, the press played an important role in shaping the *meaning* of affirmative action. For the media portion of my research, I reviewed and analyzed newspaper articles, editorials, and letters to the editor about affirmative action in *The New York Times* and the *San Francisco Chronicle* between 1990 and 2000. I focused on these two papers not only because they were readily available to the lawyers in their law library, but they also provide a local and national snapshot of the period.

At the same time, movies are particularly important as forms of collective remembering, because they offer stories and points of view Americans might not otherwise get in their daily lives. Further, cinematic codes of realism provide viewers with the sense that they actually experience what they see in the movies, thereby contributing to a sense of an "authentic" personal memory.[40] In developing a sample of Hollywood films used for this study, Wendy Leo Moore and I began by searching for all movies made between 1987 and 1999 that explored issues of race and racism. (We chose these dates because they corresponded with the time between my first and second interviews with lawyers.) We searched and analyzed plot summaries of movies and selected those in which the central storyline engaged issues of race, racism, or racial reconciliation. This search located 174 movies. Next we examined the earnings of these movies, and retained for study only those that made at least $3 million, thereby ensuring a substantial viewing audience. Sixty movies remained on our list (Appendix B).

After dividing films into different categories, such as historical drama, comedy, or romance, and determining whose perspective the story was told from (e.g., white male or black female), we conducted a discourse analysis of each one. At the outset, coding categories were generated from our theoretical questions about popular film representations of race and racism. As the research progressed, we noted important patterns that emerged, such as white male protagonists and innocence of racism as well as gendered and classed constructions of race. For each movie we produced a detailed plot summary with relevant quotes from dialogue and an analysis of six the discursive frames we found, including constructions of innocence; race in character development; gender in character development; conversion narratives by characters; whiteness; and the intersections of race, class, and gender. Of these sixty films, we identified 25 percent as falling into the category white racial progress.

In the final phase of my research, I took a number of fiction-writing classes and began work on my short story, "Small Talk." After years of academic writing, learning to write fiction was not easy. Appendix A: Reflections on Methodology describes my process in writing and revising the short story through a series of fiction workshops. Here, I discuss fiction as a method for apprehending subjectivity, feelings, longings, and innermost desires. While ethnography and fiction are often regarded as contrasting forms—realistic and imaginary—my book aims to bring them together by showing how each form complements the other and deepens our understanding of racism and sexism. As I argue, ethnography and fiction each provides unique epistemological insights. What might ethnography teach us that fiction does not? Conversely, what can fiction teach us that ethnographies cannot?

The limits of ethnographic methods became clear in my interviews with white male lawyers. As Chapter 3 shows, their upbeat narratives of determination, hard work, and success often stopped short with long uncomfortable silences when I posed questions about racial dynamics at work. In probing for details, I often came up against a reluctance to provide specific examples. What is striking in these interviews is how these otherwise articulate and highly educated middle-class men, whose very profession as trial attorneys requires that they make forceful arguments, suddenly become hesitant and inarticulate. In fact, I often had the sense that the lawyers wanted to say much more but were afraid of saying the wrong thing, of saying something that might be construed as racist. Because ethnographers rely on what people tell them as well as what they are able to observe in the field, they often do not have access to inner feelings and thoughts that may lie behind these silences.[41]

To address this gap in knowledge, I used fiction as a method for apprehending the meaning of these silences and hesitations. While a number of ethnographers have also written fiction, the general tendency is to write academic monographs and fictional works as separate books.[42] One important exception is the anthropologist Marjorie Wolf whose 1992 volume, *A Thrice Told Tale*, presents the same set of facts from her fieldwork in Taiwan in three different forms: a short story, a set of field notes, and an academic article. Writing twenty years ago in response to the "crisis of representation" in anthropology, Wolf argued against blurring the line between ethnography and fiction. In her view, experimenting with form undermined the value and legitimacy of carefully conducted research and analysis.[43]

My argument for bringing fiction and ethnography together in the same volume is slightly different. Like Wolf, I recognize that ethnography and fiction take different forms and that the content of the former has a different kind of legitimacy than the latter. At the same time, however, I argue that each form provides distinct epistemological insights which can enhance and enrich one other. The expressive dimensions of fiction can provide insights into the feelings and thoughts that might lie behind the discomfort in conversations about race. In turn, ethnographies provide a way of reading characters and situations in fiction. Too often novels are treated as revealing generalizations about members of a particular race or ethnic group, whereas it is the work of anthropological research to document cultural patterns and variations. In this light, ethnography not only helps to provide a social and cultural context for interpreting a short story, but also serves as a caution against interpreting fictional characters as representative of a group.

This project also counters weaknesses in interdisciplinary work, where the frameworks and assumptions of one discipline are used to evaluate texts from another. For instance, when social science criteria are applied to fiction, novels are dismissed as evidence because they are not "true" or "verifiable" stories. However, a "faithful interdisciplinarity" requires not only that texts from different disciplines be read side by side, but also that we study the critical tools of each discipline.[44] This means clarifying the distinctive truth claims that fiction and ethnography can make and their divergent strategies for assessment and critique. From this perspective, fiction writers are not guided by anthropology's rules of evidence, but rather aspire to verisimilitude in developing characters and settings. They write true stories in the sense that they draw from actual people and events to create believable fictional characters and plots.[45] Thus, truth has a different indexical claim in fiction.

Certainly, introducing fiction into a book based on ethnographic research and cultural analysis is an unusual methodological strategy. My point here is for readers to take seriously my argument about the epistemological value of fiction. Unlike my interviews and ethnography, the short story enables me both to move into a social situation that was not part of my fieldwork (i.e., a dinner following a job interview) and to consider what the characters might be feeling in addition to what they are saying and doing. By taking fiction seriously as an epistemological vantage point, I am hoping that readers will take the risk of entering the muddy terrain of human subjectivity in thinking about the complexity of interracial interactions.[46] In fully considering these issues, we can perhaps move beyond the gap between our ideals of colorblindness and the material reality of racial and gender inequality in the United States.

1

Innocence and Injury

The Politics of Cultural Memory in Print News Media

In the mid-1970s, Allan Bakke, a white applicant, was twice denied admission to the School of Medicine at the University of California, Davis, and subsequently filed a discrimination lawsuit on the basis of race. At the time, the School of Medicine had "set aside" 16 of its 100 slots for racial and ethnic minorities, and Bakke claimed that "less qualified minorities" were admitted over him. In 1978, the U.S. Supreme Court ruled in Bakke's favor in a sharply divided decision. Five of the nine Justices found that the UC Davis School of Medicine had violated the equal protection clause of the Constitution by denying access to whites "solely because of their race."[1] In the Court's ruling, the quota system was considered unconstitutional, because there was no history of discrimination at UC Davis that required a remedy; the School of Medicine, which was established in 1968, was only ten years old at the time.

The *Regents of the University of California v. Bakke* case was of enormous significance in bringing to national attention a number of terms and legal principles, such as "reverse discrimination," "racial quotas," and "strict scrutiny," which reverberated through other rulings and court decisions in the 1980s and 1990s.[2] In addition to its legal import, the *Bakke* decision also created a "new class of victims" in American culture.[3] While the civil rights movement, the women's movement, and Lyndon Johnson's Great Society programs of the 1960s all gave greater public currency to narratives emphasizing the historical legacy of discrimination for people of color and white women, they also placed the onus of responsibility on the federal government for restoring civil rights to victims. In adopting the logic of this narrative by treating white men as victims and calling for relief (the Court ordered that Bakke, age 37, be admitted to the medical school), the Supreme Court case also introduced what I refer to throughout this chapter as "the innocent white male."[4]

Innocence in this social and historical context means innocent of prejudice or racism. The rhetorical use of innocence appears several times in Justice Powell's opinion in reference to Allan Bakke. He writes, for example, "[T]here is a measure of inequity in forcing *innocent persons* in the respondent's position [Bakke] to bear the burdens of redressing grievances not of their making" (emphasis added).[5] In other words, Powell maintains that it is unfair that Bakke, as a white man, should bear the "burdens" of a remedial policy, such as affirmative action, that aims to correct the legacy of historical discrimination against people of color because he, as an individual, is not complicit in that history. In this interpretation, Bakke is not guilty of racism, he is innocent.

For legal scholar Thomas Ross, the notion of white innocence, which he defines as "the insistence on the . . . absence of responsibility of the contemporary white person," has a long history in legal reasoning.[6] Because innocence is also linked to cultural notions of innocence and defilement as well as white and black, he maintains that the theme of white innocence in this legal rhetoric also draws its power from these metaphors.[7] Put another way, "whiteness" evokes innocence and purity; conversely, "blackness" connotes guilt and defilement. Innocence, then, is not only an important element of legal rhetoric, but also a powerful ideological image in American culture. Indeed, stories of innocence have long been part of the mythology about America's heritage. In academic American studies, the theme of innocence is central to early historiography that depicts America as "Edenic," an exceptional nation unspoiled by European class hierarchies and aristocratic excess.[8]

This chapter charts tropes of white male innocence from the late 1980s through the 1990s in the backlash against affirmative action by focusing is on print news media as a form of cultural memory. This form of collective remembering is important for several reasons. First, in bringing the issue to national attention, the press played an important role in shaping the *meaning* of affirmative action. As scholars have long recognized, the media is a powerful institution in framing how debates about social policy such as affirmative action are likely to be understood by the general public.[9] This is not to say that people uncritically accept whatever they read in newspapers, but rather to underscore the role such sources play in providing stories that help the general public make sense of particular issues and the key players, arguments, and political stakes surrounding them. In doing so, the media "facilitates" people's understanding of affirmative action by supplying the language, such as special terminology, legal terms and concepts, and rhetoric, that revolve around the debate.[10]

As this chapter demonstrates, journalistic conventions and practices helped to frame the trope of white male innocence. In "making news," journalists and their editors are expected to construct attention-grabbing headlines and lead paragraphs in their stories to garner readers' attention—a rhetorical practice that seldom reflects the complexity of positions on affirmative action—thereby guaranteeing profits for their news organizations. In addition, ethically, journalists are expected to write news stories based on the principle of "fair and balanced reporting," meaning that they are required to be objective by presenting two sides to any story.[11]

As my close reading of these accounts shows, narratives of white male innocence in this medium became predominant in the late 1980s and throughout the 1990s. Although other kinds of narratives about people of color and white women existed during this period, their numbers were far fewer. As media scholar Marita Sturken observes, cultural memories about historical events tell us about the political "stakes held by individuals and institutions in attributing meaning to the past."[12] As I argue, the dominance of narratives about white male innocence works to both construct a particular cultural memory about the meaning of affirmative action and race in America, and to suppress stories that counter that it. Specifically, stories about discrimination against people of color and the problems the economy posed for them receive little attention in the news media, while accounts of "reverse discrimination," "angry white males," and "white male victims" took center stage—narratives that helped turn the majority of California voters against affirmative action.

In making this argument, I intervene in the historiography about the political effects of the 1973 economic downturn for white working-class men. As some scholars argue, the pain of the recession turned those men against the Democrats and fueled a backlash against welfare, affirmative action, and other federal forms of assistance.[13] By contrast, my argument is that the news media as well as a number of anti-affirmative-action intellectuals played important roles in constructing and circulating a set of ideas about white male innocence and injury that ultimately supported neoconservative and neoliberal political agendas.

White Male Innocence, American Culture, and Backlash in the '80s and '90s

In 1976, the same year that Allan Bakke's lawsuit was first decided by California's Supreme Court (the case was later appealed at higher levels of the court system), the first *Rocky* film starring Sylvester Stallone was released across the country. The film, which focuses on the life of a small-time boxer who gets the chance to fight the heavyweight champion, was immensely popular and earned record box office receipts. The movie's director, John Avildsen, received an Oscar for his work; four of the film's actors were also nominated for awards (including Sylvester Stallone, Talia Shire, Burgess Meredith, and Burt Young); and Stallone, who wrote the screenplay, was also nominated for the Best Screenplay category.[14] Critics praised the movie. When it first came out, *Chicago Sun-Times'* Roger Ebert wrote:

> It's about heroism and realizing your potential, about taking your best shot and sticking by your girl. It sounds not only clichéd but corny—and yet it's not, not a bit, because it really does work on those levels. It involves us emotionally, it makes us commit ourselves: We find, maybe to our surprise after remaining detached during so many movies, that this time we care.[15]

While the storyline of the underdog who through his own skill and ambition is able to work his way to the top resonates with a familiar American narrative about the value of individualism and the rewards of upward mobility, the film also adds a number of twists to this Horatio-Alger-like plot. Unlike the fictional character Horatio Alger, who gets the job and the girl at the end of the story, Rocky makes it to the championship and gets the girl, but he doesn't win the final match. Despite the crushing blows he delivers that literally lift his opponent Apollo Creed off his feet and result in breaking one of his ribs, the ring announcer calls the fight, in what the audience can only see as unfair—a split decision for Creed. The injustice of this decision also has a racial dimension. Rocky is a not only the underdog in the match, but also a white underdog who fights against a black champion, the highly successful and arrogant Apollo Creed, who has the power to insist that his promoters to find a "snow white" opponent. Historian Matthew Frye Jacobson argues that the *Bakke* decision and Stallone's movie share a particular historical moment as well as a way of "understanding the respective meanings of 'whiteness' and 'blackness' in post-Civil Rights America."[16] In other words, the film suggests, as does the Supreme Court decision, that whites are disadvantaged vis-à-vis black Americans.[17]

While the themes of black advantage, on one hand, and white innocence and injury, on the other, emerge both in the Supreme Court ruling and in the film, this cultural memory did not become dominant until the late 1980s.[18] As sociologist William Gamson found in his study of Americans' talk about politics, in 1969 most media stories framed affirmative action as a remedy for the continuing effects of historical discrimination. In those stories, people of color were depicted as innocent victims deserving of compensation. In the 1980s, with the resurgence of a conservative agenda with Presidents Reagan and the first George Bush and their assault against all federal forms of assistance, the dominant narrative began to shift and was supplanted by a new one calling for the end of affirmative action.[19] Here, cultural memory about victimhood reversed itself: white men became innocent victims, while people of color were painted as advantaged and thus undeserving. In what follows, I outline the elements of each of these narratives, highlighting the neoconservative and neoliberal assumptions that bolster them.

White Male Innocence and Injury: Print News Media Accounts

In 1989, a white sociologist, Frederick Lynch, published a book funded by the conservative Institute for Educational Affairs and the Earhart Foundation titled, *Invisible Victims: White Males and the Crisis of Affirmative Action.*[20] Based on interviews with thirty-two white men from around the United States who claimed to be victims of reverse discrimination, either through loss of promotions, job reassignments, or terminations (none complained of discrimination in hiring), Lynch argued that affirmative action hurt white men. The following year, Lynch co-authored another article in *Policy Review*, a publication of the conservative Heritage Foundation, with the title "'You Ain't The Right Color, Pal': White Resentment of Affirmative Action," and in a *Commentary* piece published the same year, he declared, "One of the sleeper political forces in America is the growing sense of grievance among younger working-class and middle-class white males."[21] Lynch found that many of these men who were the first to be hurt by the recession were not college graduates and worried about declining job opportunities following the economic downturn of the mid-1970s. Moreover, they believed they were losing economic and political ground to people of color and women. According to Lynch, newspaper articles, polling data, and social science research bolstered his argument that white men felt "frustrated and unfairly victimized by affirmative action."[22]

Conservatives lauded Lynch's book. For example, psychologist Joseph Adelson painted Lynch as a hero unafraid to take on such an unpopular and "taboo topic" and described *Invisible Victims* as "an excellent volume about real rather than potential victims, individuals who have suffered directly because racial preferences have disrupted or ended their careers." According to Adelson, these men were aptly described as "invisible" because "No one calls attention to them, no one speaks on their behalf . . . They find few outside their families are much troubled by their misfortune, not even their friends."[23] Significantly, what this reviewer did not point out is that while Lynch's interviews showed that these white men *perceived* themselves to be victims of discrimination, there was no additional evidence to either support or negate their claims. Instead, Lynch treated their accounts, as did his conservative audience, as if they were material reality.

In 1991, Shelby Steele, another scholar, came to national attention through a series of articles that argued against affirmative action, which were published in a book of essays titled, *The Content of Our Character: A New Vision of Race in America*. What gave Steele, then an English professor at San Jose State University, a particular notoriety at the time was that he, unlike Lynch, was African American. In a *New York Times* article that drew from his book, Steele described affirmative action as a "mandate" through which whites can atone for their "past racial sins" and thereby "achieve a new racial innocence."[24] However, in Steele's view, the resolve for this mandate has weakened since the 1980s. Like Lynch, he believed that "[w]hites are now less willing to endure the unfairness to themselves in order to grant special entitlements to blacks even when those entitlements are justified in the name of past suffering." For blacks, on the other hand, Steele argued that racial preferences lower standards "to increase black representation"—which not only reinforces the myth of white superiority/black inferiority, but also serves to create "stigma" and "doubt" for African Americans. He concluded with an emphasis on individual responsibility:

> Blacks can have no real power without taking responsibility for their own educational and economic development. Whites can have no racial innocence without earning it by eradicating discrimination and helping the disadvantaged to develop. Because we ignored the means [affirmative action], the goals had not been reached and the real work remains to be done.[25]

In Steele's view, then, for blacks to become successful in American society, they must embrace the values of individual responsibility and hard work. Conversely, until Anglo Americans do the work of challenging their own racial prejudice, they must give up the dream of "racial innocence" that affirmative action policy proffers by taking individual responsibility to bring about the end of racial prejudice.

Steele's politics of the period were emblematic of what historian Angela Dillard termed "multicultural conservatism." As she argued, in the 1980s neoconservatives began to reject what they saw as the excessive egalitarianism of American culture and opposed programs such as affirmative action and many of the Great Society program's federal initiatives which, in their view, constituted government interventions that undermined the importance of individual achievement, personal responsibility, and hard work.[26] Sociologist Howard Winant described these "new racial politics" as a "neoconservative white racial project." In his view, such a project "seeks to preserve white advantage through denial of racial difference."[27] As noted in the Introduction, other scholars locate the backlash against affirmative action within the broader discourse of neoliberalism.[28] While both discourses assume that individuals make relatively unconstrained "choices," they each contribute to the affirmative action debate in distinctive ways. The notion that white men are disadvantaged by affirmative action, and hence are unable to make unconstrained employment choices, derives from neoliberal assumptions about the "free market," while assumptions that blacks are unworthy of affirmative because they are "unqualified" draws from moral assumptions of neoconservatism.

As these neoconservative discourses reinvigorated Horatio Alger myths about the importance of self-reliance and hard work, Americans were facing grave economic realities by the late 1980s. Neoliberal economic policies and processes that began in the mid-1970s, such as deregulation, foreign competition, deindustrialization, restructuring, and plant closings, reverberated in the 1980s as trade deficits overseas increased, unemployment rates rose higher, and stable, well-paying manufacturing jobs with benefits were replaced with part-time, low-wage service jobs.[29] Further, policy reforms under Presidents Reagan and Bush encouraged predatory capital, crippled organized labor, and dismantled social supports such as the welfare system, federal loans for education, and other federally subsidized programs, thereby deepening economic inequality.[30]

Labor market statistics provide a portrait of how these broader trends played out along racial lines. Between 1979 and 1992, 4.4 percent of jobs disappeared for all men in the full-time civilian labor force. During the same period, employment among African American men dropped 5.5 percent and among Latinos dropped 6.9 percent.[31] In the elite positions of the corporate world, the small gains African Americans made through affirmative action policies of the

1960s and 1970s were eroded by the decisions of a more conservative Supreme Court during the Reagan and Bush years. By the 1980s and early 1990s, the numbers of African Americans in corporate managerial positions in the United States also declined sharply. Sociologist Sharon Collins's study of black corporate executives found, for example, that African Americans who had accepted managerial positions as affirmative action recruitment officers in large corporations in labor relations or urban affairs lost their jobs by the 1980s. These management positions, though highly visible to the general public, did not wield any real power in the corporate world because they fell outside mainstream managerial tracks, and consequently did not promise a long-term career of upward mobility. Those African Americans who accepted other kinds of managerial positions fared somewhat better, but as Collins demonstrated, they too lost jobs during economic restructuring.[32]

Collins's findings for the 1980s and early 1990s correspond with labor market statistics for this period that showed a division along racial lines. White men constituted 45.0 percent of the American labor market, yet they occupied 95.0 percent of top management positions in Fortune 500 companies. By contrast, 0.6 percent of men in those positions were African American, 0.3 percent were Asian American, and 0.4 were Latino. Furthermore, other studies consistently found high levels of racial discrimination against blacks and other racial or ethnic groups in employment, earnings, and housing, and other areas of social life.[33] As these statistics demonstrated, the economic transformation had uneven effects: White men in general were not hit as hard as other groups, and though the loss of union jobs in the manufacturing sector made life more difficult for working-class white men, conditions were much worse for people of color.

At the same time, in colleges and universities across the country, affirmative action yielded only modest gains for people of color. As William Bowen and Derek Bok pointed out in their influential study, *The Shape of the River: Long-Term Consequences of Considering Race in College and University Admission*, affirmative action only made a difference in highly selective colleges and universities, such as Harvard, Stanford, and Princeton.[34] In elite schools, however, the best factor for predicting admission was not race but legacy status. Children of alumni were three times more likely than non-legacy applicants to be accepted to Harvard, for example.[35] Moreover, even in highly selective schools where affirmative action mattered, the numbers of students of color accepted were quite small. For instance, at the University of California at Berkeley in 1995, one of the nation's former leaders in promoting affirmative action in undergraduate education, only 5.5 percent of the campus's undergraduates were

African American. Nationwide at that time, the percentage of blacks in law schools was 7.5 percent, and in medical schools, 8.1 percent.[36] These are hardly impressive numbers, given that their proportion in the general U.S. population during the same year was 11.0 percent.[37]

Against this backdrop of a dire economy, continuing discrimination against African Americans and other people of color, and the small numbers of student applicants actually affected by affirmative action, newspaper and magazine stories focusing on anxiety about affirmative action and white male injury began to increase. An April 1990 cover of *TIME* magazine declared that America's colors are "changing" and asked ominously, "What will the U.S. look like when whites are no longer the majority?" A 1994 cover of *Businessweek* declared, "White, Male, and Worried," adding, "White men still dominate corporate America. But in companies with aggressive diversity programs, white males are starting to feel angry and resentful."[38] By 1995, beneath the headline, "Race and Rage," *Newsweek* featured a cover with a black fist and a white fist pushing against each other. This was the mood of the nation during the spring 1995, declared the weekly news magazine. The accompanying article noted that ". . . the most profound fight—the one tapping deepest into the emotions of everyday American life—is affirmative action. It's setting the lights blinking on studio consoles, igniting angry rhetoric in state legislatures and focusing new attention on the word 'fairness.'"[39] In July of the same year that President Clinton began the federal review of affirmative action programs, Tom Brokaw announced on the *NBC Nightly News*, "Affirmative action: two words that can start an argument just about anywhere in America. . . . We'll be hearing a lot more about this in the months leading to the 1996 election."[40]

From the 1990 to 1996, white men appeared frequently in newspaper articles, editorials, and letters to the editor in the *San Francisco Chronicle* and *New York Times* accompanying claims about "reverse discrimination" and "white victimhood." Some claims appeared as headlines to articles with sensational phrases such as "Don't Forget about White Males," "Many Whites Say They Feel Cheated," "White Men's Eroding Economic Clout Contributes to Backlash," "White Firefighters Say San Jose Rigged Examination, Suit Claims Test Favored Minorities," and "Affirmative Action Facing Hard Times, Whites Take Initiative against Preferential Hiring"; while others argued in letters to the editor that initiatives against affirmative action were a justifiable "White Guy's Revenge."[41] (The year 1996 is used as the endpoint here because it is the same year that Proposition 209, the initiative banning affirmative action in state employment and contracts, passed.) Between 1990 and 1995, the overall number

Table 1.1 Number of articles on affirmative action between 1990 and 1996

Year	New York Times	San Francisco Chronicle	Total
1990	206	58	264
1991	275	80	355
1992	91	41	132
1993	105	33	138
1994	105	43	148
1995	411	339	750
1996	346	332	678

of articles on affirmative action in the *San Francisco Chronicle* alone increased fivefold, from 58 in 1990 to 339 articles in 1995, while in *The New York Times* the number of articles almost doubled, from 206 to 411 (see Table 1.1).

In this cultural trope of white male innocence and injury, discrimination was no longer a social problem; consequently, remedial programs like affirmative action were unnecessary. As Ward Connerly, an African American businessman and Governor Pete Wilson's appointee to the University of California Board of Regents, put it, affirmative action had "outlived its usefulness."[42] Articles featuring this storyline followed a simple formulaic plot. A white male who was denied a job or a promotion heard an anecdote about an "unqualified" black (or Latino) who got the job instead. (News stories also focused on denied university admissions.) Affirmative action was blamed for his failure to acquire the job, because it supposedly granted minorities an unfair advantage solely on the basis of race or ethnicity. Here, the issue of fairness was implicitly linked to the ideal of meritocracy. Presumably, hard work and individual achievement would be rewarded by a fair and just outcome. Because the white male was denied the job or promotion, he felt he was being discriminated against and claimed victim status.

The victimization argument was not only made about whites, but also in a few cases about Asian Americans. Benjamin Lu, for example, wrote in *New York Times* letter to the editor in response to a Bowen and Bok's study about the benefits of affirmative action:

> While it is nice to read about the achievements of students who gained admission to elite universities because of their skin color, is any thought given to those who were turned away to make space for them? There are thousands of bright white and Asian American students who are turned away from our universities every year because they were born with the wrong skin color. Are there any studies showing how this non-preferred group fares under affirmative action?[43]

Lu maintained that affirmative action was unfair in individual terms. Further, he assumed that that affirmative action created a "zero-sum calculus."[44] In other words, the letter writer assumed that race was the sole factor determining college admissions and that admitting person of one race or ethnicity (e.g., black) would automatically result in excluding one of another group (e.g., white or Asian American). What was seldom considered in this narrative was the fact that a variety of factors unrelated to race also influenced college admissions, such as "alumni relations, parental wealth, connections and donations, geographic diversity, and athletic skills [which] have long helped some whites gain admission over other whites and blacks with stronger test scores, grades, and extracurricular activities."[45]

Invoking a similar argument, the writer of a 1995 *San Francisco Chronicle* letter to the editor described the injuries of affirmative action in this way:

> For every minority person who gains through affirmative action, there is a white male who pays the price. It happened to me, and I ask, "Why is it that I, who have never discriminated, should be pushed aside by one who was never a slave and had, in fact, more advantages than I."[46]

Interestingly, the letter writer not only painted himself as a victim of affirmative action, but also as a person who was innocent of racism—someone who had "never discriminated" against people of color. Presumably, because he had not had a personal hand in the oppression of others, affirmative action was unfair to him. As in the broader anti-affirmative-action discourse, in this letter discrimination was presumed to be lodged firmly in the past (i.e., the reference to slavery) while fairness and history itself were understood in individual terms. Racism was not understood as structural or institutional. Further, the writer's implicit characterization of the typical African American as "one who has never been a slave" implied that contemporary blacks did not experience discrimination. In fact, he insisted they had "more advantages" than he did, and thus were undeserving.

The notion that blacks were undeserving of federal forms of assistance was echoed in a *New York Times* article quoting Republican Newt Gingrich, the 1994 Speaker of the House and architect of "Contract with America," a program he and other Republicans dedicated to the principles of "accountability, responsibility and opportunity" and designed to eradicate federal forms of assistance, such as welfare.[47] In his view, "poor people need to learn new habits," the implication being that they were lazy and therefore unworthy of assistance. Instead, "women and minorities who rely on affirmative action should . . . take advantage of enormous avenues of opportunity that ignore race and sex." For Gingrich, in a "backward-looking, grievance-looking system [such as affirmative action], you teach people exactly the wrong habits. They end up spending their lives waiting for the lawsuit instead of spending their lives seeking opportunity."[48] Drawing from neoliberal rhetoric about unconstrained "choices" in the "free market," Gingrich also deployed neoconservative moralistic understandings of poor people of color as unworthy.

The themes of white male victimhood and black advantage also played out in the lead paragraphs of many 1995 newspaper articles. Here are some examples:

> Mr. Pech said he was aware of the history of discrimination that underlay minority preferences, but like others [white men] who found their careers or businesses hurt by affirmative action, he found himself asking, why me? "If you were standing in my shoes," he said, "you would feel like there's a great arrow pointing at you and saying, 'This is the guy who's paying, when it comes to the guardrail business in Colorado.'"[49]

> Shortly after the Vietnam War, Robert Pollack of Hayward applied for a loan to fulfill his dream of owning a machinery shop. He never got that loan. And to this day, Pollack believes that he would have had he not been white . . . Pollack—like some white men surveyed—says he has suffered as a result of affirmative action.[50]

> After losing a coveted teaching job to a minority woman, Tom Wood has turned his private frustration into a public crusade that threatens to end America's 30-year experiment with affirmative action. . . . he was a candidate for a job teaching philosophy at a California university. He had no doubt that he was the most qualified for the post. Then came a development he had considered unthinkable. . . . a member of the search committee told him . . . "You know, Tom, it sounds to me as though you'd probably just waltz into this job if you were the right race or the right sex."[51]

Interestingly, in the case of Wood, when he told the media that he was the most qualified candidate for the job he didn't get, he failed to mention the fact that he had not published articles in any academic journal in the first fifteen years after receiving his Ph.D.—"a record of productivity that would disqualify him from employment in any serious research university."[52] Moreover, Wood did not mention that he had never been employed in a permanent teaching position; the actual job he had held was as a computer programmer. He held only a part-time adjunct position as an instructor. The television news program *Date-line* later revealed that of the five jobs Wood might have applied for, four went to white male candidates. "The fifth went to a woman who was far superior to Wood in academic achievement."[53] Interestingly, none of this information about Wood's background appeared in either the *Chronicle* or in the *New York Times*.

The fact that the print media failed to fully investigate Wood's claims suggests not only sloppy research, but also the media's willingness to grant legitimacy to white statements about affirmative action and their eagerness to construct sensational headlines about white male injury. (Wood himself was mentioned in numerous articles both locally in San Francisco and in national publications, such as *TIME* magazine and *The Washington Post*.)[54] In their influential book, *Black Image in the White Mind*, media scholars Robert Entman and Andrew Rojeki suggested that one of the reasons for this media bias might be that "journalists themselves may be one of the groups most hostile to affirmative action." Further, they observed that it was psychologically comforting for white professionals to blame their failure to gain promotions on something other than themselves—and affirmative action served as a convenient scapegoat for their thwarted desires in a highly competitive field.[55]

Of course, not all the new stories on affirmative action focused on white male injury. Following the journalistic convention of "fair and balanced reporting," the media constructed two sides to the debate. The second storyline supported affirmative action by underscoring the benefits of this policy for society.[56] Some of its proponents depicted affirmative action as a means for guaranteeing equal opportunity and remedying discrimination, while others celebrated the advantages of racial and ethnic diversity in education and employment. The media often asserted that discrimination against people of color, and very rarely women, continued to exist and must be addressed. (See Chapter 4 for a discussion of women in the media.) In many articles this assertion was made with references to the "glass ceiling," "chilly climate," "hostile environment," "institutionalized racism," "residual racism," or simply "racism," and in others was supported with statistical evidence from government reports or social science research.[57] For example, a 1993 *San Francisco Chronicle* article, titled "Gains for Minority Attorneys in SF: But They Cite Frustration of Institutional Racism . . . ," highlighted the work law firms were doing to improve the numbers of minority attorneys and provided statistical data about changes that came through about through the American Bar Association's voluntary affirmative action program. The article went on to point out, however, that minority retention remained a problem in many firms:

Minority [lawyers] believe that longstanding inadequacies in law firm systems combining with subtle patterns of institutional racism produce an often fatally inhospitable work environment. "It's one thing to let me in the door. It's another to say let my life be bearable once I am in the door." Many of those interviewed said white male attorneys tend to help only junior attorneys like themselves. "One of the greatest affirmative action programs is for white males," one minority partner commented.[58]

In addition to emphasizing the continuing existence of discrimination, the proponents' narrative also operated on a different understanding of fairness and equity: Whereas affirmative action opponents emphasized fairness for the individual, proponents emphasized the good for broader society. Affirmative action, in this argument, was regarded as an institutional remedy for discrimination as well as for the structural legacies of past mistreatment to help level an uneven playing field and guarantee fairness. The following editorial and letter to the editor from *The New York Times* illustrate this point:

I strongly support affirmative action and believe it is necessary to help level the playing field of economic opportunity. However, the assault on affirmative action by the conservative right has reframed the debate. Affirmative action, instead of being viewed as a partial remedy to past and present discrimination, is itself attacked as discriminatory. Under this logic, it has been suggested that affirmative action is a disservice to African-Americans because it taints our accomplishments as "handouts." In the business circles that Black Enterprise magazine covers, this is understood by both black and white businesspeople to be racially polarizing rhetoric that it is.[59]

[M]ost Americans will take issue with what they perceive as unfair privilege based on race. Affirmative action was designed to give minority- and female-owned businesses an equal opportunity to compete for government contracts, while at the same time redressing centuries of discrimination.[60]

Proponents also pointed to the existence of legacy admission, special admissions for athletes, the children of wealthy donors, political figures, or friends of university presidents and deans, and other cases that benefited white Americans. Here the argument was that affirmative action came in many guises wherein whites, and not people of color, were the preferred group. For example, former President Bill Clinton was described in a *New York Times* article as being "tickled" that California's Proposition 209, which restricted affirmative action in state education and employment, exempted athletes.

"So, you can give a preference for athletes to get into Berkeley, so Berkeley can have a nice football teach and a nice basketball team," Mr. Clinton said. . . . Clinton said an A student could now be denied admission because the spot went to an athlete, rather than to a minority student who might have benefited from a banned affirmative action program. "He just loses it to a basketball player instead of a kid with thick glasses who struggled late at night in Oakland to make good grades, but didn't quite make a high enough college board score to get in," he said. "What's the difference?"[61]

A related argument in favor of affirmative action that emphasizes its good for the broader society is one that underscores the value of diversity. This argument began to appear with more frequency in the late 1990s and by 1997 had supplanted the remedial logic argument.[62] In education, the general idea is that a racial and ethnically diverse student body contributes to a better educational experience through the "robust interchange of ideas" and perspectives.[63] In some articles it was deployed on its own to defend affirmative action, and in others it was used along with the remedial logic argument. One article, for example, detailed social scientists William Bowen's and Derek Bok's study on the consequences of affirmative action in elite colleges, which maintained that diversity was good for minorities, for higher education, and for society. As Derek Bok argued in this *New York Times* article, "In the case of universities and colleges, race turns out to be very relevant because we are interested in what students can teach one another and race is a part of that in an increasingly diverse society."[64] Letters to the editor responding to the article made similar points:

When the question is posed this way, we are invited to view affirmative action in terms of a broad societal question: Whom do we, as a society, prefer to place in our elite universities? The deck has been stacked, and diversity is the only humane option."[65]

Former President Bill Clinton also supported diversity in higher education as well as in employment; but compared to the letter writer above, he advanced a moderate position, what he called his promise "to mend, not end affirmative action." Simply put, Clinton supported affirmative action in principle but was troubled by some of its "abuses." His hope was to balance the goals of diversity with those of individual merit.[66]

As Clinton's position suggests, the diversity argument was also invoked as a social good for workplaces and the economy. In this argument, jobs in an increasingly global economy require knowledge and understanding of diverse cultural viewpoints. As one *New York Times* letter writer put it, "It is estimated that by 2030, 40 percent of all Americans will belong to various racial minorities. Already, the global economy requires an unprecedented grasp of diverse viewpoints and cultural traditions. . . ."[67] Here, the assumption was that hiring people of diverse racial and ethnic backgrounds would contribute to financial success in business in terms of higher profits, thereby creating a competitive edge in the global economy. Similarly, an article in the *San Francisco Chronicle* reported that the California Business Roundtable, a group including the heads of Chevron, Bank of America, Levi Strauss, and other companies, released a statement asserting that "a diverse workforce . . . must be used to our competitive advantage."[68] And, in another article in the *Times*, Richard McCormick, chairman and chief executive officer of US West, argued that diversity was what gave his company a "strategic advantage" and that it provided that advantage regardless of federal regulation.[69]

Significantly, in these news articles, the argument for hiring a racial or ethnic minority was made in economic terms; diversity was viewed as a prized commodity for corporate America. Here, the rhetoric of diversity was informed by neoliberal understandings of the "free market." Hiring an individual from a non-dominant group provide a "competitive advantage."[70] For business leaders, diversity was not about leveling the playing field or fairness as the remedial logic argument suggests; it was about individual inclusion. As we see in Chapter 3, the inclusion of token individuals does not create a diverse workplace, but actually serves to reproduce racial inequality.

Despite the journalistic convention of "two sides to every story," the proponents' argument was given less weight in news stories between 1990 and 1996. As my analysis reveals, coverage was slanted toward statements and arguments about white male victimhood. Table 1.2 summarizes the data from newspaper articles, editorials, and letters to the editor from 1990 to 1996 that I analyzed for both *The New York Times* and the *San Francisco Chronicle*. During this period, there was a consistent slant in coverage *against* affirmative action. In other words, I found more statements and arguments in newspaper articles—even those that clearly identified "two sides" to the story—that opposed affirmative action than those that supported it. For instance, an article might begin by suggesting there were two sides to the issue, but anti-affirmative-action arguments, particularly those emphasizing "reverse discrimination" and "white male resentment and victimhood," would be mentioned with greater frequency.[71] The one exception was in 1993, when the slant reversed itself to a ratio of 3:2, and there were more articles emphasizing the continuing existence of

Table 1.2   Ratio of statements/arguments slanted against affirmative action and for affirmative action, 1990–2000

Year	Slant
1990	3:1 tilted against affirmative action
1991	3:2 tilted against affirmative action
1992	3:2 tilted against affirmative action
1993	3:2 more emphasis on continuing discrimination in employment
1994	2:1 tilted against affirmative action
1995	3:2 tilted against affirmative action
1996	8:5 tilted against affirmative action

discrimination. This was the same year that a number of anti-discrimination lawsuits were either settled or filed, including the grocery store suits against Lucky's and Safeway, and suits against the Federal Reserve Bank, Princeton University, and several others.[72]

Research using other news sources, such as weekly news magazines like *TIME* and *Newsweek*, confirms my findings. Using these sources for 1995, when the Regents voted to end affirmative action in the University of California, Entman and Rojeki found that the print news media slanted 3:1 against affirmative action.[73] (Relying on data from the *San Francisco Chronicle* and *New York Times* in the same year, my research reveals a 3:2 slant.) Their content analysis further revealed that the media tended to magnify the degree of conflict and drama over this issue and to portray it as a black–white issue—even though affirmative action is designed to protect other minorities and white women from discrimination.

Headlines and lead paragraphs in the *Chronicle* and the *New York Times* also amplified the conflict. They characterized the affirmative action debate repeatedly as "contentious" and "acrimonious," opinions as "sharply divided," and "the mood of the country" as "increasingly impatient, skeptical at best, and not persuaded that there is a single, easy answer to the questions posed by awarding public benefits on the bases of race . . ." The debate was alternately described as a great "rift," a "storm," "a showdown," or "a brawl" that contributed to "unease and hostility" and "resentment," "poisons American race relations," "victimizes white men," and provokes "white guy's revenge."[74]

Further, news stories typically presented the conflict in racial terms in lead sentences and paragraphs:

> Firefighters are color-blind in the smoke. The black and white faces are hidden behind oxygen masks, and any resentment they carry inside a burning building is melted away by the heat. . . . When the fire is out and the danger is over, when

tired firefighters flop down to rest or joke, the old resentments bubble up. Then, the firefighters often split off into groups by color. . . . it is a byproduct of one of the remedies of Jim Crow rule: affirmative action.[75]

Two schoolteachers are equally qualified and equally experienced. One must be laid off. One is the only minority teacher in an otherwise all-white department; the other is white. Is it permissible to make race the deciding factor, laying off the white teacher and retaining the minority teacher? [a reference to Sharon Taxman, the white plaintiff, who planned to sue the Piscataway, New Jersey, School Board.][76]

Another article on the front page of the *San Francisco Chronicle*, titled, "UC Campus Debates Affirmative Action, Some Say Success in Diversifying Berkeley Student Body Back," began with a glimpse of the "appealing" racial diversity in a University of California at Berkeley undergraduate philosophy classroom. Professor John Searle, who taught the course, was quoted as saying, "You look out at the class and you think, 'This is wonderful. I've got the whole United Nations in this classroom.'" Significantly, diversity here was described much like a commodity, as something "appealing." In the very next line of the article, this seemingly positive endorsement of diversity was countered by pointing out that black and Latino students did not do well in Professor Searle's course—either they dropped out by mid-semester or they did poorly in the class. Rather than asking why these students dropped out or whether they were in fact the only ones to do so, the narrative quickly moved to turn this one professor's personal observation into it a social problem with a hyperbolic assertion about affirmative action and racial discord. "At Berkeley and across the nation, affirmative action is under assault. And Searle's disenchanted view from the lectern is just one glimpse into the deep undercurrent of racial tension ripping across American's campuses as they struggle anew with issues of fairness and merit."[77]

This news story went on to follow the journalistic convention of "fair and balanced" reporting by presenting the "other side" of the debate. Upon closer reading, however, the clarity and logic of the proponents' argument appeared at times to be ambiguous, less detailed, and not as persuasive. To take one example: Professor David Kirp in Berkeley's School of Public Policy was named as a proponent who endorsed affirmative action by saying it contributed to diversity. But there is no space for an explanation of what he meant by that statement or precisely what he thought diversity contributed to higher education. Further, while Kirp described black and Latino students as "smart" and "hungry to learn," he acknowledged that they were weaker academically than other students, a point that could be interpreted by critics as giving credence to the "lowered standards" argument against affirmative action. By contrast, Kevin Nguyen, a Vietnamese student who was quoted four times in the article, compared to once or twice for the other students, provided far more detail for the anti-affirmative-action position. He argued, for instance, that affirmative action worked to create stereotypes about minorities—the stigma argument. He maintained that admissions criteria based solely on race were exclusionary to other people of other races—the white male injury argument. Finally, he contended that race-based preferences violated the ideals of meritocracy. Combined with the statements from a white student, another student of color, and Professor Searle, the argument against affirmative action was given more space and detail, enabling greater clarity of explanation for each point. As in the other articles I analyzed, this one followed the pattern of slanting against affirmative action.

In addition to providing more detail about the anti-affirmative-action argument, the article also provided different kinds of information about each Berkeley student. Grades and test scores were mentioned for both Pacheco and Manuel, the Latino and black students, but not for Weingarten, the white student. While Nguyen, the Vietnamese American student, was described as having "near perfect grades," his test scores were not mentioned. It is possible that the reporter simply did not ask each student the same set of questions or, if he did, the students refused to provide details. Nevertheless, by leaving this information out with no explanation, the article gave the impression that the only students whose qualifications demanded scrutiny were black and Latino students. White and Asian American students were granted automatic legitimacy, just as Thomas Wood and other white men's assertions of reverse discrimination were in other news articles. The underlying assumption was that white students (and some Asian Americans) got in for the "right" reasons—that is, for their grades and test scores—while African Americans and Latinos did not. Here, the omission of test scores and grades for white students suggested an implicit acceptance of the logic of the anti-affirmative-action argument, that students of color were "less qualified" than white students and hence undeserving.

Another way the media slanted news stories against affirmative action had to do with the way they used polling data. For instance, a 1993 *Newsweek* poll reported that about 50 percent of white men interviewed said that they felt they should fight against affirmative action; two years later, 57 percent agreed that affirmative action had resulted in "less opportunities" for white men.[78]

Another poll conducted by the *San Francisco Chronicle* in March 1995 reported that 65 percent of whites favored Proposition 209, the initiative designed to ban affirmative action.[79] Still another poll in the same month reported that 59 percent of white women in California favored the initiative.[80] However, as other polling and survey data conducted during this time demonstrates, the way questions were posed—either as "affirmative action" or as "preferential treatment"—often influenced the way people responded. Asking about "racial preferences" tended to evoke negative responses, while asking about affirmative action yielded positive responses.[81] In fact, despite media and conservative politicians' claims of a massive shift in attitudes in the mid-1990s, the most comprehensive review of survey data conducted by sociologists Charlotte Steeh and Maria Krysan concluded that white attitudes on affirmative action remained virtually unchanged between 1970 and 1990. When the issue was not framed as a racial preference, most Americans supported the policy.[82]

These survey findings raise the question as to whether a demographic category of "angry white males" ever existed. Significantly, a 1995 government study conducted by the U.S. Labor Department revealed that actual cases of reverse discrimination against white men were rare. Of the 300 cases filed with the Equal Employment Opportunity Commission, "Reverse discrimination was established in *six cases*, and the courts provided appropriate relief in those cases" (emphasis added). The study concluded that many of the cases were "the result of a disappointed applicant failing to examine his or her own qualifications and erroneously assuming that when a women or minority got a job, it was because of their race or sex, not qualifications."[83]

The news media paid scant attention to these relevant facts and continued to report on white male resentment. "Angry white men is a phrase with a certain ring to it," declared one national newspaper after the midterm elections in 1994. "They've changed the political face of America by voting disproportionately GOP. . . . They've had it with Democrats."[84] Indeed, many Democratic white men, dissatisfied with Clinton's policies, particularly on crime, school busing, welfare, and affirmative action, voted in droves for Republicans in the midterm elections.[85] However, in contrast to the historiography which argues that working-class white men fueled the backlash against federal forms of assistance, I argue that the news media slant played an important role in constructing the *perception* of the white male resentment and victimhood.[86]

The fact that the perception of white male resentment and injury had become dominant underscored the news media's success in promulgating an anti-affirmative-action message. Moreover, by seeking out and dramatizing racial conflict, the news media also created the impression that there were clear divisions between whites and blacks on the issue. At the same time, it suggested that African Americans were advantaged through affirmative action, often "unqualified" for jobs or college admissions slots, and hence undeserving. Furthermore, because less attention was granted to the benefits of affirmative action or to continuing discrimination against people of color, it created the impression that affirmative action was no longer necessary.

Why did the media slant stories in this way, especially in light of facts from reputable sources that demonstrated continuing discrimination? Part of the answer lies in news media organizations' incentive for profits. As sociologist Gay Tuchman has argued, in order to "make news" and increase sales of newspapers, journalists are expected to write sensationalist headlines and lead paragraphs to grab readers' attention.[87] While this practice helps us to understand why news story headlines dramatized the conflict in ways that were not entirely accurate, it does not explain why these accounts reduced the affirmative action debate to two simplistic positions. Here, another media practice, the convention of two, and only, two sides to the story obscures the fact that there may be more than two sides to any issue. As Chapter 4 shows, many of the women lawyers I interviewed expressed ambivalence about this policy. In other words, they recognized both good and bad things about affirmative action—a position that was rarely articulated in news articles or editorials in either the *San Francisco Chronicle* or *The New York Times*.[88] Similarly, Entman and Rojeki found that, when interviewed, both blacks and whites expressed far more ambivalence about this policy than was portrayed in the news media.[89] What this suggests is that the media convention of "fair and balanced reporting" contributed to the perception of stark divisions when, in fact, the actual story about American attitudes was more complicated.

In focusing on two sides to any story, the media also tends to treat both sides as if they were equivalent accounts. To give one example, in the story about UC Berkeley and affirmative action, Professors Kirp and Searle were treated as holding two different but equivalent positions on the issue. What was not mentioned was the fact that David Kirp, a professor of public policy, had conducted research on race and education, while John Searle, a philosophy professor, was an anti-affirmative-action spokesperson.[90] Their "opinions" did not have equal weight. One was the position of a knowledgeable expert who had conducted years of research and the other was an activist who provided anecdotal evidence. Part of the problem here was that journalists typically failed to provide a context for their "facts."[91] By contextualizing these facts, the journalists might have given their audiences a better understanding of the difference between an anecdote from a politically motivated individual and another based on solid research.

Significantly, other important research that cast significant doubt on the opponents' position—the Labor Department's findings about the small number of actual cases of "reverse discrimination," the Glass Ceiling Commission's report on discrimination against women and people of color in employment, and Derek Bok's and William Bowen's comprehensive study on affirmative action policy in selective colleges and universities—received little or no attention in *The New York Times* and the *San Francisco Chronicle*. The *Times* devoted only one article to Bok's and Bowen's book and another to the findings of the Glass Ceiling Commission; while the *Chronicle* failed to print an article on either one.[92] The fact that such credible sources were given little attention suggests that the media chose to downplay or ignore research that would contradict an anti-affirmative-action message.

As pointed out earlier, journalists may have strong feelings about affirmative action policy that slant their news reporting. The conventions and practices in newsrooms had serious political consequence. News stories focusing on proponents' arguments, continuing discrimination against people of color and white women, and the rarity of actual cases of reverse discrimination were given far less attention throughout the 1990s. As I have argued, the predominance of accounts emphasizing affirmative action opponents worked collectively to create a cultural memory of white male innocence and injury and suppress others.

Conclusion

As I have argued in this chapter, the print new media is a collective form of remembering for many Americans, and in the late 1980s and throughout the 1990s, the news media established a dominant narrative about white male innocence and injury. Furthermore, cultural memories often become conflated with official history. As Marita Sturken points out, "cultural memory and all history are forged in a context in which details, voices, and impressions of the past are forgotten."[93] As we have seen, cultural tropes of white male innocence serve to obscure the actual fact of white privilege, continuing racial discrimination against people of color, and the small numbers of students of color actually admitted to colleges and universities.

While news media accounts worked to construct white male victims whose choices were constrained by policies such as affirmative action and undeserving black recipients, they also reinvigorated neoliberal and neoconservative assumptions about "choice," "free markets" as good for society, and moralistic understanding of who is "most worthy" of federal assistance. The power of the media to define this reality and, in the case of Proposition 209 and the ban of affirmative action in the UC system, the power of politicians to construct policy that benefited whites was far from innocent. In constructing a new cultural memory of the innocent white male, they also contributed to dismantling a policy that promised to transform racial inequality.

2

Filming Racial Progress

The Transformation of White Male Innocence

Was blind, but now I see.
—*Anonymous, "Amazing Grace"*

Once memory enters into our consciousness, it is hard to
circumvent, harder to stop, and impossible to run from.
—*Teshome Gabriel, "Third Cinema as Guardian of Popular Memory"*

In 1996, the same year that the majority of California residents voted to end affirmative action in their state, director Joel Schumacher released his film, *A Time to Kill*. Based on John Grisham's novel, the story is about Jake Brigance, a young white lawyer (played by Matthew McConaughey) who defends Carl Lee Hailey, a black man (played by Samuel Jackson) who murdered the white men who brutally beat and raped his ten-year-old daughter. Brigance's understanding of how racism operates in this historical moment is established early in the movie when a reporter asks him whether Carl Lee Hailey can get a fair trial in Clanton, Mississippi. "Some folks believe Black folks can't get a fair trial," he says, "but in the New South justice will be colorblind." From this point, the central focus of the movie is the growth of Brigance from racial innocent to anti-racist white hero. Because Brigance agrees to take the case, a newly constructed branch of the Ku Klux Klan begins a spree of hate crimes against his home and his co-workers. Fearing for their safety, his wife leaves town with their daughter in tow. In the next series of events, the Klan attacks and beats his legal secretary's husband, kidnaps and tortures the law student assisting him, and burns his house to the ground. Despite the suffering he endures, Brigance moves forward with the case and in the end, through an emotional appeal to the jury where he asks them to imagine that Tonya is white, wins Carl Lee Hailey's case. The transformation of Brigance from a white man who espouses "colorblindness" to one who comes to understand racism and becomes an advocate for people of color through normative systems of justice is complete by the end of the film.

Of the novel and movie, *New York Times* film critic Janet Maslin writes: What makes John Grisham's "most interesting novel is the gray area into which this black-and-white case wanders. In Clanton, where the jury will be mostly white, can Jake really play by the rules? Or should he recognize the realities of small-town Southern justice and try more unconventional means of saving his client's life?" She concludes by saying, "If the film doesn't add up to a cogent legal argument, neither does it have trouble delivering 2 hours and 20 minutes of sturdy, highly charged drama."[1] By contrast, Gene Siskel, of *Siskel and Ebert*, describes the movie as "boring," the final summation as "cornball," and finds the violent Klan scenes which appear every ten or fifteen minutes "offensive" because they were "goosed for entertainment value." Though Roger Ebert of the *Chicago Sun-Times* agrees with some of Siskel's points, he ultimately recommends the film because he thinks Jackson's and McConaughey's performances carry the movie. He does, however, acknowledge that one of its weaknesses lies in its inability to imagine blacks as complex individuals, and he wonders why more screen time wasn't given to characters such as Hailey's wife. He adds: "Maybe the answer is the movie is interested in the white characters as people and the black characters . . . as atmosphere. My advice to the filmmakers about the black people in town: Try imagining they're white."[2]

Despite these mixed reviews, *A Time to Kill* was an enormous box office success, making $20 million in the United States alone and over $145 million worldwide. Samuel L. Jackson was nominated for a Golden Globe, the young actress Rae'Ven Larrymore Kelly received a Young Star Award for her portrayal of Tonya, and Matthew McConaughey won an MTV Award for Best Breakthrough Performance.[3] The immense popularity of the film suggests that its central story line about white racial progress, that is, the movement from white ignorance about people of color to understanding, acceptance, and advocacy, is an appealing one. As I show in this chapter, this story appeared in many late 1980s and 1990s Hollywood films. Unlike the dominant print news media accounts discussed in the last chapter, which highlighted the themes of white male innocence and injury throughout the 1990s, these movies revolve around a different kind of protagonist, one whose consciousness transforms from innocence of racism's pernicious effects to one who, through hardship and struggle, comes to understand racial injustice, fights against it, and ultimately triumphs.

Just as the print news media served as a powerful form of cultural memory in facilitating American understandings of affirmative action, here I argue that mainstream Hollywood films serve a similar function by providing audiences with stories about their own lives and those of racial "others."[4] Of course, as forms of cultural memory, movies are not mirror reflections of reality, but they perform important work by providing occasions for identification with characters and exposing audiences to new narratives.[5] In the case of race, the expansive reach of movies also makes them an especially important means of examining cultural constructions of social issues. Because the United States is racially segregated socially and culturally, most Americans, particularly white Americans, spend the majority of their time socially interacting with people of their own race.[6] This means that films with racial themes offer Americans viewpoints and stories they might not otherwise get in their daily lives. Further, cinematic codes of realism give viewers the sense that they actually experience what they see in the movies, thereby contributing to a sense of an "authentic" personal memory. For example, Marita Sturken found that Vietnam veterans' expectations of what that war would be like were based on the films they had seen about World War II, and they were surprised when the Vietnam war did not live up to their expectations.[7] To paraphrase media scholar Teshome Gabriel, who is quoted in the second epigraph, once *cultural memory* enters our consciousness, it is "harder to stop, and impossible to run from."[8]

As this chapter shows, the dominant trope of white male innocence takes a slightly different form in Hollywood films than it did in the print news media. This is not surprising, as each one operates according to a different set of conventions. While journalists are expected to write news stories based on the principle of "fair and balanced reporting" by providing two opposing perspectives on an issue, Hollywood directors draw from stories typically focusing on one point of view within filmic codes of realism. While a number of other movie genres about whites and people of color existed during this time period, such as historical dramas, the black–white buddy formula, and romances, the narrative of white transformation served a particular function in this historical moment that other films did not (see Appendix B). By underscoring racial progress, it redeemed white Americans from past "racial sins."

My use of the word "sin" is intentional. Historically, American stories of re-demption are predicated on Puritan spiritual autobiographies wherein authors describe moving from a state of sin to a state of grace by accepting the word of God. To give one well-known instance, in the original song "Amazing Grace," the line, "Was blind, but now I see" refers to the religious conversion of John Newton, an eighteenth-century white sailor involved in the slave trade who, in coming to accept God's grace, understood his "wretchedness" in participat-ing in the horrific trafficking of African people and found forgiveness.[9] As literary scholar Ann duCille argues, in the 1980s and 1990s in a more secular context, white feminists drew from a similar kind of narrative, in what duCille terms, "I was blind once, but now I see—you." Here, white women confess past racist beliefs and proffer new, transformed selves as unencumbered by racism. As duCille and other feminist scholars have argued, these declarations of "un-derstanding, and empathy" among white women often work paradoxically by recapitulating the very patterns they sought to replace. In other words, their as-sertions of personal transformation "foster the continued production of scripts in which white remains the center, the defining core, in opposition to the other, which remains at the margins."[10]

My central argument in this chapter is that stories of white redemption in Hollywood films served a similar purpose in the late 1980s and throughout the 1990s. In telling stories about race relations, these movies remain fixed on white, elite, and predominantly male experiences and understandings. People of color became background figures, though their relationship to the white central character often served to support and "anoint" the protagonist as a sav-ior; and working-class whites were demonized as the "true" racists. In addition, these films became a much repeated genre at precisely the moment that poli-cies designed to ameliorate racial discrimination in California and other states were being dismantled, and stories of white male innocence and injury were circulating in the news media. I read these films in light of these historical events as well as in the context of the dominant news media discourse dis-cussed in the previous chapter.

As I show, at the same time that the news media proffered accounts of white men who unfairly lost promotions and jobs to African Americans, Hollywood films told stories about elite white men who underwent a transformation from racial innocence to racial understanding and became advocates who fought for racial justice. In doing so, these benevolent white men typically "saved" people of color from the ignorant violence of white, working-class vigilantes. Through this process, normative whiteness was imagined as Northern, cosmopolitan, liberal, and anti-racist, while aberrant whiteness was imagined as Southern, poor, violent, and at times sexually dysfunctional.

Cinematic Narratives of Racial Progress and the "Anti-Racist White Hero"

Unlike the 1976 film *Rocky* discussed in Chapter 1 that epitomized the trope of white male innocence and injury, 1980s and '90s mainstream Hollywood films revolved around a white hero who underwent a transformation in consciousness from innocence of racism to racial understanding. This theme appeared not only in *A Time to Kill* (1996), but also in *Mississippi Burning* (1988), where Gene Hackman and Willem Dafoe played FBI agents investigating the murders of civil rights workers; and in *Ghosts of Mississippi* (1996), where Alec Baldwin played an attorney retrying the white supremacist murder suspect in the Medgar Evers case. It also surfaced in *Amistad* (1997), where McConaughey again played a lawyer, this time defending the Africans who revolted on a Spanish ship illegally engaged in the transportation of slaves; in the historical drama *Dances with Wolves*, where Kevin Costner played a military officer adopted by a Native American tribe; and in yet another historical drama, *The Long Walk Home* (1990), where Sissy Spacek portrayed a white middle-class housewife during the Birmingham, Alabama, bus boycott in the 1950s. In these movies, the triumphal narrative of racial progress suggested that white Americans could overcome their blindness to racism and become not only allies to people of color, but even heroic leaders in movements for racial justice.

Communications scholar Kelly Madson describes this genre of film "the anti-racist white hero." In her argument, the civil rights movement created a crisis of identity for whites by redefining the image of the black self for white America. African Americans asserted themselves as a positive and powerful force against racial oppression and publicly voiced the fact that that discrimination was rooted in a continuing history of white supremacy. This, Madson suggests, led to a need among white America to redefine itself in order to maintain the notion of whiteness as good, civilized, and just. In her view, the emergence of the beneficent white hero, savior of racial minorities in America, worked to create a new cultural memory in which whites became the heroes of the civil rights movement and leaders in the historic fight for racial justice.[11]

While Madson's argument about the "legitimation crisis" that the civil rights movement posed for white America is a compelling one, the beneficent white hero did not emerge in post-civil-rights American popular culture.

The film *To Kill a Mockingbird*, in which small-town Southern lawyer, Atticus Finch, defended a black man wrongly accused of rape, illustrated that the project began at least as early as the 1960s.[12] *To Kill a Mockingbird* and the book upon which it was based were immediately and immensely successful. Harper Lee's book won instant acclaim with the Pulitzer Prize, and the movie released in 1962, only two years after publication of the book, received eight Academy Award nominations and three Oscars.[13]

Written and produced in early 1960s, in the midst of the civil rights movement, the popularity of *To Kill a Mockingbird* suggests that the role of an antiracist white hero was ripe for the American imagination much earlier than Madson proposes. As sociologist Wendy Leo Moore and I argue, this movie set up a new genre for films about race, one which outlasted the civil rights movement and continued in the late 1980s and the 1990s.[14] While there is no question that many of these post-civil-rights films have a "feel good," even recuperative element for whiteness as Madson suggests, here I complicate her reading of these films by locating them within the historical context of the backlash against affirmative action and, more specifically, within the dominant print news media trope of white male innocence and injury. As I argue, the narrative of white racial progress not only registers with the media's dominant trope about white male innocence and injury by focusing films about race on white Americans, but also adds several new and important elements to it. Specifically, though white innocence is also a theme, these films suggest that *elite* white men lose their innocence of racism and become advocates for people of color. Further, like the white men in the news media who are "injured" by affirmative action, these men too experience injury. In the film genre, however, the violence committed against them comes from white working-class men who are depicted as the "real" racists.

My argument is based on research that Moore and I conducted on Hollywood films focusing on race or racial inequality that were produced between 1987 and 1999. (See Appendix B for the complete list of movies in our sample.) Of the sixty films addressing these topics, we identified twenty-five percent as falling into the category of white racial progress. In chronological order, they include: *Cry Freedom* (1987), *Mississippi Burning* (1988), *Stand and Deliver* (1988), *Dry White Season* (1989), *Glory* (1989), *The Long Walk Home* (1990), *Dances with Wolves* (1990), *Thunderheart* (1993), *Dangerous Minds* (1995), *Losing Isaiah* (1995), *A Walk in the Clouds* (1995), *Ghosts of Mississippi* (1996), *A Time to Kill* (1996), *Amistad* (1997), *American History X* (1998), and *Bullworth* (1998).

Most of the films in this genre were told from the perspective of the white male hero in a position of professional influence who was initially presented as innocent of racism.[15] In contrast to the media trope that depicted white men of various class backgrounds as innocent victims of affirmative action, these films represented white men (or in a few cases white women and people of color) in middle- to upper-middle-class occupations as innocent. In *Ghosts of Mississippi, A Time to Kill, Amistad,* and *Dry White Season,* the white hero was a lawyer; while in *Mississippi Burning, Thunderheart, Dances with Wolves, Glory,* and *Dangerous Minds,* the focus, respectively, was on high-profile FBI agents, military officers, and a high school teacher. Significantly, innocence took on a slightly different meaning in these filmic representations than in the dominant print news media trope. These white men were not innocent victims who had never done anything racist; instead they were often unaware of or uncritical of racism. For example, in *Mississippi Burning, Ghosts of Mississippi,* and *A Time to Kill,* the protagonists believed racism was no longer a problem, while in *Dances with Wolves* and *American History X,* the main characters initially accepted racism as normative.

The second twist on the print media narrative that these movies offered has to do with white injury. Whereas the media narrative depicted white men as injured by affirmative action, in the majority of these films white men experienced harm at the hands of white working-class racists.[16] The implication here is that the real racist villains in American culture were not white people in general, but a more restricted and less educated subset. For example, in *A Time to Kill, Mississippi Burning, Ghosts of Mississippi,* and *American History X,* racism was attributed to working-class white men. Moreover, racism in these films was represented by extreme forms of violence—bomb threats, house burnings, beatings, torture, and even murder. On the surface, then, in most of these movies, it wasn't affirmative action that hurt or thwarted elite white men, but white working-class vigilantes.

In a final twist on the media narrative, the white hero "saved" the person of color through his relentless work in normative systems of justice. In this way, elite whites who were once blind to racism, over time became relentless advocates of racial justice through a system that was portrayed as fundamentally fair. We see this narrative of racial progress through the characters played by Matthew McConaughey in *A Time to Kill,* Alec Baldwin in *Ghosts of Mississippi,* Gene Hackman and Willem Dafoe in *Mississippi Burning,* Matthew McConaughey (again) in *Amistad,* Kevin Costner in *Dances with Wolves,* Sissy Spacek in *The Long Walk Home,* and Michelle Pfeiffer in *Dangerous Minds.* Significantly, the success of these heroes and heroines also differed from Atticus Finch, the lawyer in *To Kill a Mockingbird*, who despite his valiant efforts lost the case for Tom Robinson, the black defendant who was wrongly accused of rape. While the conclusion of the legal case for Tom Robinson could be interpreted as an indictment of institutionalized structures of racism in the Depression-era Southern legal system, in these newer films, produced in our post-civil-rights era, the legal system was portrayed as just and fair.

In what follows, I provide a close reading of two films that best exemplify the broader genre: director Rob Reiner's *Ghosts of Mississippi* and Joel Schumacher's *A Time to Kill*. Both movies were directed by acclaimed Hollywood directors and both focus on white attorneys. This lawyer-driven narrative is important for several reasons. As discussed in the Introduction, attorneys as professional elites have considerable power and influence in the United States. Unlike the central characters in other white racial progress films, these cinematic lawyers had a different kind of authority; they were arbiters of the law, justice, and morality.[17] As such, they served as "civilizing" figures who worked to bring order to social upheaval through the law. In addition, both movies were produced in 1996—a significant historical moment, given that it was the same year that affirmative action was abolished in California. What these films shared with this particular moment in the "Golden State" was an understanding that racial progress had been achieved. California voters endorsed the principle of colorblindness by voting against affirmative action, and these filmic representations suggested that racial progress among white Americans was a *fait accompli*. Although neither film was as widely acclaimed as *To Kill a Mockingbird*, they served as important forms of cultural memory in highlighting the ways the white anti-racist-hero genre continued in the 1990s. In its more recent incarnation, however, the storyline differs in important ways from the plot of the 1962 film, which I discuss later in the chapter.

In *Ghosts of Mississippi*, the central focus is on a white lawyer who retries the murder case of a black civil rights advocate who was murdered by a white man. The film is based on an actual events—the murder case of civil rights leader Medgar Evers. The movie begins with a rousing montage of scenes from the civil rights movement in the 1960s set to protest music of the era. Scenes of African American protestors being beaten by white police, of black soldiers fighting in Vietnam, and black athletes winning major competitions are shown along with photos of Martin Luther King, Jr. and Malcolm X. African American women picking cotton are juxtaposed with photos of crosses burning in front of homes. A printed legend on the screen reads, "Mississippi Delta in 1963." Then it reads, "This story is true."

Following this montage of African American history, the first action scene depicts a white man shooting and killing Medgar Evers in the driveway of his home. As the murder unfolds, we hear John F. Kennedy's civil rights speech in the background. In the next scene, Byron De La Beckwith, the white man who shot Evers (played by James Woods), enters the courthouse as white law officials approach him and shake his hand. While Evers' wife Myrlie (played by Whoopi Goldberg) testifies on the witness stand, the former governor of Mississippi walks up to Beckwith in front of the entire courtroom and jury. After two hung juries, Beckwith is released, and when he leaves the courthouse, he is greeted by a street full of whites, cheering his release. Juxtaposed against this scene, Myrlie Evers is on her knees trying to scrub the blood off of the carport cement outside her home where her husband was shot. These scenes work not only to set up the legal challenge for the rest of the film, but also to evoke sympathy for Myrlie Evers, who is compelled to live with this grotesque injustice.

The film then jumps forward to 1989 when Bobby DeLaughter (played by Alec Baldwin), a white prosecutor for the district attorney's office, is introduced when his boss asks him to check the files on the Medgar Evers case. Initially, DeLaughter resists, pointing out that the case is nearly twenty-five years old. His boss replies, "Sure it is, but if we try to bury this, Myrlie Evers is gonna' have every black politician in Jackson climbing all over me." While DeLaughter's initial resistance appears reasonable, Evers, by contrast, is represented as a political operator fixated on racism of the past. At the same time, African American politicians are depicted as a group with "special rights" giving them more power than whites, a theme that resonates with print news media stories about blacks as advantaged through affirmative action. To appease Evers, DeLaughter looks into the murder case file and in the process of doing so uncovers evidence of corruption from the first trial. He is angered by the blatant racism he finds, a shift suggesting an earlier innocence of racism. His gradual transformation begins when he decides to reopen the case and reprosecute Beckwith for the murder of Medgar Evers. Soon thereafter, he begins to pay the price for his decision. His in-laws express embarrassment that he has taken this case; his wife, who is unhappy with his decision, leaves him; and his house becomes the target of hate crimes. Like Atticus Finch in *To Kill a Mockingbird*, DeLaughter and his family experience injury at the hands of other whites. His van is vandalized, his son gets in a fight with a boy who calls his father a "nigger lover," and he receives a number of threatening phone calls including a bomb threat to his home. Unlike Atticus Finch, however, who anticipates the consequences of taking on an unpopular case, DeLaughter is surprised and confused by these events. He is still a racial innocent.

Near the conclusion of the film, the press learns that through DeLaughter's dogged investigative work, he has found the old murder weapon. They publish a story about it, and Evers is furious with DeLaughter because she was not informed. In the next scene, two African American men stand at a podium at a press conference. One of them says, ". . . as far as I'm concerned, they're [Bobby DeLaughter and his boss] nothin' but a pair of lying racists who never, I repeat never, had any intention of prosecuting the case." Like the comments about Evers' efforts to reopen the case, this representation of black community leaders invokes stereotypical images of African Americans as quick to exert pressure by playing the "race card." The next day, DeLaughter's boss takes him off the case, and replaces him with an African American prosecutor. This scene is presented as deeply painful and grossly unfair to DeLaughter: a portrayal that resonates with the news media trope of the innocent white person who is being unfairly harmed by affirmative action.

The night after his boss takes him off the case, DeLaughter calls Evers, telling her that he is fully committed to the case and asks that she make a commitment in return by telling his boss to put him back on the case. The next day Evers shows up at the district attorney's office and gives DeLaughter the transcript to the original trial—noting that she has kept it for many years and tells him he will not find any more opposition to his handling of the case. De-Laughter says, "Thank you, ma'am, it's truly appreciated." Evers replies, "Let's get the son of a bitch." Evers' pronouncement not only works to "anoint" DeLaughter as a savior for racial justice, but also completes his transformation from racial innocent to anti-racist white hero. He moves forward to win the case with the full trust and support of Evers. Justice prevails through the legal system, and DeLaughter is redeemed as a good white person. Significantly, un-like Atticus Finch who loses his case, in this post-civil-rights moment, victory is possible through a fair and judicious legal system.

By contrast, director Joel Schumacher's motion picture adaptation of John Grisham's novel, *A Time to Kill*, stands apart from other Hollywood narratives of white racial progress in this era in that it does not return to some horrific moment in the past, as do films such as *Ghosts of Mississippi, Mississippi Burning, Amistad, Dances with Wolves*, and *Glory*. Instead, the central character and the ethical dilemmas he confronts play out in Mississippi in the 1990s. The movie opens with a dramatic setup for the legal challenge for the film's anti-racist white lawyer hero: Foreboding music plays as two white working-class men

in a pickup truck with a confederate flag ride around yelling loudly and making dirt fly off the road. This scene is juxtaposed with one of a young African
America girl, ten-year-old Tonya, buying groceries at a small store. After Tonya
leaves the store, one of the white men driving by in the truck throws a can of
beer at her head, hitting her. In the next scene, Tonya is displayed screaming
with her arms and legs tied up and spread as she dangles just above the ground.
The audience sees the face of one of the white men laughing and blood is
shown on the ground beneath her feet. She has been brutally beaten and raped.
As in *Ghosts of Mississippi*, extreme violence against African Americans is deployed to evoke audience sympathy with the victim—this time a sexually innocent young girl. Audience identification and empathy are heightened in the
next scene, when her father, Carl Lee Hailey (played by Samuel Jackson) comes
home from work and sits on the couch beside Tonya, whose face is badly swol-
len and bloody, and she says, "Daddy, I'm sorry I dropped the groceries." Here,
Tonya's innocent victimhood is not only reinforced, but also the close-up of
Hailey's face lined with misery invites viewers to identify with his position as
a father who has been compelled to witness the consequences of this horrific
violence.

The two white men who later brag in a bar about the rape and beating are
arrested, and in the next scene Hailey meets with Jake Brigance, a white lawyer (played by Matthew McConaughey). Hailey asks Brigance what sentence
the men who raped his daughter are likely to get. Brigance responds with
uncertainty, but acknowledges that in a nearby town a white man who raped
a black girl managed to evade the charge. Hailey asks, "If I was in a jam, you'd
help me?" Brigance agrees that he would. The next day when the two white
men are scheduled to attend their arraignment in court, Hailey shoots and
kills them. He is arrested, charged with the murder, and requests that Brigance
represent him.

From this point, the central focus of movie is the growth of Brigance from
racial innocent to anti-racist white hero. We learn little of Hailey's perspective
and nothing of the ten-year-old Tonya. Because Brigance agrees to take the
case, a newly constructed branch of the Ku Klux Klan begins a spree of hate
crimes against his home and his co-workers. A cross is burned on the lawn in
front of his home, and his daughter, Hannah, is called a "nigger lover" at school.
When his wife tells him of these incidents, Brigance, like Bobby DeLaughter
in *Ghosts of Mississippi*, is stunned and confused. Fearing for their safety, his wife
decides to leave town with their daughter in tow, a move that clearly places
their marriage is in jeopardy. When Brigance's legal secretary tells him that she

has been receiving phone threats, he responds with concern and confusion, "Why didn't you tell me?" She responds indignantly, "Why? Would you have dropped the case?" Here, like DeLaughter in *Ghosts of Mississippi*, Brigance is initially represented as a racial innocent.

As the story moves forward, Klan violence escalates. First, they beat his secretary's husband, while holding her down and forcing her to watch, and he dies later of a heart attack. After the funeral, Brigance tells her he is sorry, that he never wanted any of this to happen. She responds, "I know you didn't want any of this to happen, but it happened all the same. You wagered all our lives on this, you just went ahead and did what you thought was best, regardless of the cost. Some folks think that's brave. Not me, Jake. Now, you may win, but I think we've all lost here." Next, the Klan burns Brigance's home to the ground, and another lawyer and friend tells him, "Your marriage is on the rocks . . . Your career is ruined, if you're lucky, and if you're not, you're dead. Do everyone a favor, though. Drop the case." Brigance ignores the advice, sitting forlornly in the rubble of his house, calling for his dog.

Despite his suffering at the hands of the vigilante white supremacists, Brigance moves forward with the case. Like DeLaughter in *Ghosts of Mississippi*, the next obstacle he encounters comes not from the Klan, but from crooked black political and religious leaders. Hailey's minister tells him that he should hire an NAACP-sponsored lawyer who is sensitive to "the needs of the movement." The organizers ostensibly raise funds for Hailey's case and for his family, but actually use it to line their coffers and those of Hailey's minister. Like Myrlie Evers in *Ghosts of Mississippi*, Hailey ultimately refuses their offers of help, condemns their politics, and chooses Brigance to represent him. Here again, African American political organizations are indicted as crooked and politically opportunistic and a white individual is chosen to wage the battle alone. This theme not only resonates with the news media's portrayal of black advantage, but also reinforces neoliberal assumptions about the ineffectiveness of collective action and federal bureaucracy and the importance of individual responsibility.

As Brigance continues to work on Hailey's case while his wife and daughter are out of town, a star law student from a nearby university (played by Sandra Bullock) appears in Clanton and offers her assistance on the case. Brigance is initially reluctant to accept but finally agrees. Though a romantic attraction develops between the two, Brigance, as the virtuous married hero, ultimately resists. In the meantime, the law student's relentless work on the case comes to the attention of the Klan and they kidnap and beat her, strip her down to her camisole and panties, and tie her to a pole where she is displayed during a nighttime Klan meeting with white hooded figures carrying brightly burning torches. She is later freed by one of the Klan members and ends up in the hospital where Brigance comes to visit her. At this point, he feels demoralized and wonders, after all the violence, whether the case is really worth it. She encourages him to continue.

Later, Brigance's wife comes back with their daughter and apologizes for leaving, telling him now she now understands he took to case because she knows that if the men had hurt their daughter, he too would have murdered them. After their reunion and the night before Jake is scheduled to make his closing statement in court, he goes to see Hailey in jail to tell him that the trial is going badly and he fears that they will lose. Hailey counters by saying, "I picked you because you think like them. You one of them. Don't you see?" Brigance protests that he is not "one of them," arguing that the two of them are friends. Hailey says, "We ain't no friends. America is a war, and you on the other side. How a black man ever going to get a fair trial? You, you one of the bad guys. You see me as different. You see me as the jury sees me. If you was on the jury, what would it take to convince you to set me free?" In this dramatic scene, Hailey shatters the last remnants of Brigance's innocence. Further, Hailey's rationale for choosing a white attorney to "save" him resonates with Myrlie Evers's decision to reappoint Bobby DeLaughter. Brigance has been appointed by Hailey to become the white savior.

In the end and despite the incredible odds, Brigance wins Hailey's case. However, it is not through the solid legal investigative work that DeLaughter conducts in *Ghosts of Mississippi*, but through an emotional appeal to the jury. At the end of his closing statement, Brigance asks the jury members to close their eyes as he provides all the graphic details of Tonya's brutal rape. When he has finished his dramatic soliloquy, he pauses for emphasis and says, "Now imagine she was white." Jury members' eyes flutter open in confusion, some with tears streaming down their cheeks. Presumably, by asking the jury members to invert the racial circumstances of the case, Brigance is able to win a positive judgment for Hailey. The dramatic conclusion redeems Brigance as an anti-racist white hero who valiantly pursued justice.

Movie reviews in 1996 were lukewarm at best for *Ghosts of Mississippi* and a bit more enthusiastic for *A Time to Kill*; and given the timing of their respective releases, some critics compared the two. Janet Maslin, reviewer for *The New York Times*, for instance, says of *Ghosts of Mississippi*: "This film runs so true to the Hollywood view of Southern white racism that its hero's wife is the fading blonde belle who won't stay with her man when the going gets tough." She adds, its "most jaw-dropping line" comes from Myrlie Evers when she tells Bobby DeLaughter, "You remind me of Edgar," a reference to his intrepid work in reopening the case. Although the real-life Myrlie Evers was a consultant on the film, Maslin observes, "the movie's stolid hero is not seen as rivaling her husband's accomplishments."[18] In another review, Christ Hewitt begins his piece by asking: "Would somebody please shoot me if I have to sit through one more Hollywood movie in which the important story of a black character is told through the eyes of a boring white guy?" He goes on to say that in the "time-dishonored tradition of *A Time to Kill, Cry Freedom,* and *Glory* (which was, at least, good), the wretched *Ghosts of Mississippi* is the story of Medgar Evers, who helped integrate Mississippi schools . . . Not that you'd know that from the movie, because Evers dies in the opening scene without having uttered a single line of dialogue. In effect, he's been cut out of his own story." Hewitt concludes his review with the pronouncement: "[I]f the road to movie hell is paved with good intentions, *Ghosts of Mississippi* is the gutter on that road."[19]

As noted in the Introduction, *A Time to Kill* fared somewhat better among critics, though it received mixed reviews. Despite these reviews and as mentioned earlier, *A Time to Kill* was a huge box office success. By comparison, *Ghosts of Mississippi* was not nearly as successful, grossing $13.0 million. Nonetheless, together with *American History X* ($6.7 million), *Amistad* ($44.0 million), *Cry Freedom* ($5.8 million), *Dances with Wolves* ($184.0 million), *Bullworth* ($26.0 million), *Dangerous Minds* ($5.0 million), *A Dry White Season* ($3.7 million), *Glory* ($26.0 million), *The Long Walk Home* ($4.8 million), *Losing Isaiah* ($7.6 million), *Mississippi Burning* ($34.0 million), *Stand and Deliver* ($13.9 million), *Thunderheart* ($4.5 million), and *A Walk in the Clouds* ($50.0 million), these mainstream Hollywood films commanded a sizeable viewing audience as suggested by their combined total of over $400 million in box office receipts.[20] What were the political and aesthetic ingredients that made these films so appealing? And, how did they measure up to their 1962 predecessor, *To Kill a Mockingbird*?

In many ways the portrayal of white involvement in struggles for racial justice in *A Time to Kill* and *Ghosts of Mississippi* was a hopeful and progressive one. It suggested that through hard work white Americans could overcome their racial prejudices, and become political allies—and even friends with and advocates for—people of color. In this modernist narrative of progress, reasoned reflection of irrational feelings such as prejudice could bring about interracial understanding and empathy. If these two mainstream films had been the only ones with this plot formula, and all the other movies on racial themes had focused on contemporary discrimination in the United States from the perspective of characters of color, they might be read as optimistic moments in Hollywood cinema. However, there were actually very few movies on contemporary racial discrimination during this time period. Those that took up the issue of race were disproportionately likely to reiterate progressive narratives of white racial transformation (see Appendix B).

My point here is the fact that the storyline of white racial progress, and not one focusing on contemporary forms of racial discrimination, becoming a predominant genre has significant political implications for Americans' cultural memory of race relations in the late 1980s and the 1990s. As discussed in the opening to this chapter, the repeated emphasis on individual stories of white racial progress reproduced a normative framework whereby white experiences of race remained at the center and people of color's stories were marginalized. In doing so, these films neglected the history of people of color as central agents for social change in the civil rights movement and other struggles for racial justice. Indeed, in *Ghosts of Mississippi* and *A Time to Kill*, African American civil rights organizations such as the NAACP were indicted as politically opportunistic, even corrupt. At the same time that organized collectivities such as the NAACP were portrayed as bad, the lone individual was celebrated as selfless, noble, and good. As discussed earlier, this is a neoliberal iteration of anti-racism. Statist, bureaucratic interest groups like the NAACP were cast as bad, while anti-racism was redeemed through the actions of individual, self-determining anti-racists. Furthermore, within this genre of mainstream Hollywood film, people of color as central heroic characters were seldom represented, while the white experience and interpretation of racial struggles was repeated time and again.[21] In their portrayal of elite white men as saviors, such films depicted people of color as passive or ineffectual victims: a portrait that reinforced white paternalism and erased black struggles for justice.

At the same time, however, though African Americans were often treated as background characters in this genre of film, their presence and ultimate selection of white men to "save" them was necessary to the protagonist's ultimate redemption.[22] For example, in the jail scene in *A Time to Kill*, Hailey made it clear that he had chosen Brigance precisely because he was white and not African American. In a similar vein, following the political grandstanding of black politicians about Bobby DeLaughter's discovery of the murder weapon, Myrlie Evers too ultimately selected him to continue work on that case. Strikingly, then, it was a black character's "anointment" of a white hero that moved the narrative forward, leading to the lawyer's transformation as an anti-racist savior. The structure of the relationship between white and black characters in these movies paralleled that of German philosopher Georg Hegel's discussion of the master and the slave.[23] For Hegel, the master denied and negated the slave's subjectivity in his quest for self-assertion, even as he needed the slave to recognize him as the master. This paradox of recognition and domination—the master desires recognition from the very other he negates—was central to the relationship between anti-racist white heroes and the African American characters they "saved." They were redeemed, not through God as the song "Amazing Grace" suggests, but rather through their anointment as "saviors" by black subordinates.

In addition, these films also differentiated elite white men from "bad" white people as the narrative of racism was framed around explicit racial violence. In A *Time to Kill*, as in *Mississippi Burning, Ghosts of Mississippi*, and *American History X*, vigilante violence committed by working-class white supremacists emerged as the central problem facing black Americans—a trope echoing the focus of social science and historical studies of racism where working-class whites were often vilified, while white elites were rarely studied.[24] This not only promoted popular stereotypes about working-class whites as racist in the late 1980s and the 1990s, but also erased more common, subtle forms of racism and discrimination in jobs, housing, and education that people of color were experiencing in the United States at the time. Furthermore, the focus on the white savior repeated a theme common to many Hollywood movies; collective endeavors, such as the civil rights movement, were transformed into the battle of a lone individual who triumphed against evil, in this case, racism.[25]

The focus on the main character's transformation from innocence to consciousness about racism also suggested that white Americans could not only come to understand racial discrimination, but also would work against all odds to dismantle it. By contrast, surveys conducted by sociologists and political scientists in this time period found that the majority of white Americans believed that people of color and, more specifically, African Americans, no longer experienced discrimination.[26] Furthermore, as noted in the Introduction, most white Americans still live in racially segregated neighborhoods, marry people of their own racial and ethnic group, work in racially segregated occupations, and when given the opportunity, will hire other whites rather than African Americans or Latinos.[27] In this way, the films provide a convenient fiction glossing over the actual beliefs and practices of most white Americans.

At the same time, by emphasizing the victimhood of white men who tirelessly worked to combat racial injustice, these films played into and reinforced the news media trope of the innocent white male. In *A Time to Kill*, Jake Brigance's house was burned down, the law student who worked for him was beaten by Klan members, and his secretary's husband was also beaten and later died at the hands of Klan. In *Ghosts of Mississippi*, Bobby DeLaughter received threatening phone calls, his vehicle was vandalized, and his family turned their backs on him. Within the historical and discursive context of the backlash against affirmative action, the signifier of white victimhood referenced the innocent white male who had been unfairly discriminated against by affirmative action. Given this context, the focus on white victimhood silently suggested that affirmative action was a form of "reverse discrimination."

In addition, the African Americans victims whom these valiant white heroes rescued in the films shared an important feature, one that became more significant given the historical moment in which they were produced: The victims were all portrayed as "deserving" or "worthy" of being saved. In *Ghosts of Mississippi*, the victim was Medgar Evers, the black civil rights activist who was gunned down in his own driveway; in *A Time to Kill*, it was Tonya, an African American, sexually innocent ten-year-old girl, who was raped, beaten, and left for dead; in *Mississippi Burning* it was civil rights workers who were violently killed by the Klan; and in *Amistad*, it was the Africans who had been unjustly captured to be sold into slavery. In each case, extreme violence worked not only to capture the attention and sympathy of viewing audiences, but also to justify the "civilizing" work the white anti-racist hero must do to bring about racial justice. Significantly, these cinematic representations resonated with the historical memory of African Americans in the civil rights movement in the 1950s and 1960s as individuals who were deserving of redress and compensation for unjust treatment. The most obvious example was the civil rights workers in *Mississippi Burning*, which was loosely based on historical events. But, they recalled other historical images as well—the four black girls fire-hosed through police chief Bull Connor's orders in Alabama, the nine African American high school students who attended Little Rock High in the face of mob violence in Arkansas in 1958, and Rosa Parks, who was unjustly refused a seat at the front of the bus.[28]

Strikingly, at the very moment that these particular filmic representations of black victims were created, the print news media was filled with messages about "undeserving" racial or ethnic minorities. In the case of affirmative action, it was "unqualified" people of color who unfairly gained from the policy and took jobs away from more "deserving" white men. In debates about welfare reform, it was African American "welfare queens" who took advantage of federal assistance while white working-class Americans struggled to make ends meet. In debates about immigration reform, it was migrants of color who were depicted as exploiting America's largesse.[29] Reading the cinematic representations against this broader neoconservative discourse suggests that some racial or ethnic minorities were considered "worthy" of white protection, specifically those who experienced brutal forms of violence, while others, such as poor, single mothers of color or other racial or ethnic minorities who faced discrimination in the labor market, were not.[30]

Finally, by focusing on the white savior's heroic and individual efforts to combat racism, these films also celebrated and reinforced the ideology of liberal individualism. This point ties in with the ways that the news media trope individualized history in its accounts of racism. Recall the anti-affirmative-action letter-to-the-editor writer in the last chapter, who claimed he was not responsible for slavery because he had never owned a slave. In such an individualized notion of history and of fairness, institutionalized racism goes unrecognized. As sociologist Troy Duster has argued, within this framework fairness is "decontextualized."

> Indeed, since there are only individuals and individual responsibility and individual entitlements are the only currency in the contemporary discourse about race policies and affirmative action policies, not having had a personal hand in the oppression of others *makes one innocent*. The mere fact that one's group has accumulated wealth 10 times that of another group is rendered irrelevant by the legerdemain of invoking individual fairness [emphasis added].[31]

By taking race relations out of context, ignoring structural inequality and the reproduction of white wealth across generations, and focusing on lone white men, these films underscored the triumph of the individual. Such a discursive move not only obscured the institutional exercise of power that funneled rewards, resources, and opportunities to white Americans, but also implicitly suggested that federal programs and policies, such as affirmative action, that aimed to dismantle structural inequality were unnecessary. In this way, the white racial progress genre in film and dominant media narratives on white innocence and injury shared similar political goals; both operated as assaults on systematic analyses of institutionalized racism.

The anti-racist white lawyer hero in the 1962 film *To Kill a Mockingbird* provided an interesting, historically significant contrast. Unlike our post-civil-rights anti-racist heroes, Atticus Finch did not prevail. Not only did he lose the case and Tom Robinson was unfairly sentenced to time in prison for a crime he did not commit, but also Robinson was killed when he tries to escape. Finch's failure can be read as a critique of a racist system of justice, especially when compared to more recent post-civil-rights films. Importantly, *To Kill a Mockingbird* was produced in the midst of the civil rights movement when dominant narratives about racial inequality were shifting and changing. Though the movement was launched in the 1950s, 1963—only one year after the film was released—is often considered its major turning point in gaining national and federal attention. At the time, the Reverend Martin Luther King, Jr. and the Southern Leadership Conference launched nonviolent demonstrations in Birmingham, Alabama, against segregation in public facilities that reverberated in protests in nearly 200 cities across the South. With television cameras from all the major networks rolling, police chief Bull Connor ordered the police to charge the peaceful protesters. Brutal scenes with German shepherds snapping at demonstrators, police with nightsticks swinging at crowds, and high-pressure fire hoses blasting protestors were captured on national television and displayed prominently on the front pages of newspaper across the country. These events finally pushed Congress to pass the Civil Rights Act of 1964.[32]

During this tumultuous period, argues political scientist Richard Pride, notions of black biological inferiority were being supplanted by narratives highlighting the historical and contemporary effects of white discrimination against African Americans.[33] Although such arguments originated with civil rights activists, Pride suggests that white liberals also drew upon these stories to explain racial inequality. In this light, white attorney hero Atticus Finch's understanding of racism reflected this broader conceptualization of history. Finch began with an awareness of institutional white racism. Further, his failure to save Tom Robinson resonated with this broader public narrative. But despite his goodness, his hard work, and his commitment to justice through the legal system, as a lone individual Finch could not change these broader structural problems.

While *To Kill a Mockingbird* offers a more serious critique of racism than white racial progress films do, the fact that the story is set in the deep South during the Depression era carries with it another set of problems. As some scholars have observed, the use of this particular setting in Hollywood movies suggests that racism is unique to the southern region of the United States.[34] In their argument, the American South is often depicted as an "uncivilized" and "backward" space that stands apart from the rest of the nation. In addition, because this film is set in the 1930s, it gives the impression that racism is something that took place long ago. Strikingly, not only are a number of films in the white racial progress genre historical dramas set in the South (e.g., *Glory, Ghosts of Mississippi, A Time to Kill, Mississippi Burning*, and *The Long Walk Home*), but also many other films with racial themes in the late 1980s and throughout the 1990s focus on historical figures and events, such as *Driving Miss Daisy, Rosewood, Malcolm X, American Me, Panther*, and *The Hurricane* (see Appendix B.) While some of these films, particularly *Rosewood*, a dramatization of the 1923 lynch mob attack on an African American community, are thoughtful and provocative, they work to create a cultural memory that lodges racism firmly in a distant and hazy past.[35]

Conclusion

In this chapter, I have argued that a genre of mainstream Hollywood films emphasizing white racial progress emerged in the late 1980s and continued throughout 1990s at the same historical moment that affirmative action came under attack by neoconservative groups and neoliberal policy makers in the United States. Such films were likely to revolve around a storyline where a white protagonist recognizes, in the words of literary scholar Anne duCille, that "I was blind once, but now I see—you." This formula simultaneously places white experiences and understandings of race relations at the center and people of color in the background, though their relationship to the white central character often functions to "anoint" the protagonist as a savior.

These films also became a much repeated genre at precisely the moment that stories of white male innocence and injury were circulating in the news media. What they shared both with the dominant news media trope and with the majority of California voters in 1996 is an understanding that the ideal of "colorblindness" had been achieved and that policies such as affirmative action were no longer necessary. Moreover, just as print news media accounts worked to reinvigorate neoliberal and neoconservative assumptions about "choice" and "free markets" as good for society as well as to promote moralistic understandings of who is most "worthy" of federal assistance, films in the white racial progress genre hyped Horatio Alger-like assumptions about heroic white men who struggled valiantly and ultimately triumphed over racism. Meanwhile, such films operated on the assumption that some people of color (i.e., young girls who were brutally beaten and raped) were more worthy of "saving" than others (i.e., those who faced discrimination in the job market).

These films reinforced notions that black politicians and political organizations, such as the NAACP, were corrupt—an image that resonated with the media trope of black unworthiness—while simultaneously demonizing white

working-class men and absolving white elites of racism. Put another way, particularly in films with lawyer-driven narratives, white elites became "civilizing"
figures that brought order to the chaos created by white working-class racists,
on one hand, and corrupt African American politicians, on the other. In the
late 1980s and throughout the 1990s, these twin cinematic themes resonated
with and reinforced news media representations of angry white working-class
men and of zealous black leaders who were quick to "play the race card." Such
a narrative both discredited African American politicians and white working-
class men and absolved white elites from accountability for their own racism.
By placing the focus on others who stirred up "racial trouble," elite white men
were "innocent"—a theme I return to in the next chapter on male lawyers
and in my short story, "Small Talk," in Chapter 5. As I argue, in "racing for innocence," the white male attorneys I interviewed, as well as my white fictional
characters, deny accountability for racism at the same that they enact racially
exclusionary practices.

Finally, as I have demonstrated, the story of an anti-racist elite white hero is
not a new one; it began as least as early as the widely acclaimed film, *To Kill a
Mockingbird*. Despite some similarities with the 1962 storyline, specifically the
emphasis on a white male hero who attempts to save a black victim, this newer
genre differed in significant ways from the 1962 film. Unlike Atticus Finch, the
white hero of *To Kill a Mockingbird* who understood the pernicious effects of
racism, these post-civil-rights white anti-racist characters began their stories in
racial innocence. Either they were unaware of racism or, in some cases, accepted
it as a normative system of racial inequality. Over the course of the narrative,
they moved from innocence of racial injustice to racial understanding, and in
the end became white saviors who, through their relentless determination and
hard work for people of color, prevailed in normative systems of justice.

These cinematic heroes' recognition and struggle against racism was not
only different from white men depicted in the news media who worked
against "race-based preferences" that unfairly disadvantaged them, but also suggested a more progressive and hopeful vision about white racism, specifically
the notion that racial prejudices can change over time. However, the fact that
these films became a dominant genre, and movies focusing on contemporary
discrimination from the perspective of characters of color were rare in this
period, demonstrates that cultural memory via mainstream Hollywood film is
about the possibility and achievement of white racial progress. As I have argued,
the greatest number of films deploying racial themes beyond those emphasizing white racial progress focused on historical figures and events which, though

important, served to render racism a relic of a hazy and distant past. What this means for most white Americans, who are unlikely to have many personal interactions with people of color, is that these movies provided not just stories about race relations, but also a significant form of cultural memory about individual notions of fairness that reject structural explanations of inequality. As historian George Lipsitz observes, "[t]he Mississippi of the 1960s that has come down to us through political discourse, popular journalism, fiction, and motion pictures (especially *Mississippi Burning* and *Ghosts of Mississippi*) . . . probably frame memory [of that period] for the greatest number of people . . ."[36]

How Americans interpret forms of cultural memory in film and in the news media is, of course, another question. Stories in print journalism do not determine individual understandings of affirmative action, but rather facilitate it by supplying the names of key players, special terminology, and rhetoric that revolve around the debate.[37] Similarly, though mainstream Hollywood films on racial progress provide stories that encourage identification with white elite characters, audiences may understand and assess these narratives in different ways. As scholars from a number of fields argue, texts—whether in the form of news media, film, or literature—do not yield a single interpretation, but rather are open to multiple interpretations because they are read through the particularities of readers' life experiences, such as race, class, gender, and age.[38] By focusing first on interviews with male attorneys, then with their female professional counterparts, and finally my short story, which considers both groups, the next three chapters examine the meanings these elite men and women attribute to affirmative action policy as well as to racial and gender inequities in the workplace.

3

Racing for Innocence

Stories of Disavowal and Exclusion

> RK: It's like they were just racing for innocence . . .
>
> JP: That's a great phrase! Tell me what you mean . . .
>
> RK: Racing for innocence? Racists for innocence. [He laughs.] It's like
> they are just working like crazy to convince me that they aren't racist
> when they know they have done something wrong. But they won't admit
> they've done anything wrong. You know, "Who me? I'm not a racist." So,
> they're racing to be the most liberal, most hip, non-racist white guy.
>
> —*Randall Kingsley, African American attorney*

While Hollywood films celebrate the transformation of a racial innocent into
a heroic leader against racial injustice, male lawyers' personal narratives tell a
different story about racism. Here, there are no "white saviors" who relentlessly
crusade against all personal odds and triumph against evil. Rather, these stories
are told in the context of a professional workplace, the Legal Department in
BC Corporation, where the principles of meritocracy are central to justifying
their success in career ladders.[1] Moreover, this is a workplace, as I mentioned
in the Introduction, that has its own historical legacy of discrimination but,
presumably through its court-ordered affirmative action program, has effectively remedied these problems. Race is understood as having no influence in
determining professional success, and in this historical moment, colorblindness
as an ideal is assumed to have been achieved. Here, white male lawyers employ

a discursive practice that I describe by borrowing from Randall Kingsley (one of the African American attorneys I interviewed) in the epigraph above and term "racing for innocence"; that is, they disavow responsibility for racist practices at the same time they practice racially exclusionary behavior. In this sense, they are like the cinematic lawyer heroes in the previous chapter who initially believe that colorblindness has been accomplished; but unlike their fictional counterparts, most do not develop a more complicated understanding. As I argue, their personal narratives not only serve to deny the experiences of lawyers of color and the existence of discrimination, but also maintain and reproduce whiteness as a structure of inequality in the workplace.[2]

As discussed in the Introduction, a number of scholars have described the post-civil-rights era as one in which overt forms of racism, such as legally segregated housing or discrimination in employment markets, have not entirely disappeared, but have reemerged through a variety of subtle practices. At the same time, a "new racial politics" has appeared that has incorporated the language of the civil rights movement and "repackaged itself as 'colorblind.'"[3] As I argued in Chapter 1, this language draws from both neoliberal and neoconservative discourses emphasizing unconstrained "choice" for individuals and notions about who is morally "undeserving." While these scholars have done important work in documenting and mapping the contours of colorblind ideology in our post-civil-rights era, there has been less attention to how it is that recipients of white privilege come to deny the role they play in reproducing racial inequality, and even less attention paid to how these practices operate among elites in contemporary workplaces.[4]

This chapter focuses on how male lawyers, as elite professionals in BC Corporation's Legal Department, understand and interpret affirmative action policy. As I show, they not only draw from themes in the dominant news media trope and the "white racial progress" film genre, but also put them together in the context of this particular workplace to tell their own stories about race at work. Moreover, just as films and print news media become forms of collective remembering, here I argue that the personal narratives white attorneys construct about themselves and others also become part of the cultural memory of this particular workplace.

Social scientists and historians have long been skeptical of personal narrative sources such as life histories, because memories are considered fallible and hence unreliable as forms of evidence. Here, Sigmund Freud's work serves as an important challenge in thinking about the significance of memory, in both its symbolic content and in its changeability. Psychoanalytic theory assumes that we cannot remember everything that happens to us, but maintains that what we do remember is nonetheless significant. For example, psychoanalyst Donald Spence makes this point in distinguishing between *historical truth* and *narrative truth*. While the former regards stories as something through which a historical truth can be discovered, narrative truth highlights the role our stories play in the creation of meaning about self and others.[5] As my co-authors Mary Jo Maynes, Barbara Laslett, and I argue in *Telling Stories*, the value of personal narratives lies precisely in their tendency to go beyond the facts because they tap into realms of meaning, subjectivity, emotion, and imagination.[6] In this light, what we do remember, even if it is not factually accurate, bears symbolic importance.[7]

Psychoanalytic theory is also relevant for thinking about how memories change over time, a process that Freud called "secondary revision," involving the relationship between fantasy and memory and the role that "screen memories" can play in blocking out other memories.[8] In Freud's understanding, we sometimes repress actual memories because they are too embarrassing or painful to remember, and then, through fantasy, substitute them with others that we come to understand as true even though they did not actually happen. As I argue, in the BC Corporation workplace screen memories among white lawyers function to create "stories" about attorneys of color, stories that operate collectively as gossip. Their gossip, in turn, serves to penalize those whose behavior does not fit workplace norms.

My focus here is on a group of mostly white attorneys whom I interviewed in my research, first in 1989, and then again in 1998 and 1999 (see Table 3.1). (Chapter 4 examines women lawyers.) It begins by exploring the discomfort that many white men experienced in talking about affirmative action at work, and then considers the few white men who became defensive in their interviews when this policy and related issues were raised. Strikingly, what some of these men do "remember" about race and gender at work is a time in the

Table 3.1 Interviews with male lawyers who stayed or left (N = 34)

Year	White men	African American men
Original number	32	2
Stayed	13	0
Left	19	2
Interviewed	23	2
Unable to interview	9	0

past when their professional workplace was predominantly white and male and they could make comments and jokes without worrying that they might offend white women or people of color. As the following section shows, the general adherence to a "colorblind" ideology in BC's Legal Department posed serious problems for the two men of color who worked there, both of whom ultimately chose to leave.

"Walking Around on Eggshells": White Men Talking About Race

The majority of white male lawyers who worked in the BC Corporation Legal Department from the late 1980s to 1999 described their work environment and their work in positive terms. Most expressed loyalty to the Legal Department and emphasized the role it played in building their careers. They described their success in terms of the legal cases they had defended and won, the increasing respect they had garnered over the years, their pride in their homes and families, and their sense of satisfaction in having worked hard and done well. This is not an especially surprising finding, as people who leave jobs are more likely to have done so because they are unhappy or recognized better opportunities elsewhere, while those who stay at the same firm are more likely to enjoy their work. These interviews took a surprising turn, however, when I asked them to talk about their employer's policy for affirmative action. Here, their upbeat, often self-congratulatory narratives of determination, hard work, and the rewards of success stopped short with long, uncomfortable silences.

The one exception to this pattern was Jason Wideman, a thirty-seven-year-old white lawyer whose wife was also an attorney, though in a different firm. In response to my question about affirmative action midway through the interview, he exclaimed:

> Wow, that's a loaded question! I mean, you know, affirmative action is such a controversial issue. I bet you have a hard time getting people to talk about this in a [pauses], a kind of straightforward way—especially here. You probably know the corporation was sued in the 1970s for race and sex discrimination and the federal court's finding of "egregious discrimination" led to a mandatory court-ordered affirmative action plan. Plus, do you know about the spin on the program for the general public?

As I had discovered in my meeting with the personnel director, promotional materials such as videos for employees and brochures for the general public indicated recognition of past mistakes, but emphasized above all the company's current efforts to redress them. In Jason's view, this public image made it difficult for people who worked at BC Corporation to publicly admit to any mistakes. As he put it:

> You know, I think just about everyone knows there are times when we have screwed up with minority lawyers, but all the talk goes on behind closed doors. Everyone is afraid of another lawsuit . . . And, we're supposed to present this united front to the general public. You know, "diversity is excellence," and all that. So, you know, people don't talk about these things in a public way. It's more like a conversation over lunch or in someone's office.

Jason's remarks help make sense of why it was so difficult for other male lawyers to move beyond silence in talking about affirmative action. The corporation's past history and its efforts to improve its image as an employer providing multiple opportunities to minorities and white women made them reluctant to discuss any problems. Moreover, his comments about what people talk about "over lunch or in someone's office" suggest that strong boundaries existed between public discourse and personal disclosures.[9] Furthermore, I suspect that conducting interviews at a historical moment when colorblindness is assumed to have been achieved made it all the more difficult to talk candidly or openly about racial matters. As sociologist Howard Winant observes, one of the hallmarks of the neoconservative construction of colorblind discourse has been that "every invocation of racial significance manifests 'race thinking,' and is thus suspect."[10] In other words, mentioning race at all suggests that one is racist.

In stark contrast to Jason's narrative about affirmative action, the most common response to my queries was silence followed by complaints in hushed tones about "having to be careful" about what was said at work. In probing for details, I often came up against either attorneys' reluctance or embarrassment to provide specific examples. Here is a typical exchange from an interview with Jonathan Galaskiewitz, a fifty-two-year-old white man.

JP: Be careful about saying what?

JG: Oh, you know, certain things, you just don't say certain things.

JP: But, like what?

JG: Just certain kinds of things, you just don't say them.

JP: But what? I really don't know what you mean. Can you be specific?

JG: Certain things, you know, you just don't say certain things, you can't make, um, [pauses] make certain comments or jokes, things that used to be, you know, okay. It makes me feel [pauses], it makes me feel like I am walking around on eggshells all the time, like I might say the wrong thing.

JP: But what would be the wrong thing? You mean a joke that might be racist or sexist?

JG: Well, no, I mean, I don't tell those kind of jokes. [pauses] But you know how it is, some people take every little thing personally—they're offended by the most innocent remark. I don't know, it's hard to say exactly, but I feel like I have to watch everything I say.

What is striking in this interview is how an otherwise articulate and highly educated white upper-middle-class man whose work required him to make forceful arguments suddenly became stumbling and inarticulate. In fact, I often had the sense in interviews like this one that lawyers wanted to say much more but were afraid, as Jonathan said, of saying the "wrong thing," of saying something that might be construed as racist. For many white Americans, color-blindness continues to be the "polite language of race," and Jonathan's oblique reference to "certain comments" is constructed in such a way that can hardly offend anyone.[11] His stumbling also suggests that he was self-conscious about talking, listening to how it might sound to others and thinking about how they might respond—a form of talk that other scholars refer to as "disrupted speech." Sociologist Susan Chase, for example, discovered this kind of talk in her research on white students who worried about what students of color might think about their opinions about diversity initiatives on a college campus.[12]

There is more than simple politeness to his response, however. His stumbling language, "certain things, you know, you just don't say certain things," contrasts with his first-person descriptions of self earlier in the interview, i.e., "I worked very hard to make senior counsel," or "I won the case hands down." Jonathan's shift to second-person subtly operated to remove him from these presumably delicate conversations, as if to imply "it's about what you all say, not me." And, when I asked directly whether he was referring to racist or sexist jokes, his immediate response was, "I don't tell jokes like that," suggesting that he was not responsible for such behavior. He further deflected responsibility from himself in the next sentence by pointing the finger of blame at others: "some people take every little thing personally." Implicit throughout is not only the difficulty and discomfort he had in talking about race and racism directly—he never actually mentioned either word—but also the sense that he, as an individual, was not responsible for such problems.

"All These Government Regulations": White Male Defensiveness

A few other white men who initially appeared uncomfortable with my questions explained the legal history of the company's policy to me in lawyerly terms and added that such a program was either unfair or no longer necessary because "things are better." Here, some of the arguments from narratives in anti-affirmative-action news media emerged. Following this logic, discrimination is a relic of the past and hence affirmative action is no longer necessary. But even in these legalistic discussions, the attorneys' reluctance to say what they really thought and their defensiveness about the company's reputation for diversity came through. Here is one exchange I had with Sam Nelson, a forty-four-year-old attorney and Randall Kingsley's former supervisor, an exchange that became more and more heated as I probed for specifics to his evasive answers.

JP: Can you tell me what about this policy is unfair?

SN: Well, sometimes positions go to people who are unqualified. So, it takes jobs away from people who are.

JP: Not qualified in what way?

SN: That they're not qualified. That they don't have the expertise.

JP: Do you have someone in mind?

SN: [long pause] Well, no, not really.

JP: So, none of the lawyers hired here lack expertise?

SN: [quietly answers] Well, no.

JP: So, you're talking about affirmative action in general as opposed to what's happened here?

SN: Uh-huh. Uh-huh.

JP: Well, let me ask again, um, in a different way. How do you feel about the program here?

SN: I guess I would have to say it's outlived its usefulness.

JP: Because?

SN: Because things are better. Things are so much better. Look, we hire minorities. That's more than you can say for a lot of firms in the city.

JP: And, you don't have any problems with their qualifications?

SN: I never said that I did! I never said that. [his tone becomes increasingly angry] Look, the problem is with all these government regulations about who were supposed to hire. I resent like hell all these regulations. [he repeats his criticism of regulations several times]. . . . Things are better here.

JP: So, about how many of the lawyers in this department are white women or people of color?

SN: I don't know. [pauses, then speaks definitively] A lot. I don't have the exact numbers at my fingertips. You'll have to check with personnel.

JP: Well, what about retention issues? Do you know how many people have stayed and how many people have left?

SN: Look, you'll have to check with personnel. I don't keep track of these things. But, I have to say, it's really not unusual for anyone to leave. It's a long haul to make senior counsel [the equivalent of partnership] and lots of young attorneys drop out along the way. They decide that corporate law is not for them, they want to move on, get different experience, better jobs, other opportunities or they just don't have what it takes.

JP: Yeah, I know that's true. I mean, I know it's difficult to make partner. But I was wondering, you know the ABA [American Bar Association] has published statistics about women and minorities in law, and the percentages who make partner are still very small nationwide. And, I was wondering, what your sense of that was here? I mean maybe not the actual numbers, but your sense of . . .

SN: [interrupts] Look, I already told you, I don't know the exact numbers.

JP: I know, but I was wondering . . .

SN: [interrupts again] But, I will say this, if these people don't want to stay here, it's not my fault. If they want to move on, there's nothing that I can do about that.

JP: So, some minorities have left?

SN: [with exasperation] I don't know the numbers.

JP: But you do know someone who left?

SN: [sighs loudly and pauses] Yes, I do remember someone who left. A young attorney named Randall. African American. And yes, he left for a better job.

And, I've heard that he's done very well for himself. Now, I am sure you can appreciate that I am a very busy man and I don't have time for any more questions.

As in the other interviews I had conducted with these white men, once I raised questions about affirmative action and the retention for people of color, the upbeat progression of the narrative was interrupted, the rapport I had worked hard to maintain broke down, and, in this case, I was summarily dismissed. Several themes in Sam's personal narrative deserve attention here. First, his criticism of "government regulations" recalls neoliberal arguments made by anti-affirmative-action advocates in the news media who argued that such policies interfered in the operation of "free markets," just as his insistence that "things are better" resonates with the idea that such policies were no longer necessary. In addition, despite his insistence that things have improved for people of color, he did not have the "exact numbers" to support his claim, suggesting either his lack of knowledge or denial of the problem. In fact, the more I probed about numbers and retention of people of color, the more defensive he became, until he finally said, "if these people don't want to stay here, it's not my fault."

As Table 3.1 shows, the turnover rate for the 1989 cohort of African Americans was 100 percent—a retention rate of zero. Furthermore, when I checked with personnel, I discovered that the percentage of litigators of color in the BC Legal Department in 1999 was 3 percent—one African American and one Latino. So, despite Sam's claim, in numerical terms at least, things were actually not better, but slightly worse.

Of additional interest in Sam's narrative are not only his use of neoliberal rhetoric or its factual inaccuracies, but also its emotional tone and construction. The defensiveness and anger and, finally, his abrupt ending of the interview all suggest that my queries about race provoked discomfort. Furthermore, like Jonathan, Sam moved quickly to absolve himself of responsibility—it wasn't not his fault if lawyers left the department. This is an interesting sleight of hand. If Sam was not the perpetrator of racism, then the blame lay elsewhere. He was innocent. This theme of innocence and blame of others resurfaced in almost all the interviews with white lawyers when I brought up questions about affirmative action or race.

There was one other exception to these evasive interviews. I had a vitriolic exchange with an older white litigator named David Cooperman who had been in the Legal Department for over twenty-five years. The interview began on a bad note because I was five minutes late. (Typically, I was always on time, and then ended up waiting anywhere from fifteen minutes to half an hour for my prescheduled appointments, but not so in this case.) He took punctuality seriously and expressed his grave disappointment with my "unprofessional behavior." Though I apologized profusely, he continued to berate me about the "irresponsibility of young people these days." (I was in my early forties at the time.) Frustrated with his seemingly gruff and inhospitable behavior, I finally said in a less contrite and loud tone of voice, "Are you sure this is a good time for the interview? I seem to have greatly inconvenienced you."

My directness seemed to mollify him, and after his initial prickliness, the interview seemed to go well as David narrated his work history of an upwardly mobile career trajectory. From his account, I learned that he was a terrifically gifted and successful litigator as well as a mentor to others—he enjoyed the parry and thrust of gamesmanship, the theatrics of the courtroom, and giving advice about strategy to his junior colleagues. The tone of the interview began to shift, however, when I asked him what he thought about affirmative action policy.

DC: Affirmative action is a government regulation that gets in the way of the good work we do here.

JP: Could you say more about how it gets in the way?

DC: I spent three years in law school, over twenty-five years in practice, and some idiot judge who doesn't even work here gets to tell me who the hell I am supposed to hire—regardless of their qualifications. I don't think I can be any clearer than that.

JP: Um, okay, I understand. Uh, but can you describe any other effects, particularly here, that affirmative action has had. I mean, I know it's supposed to influence hiring, but has it had any other effects? Like, um, some attorneys have talked about how it affects what goes on day to day, like what people feel they can talk about at work, or how people socialize outside the office or—

DC: [interrupts] Beyond *forcing* us to hire unqualified individuals, I would have to say that it has changed the nature of discussions we have in the office. When I first started in 1972, we didn't waste time talking about child care responsibilities, going part-time, or flex time or anything like that. Now, it's a constant whine. [adopts a whiney falsetto voice] "I can't take this case because I can't leave town for two weeks, my children are still young . . ." [emphasis in original]

JP: So, what you're saying is that the entrance of women attorneys into the department has had an impact on, um, these kinds of discussions?

DC: Yes.

JP: What about people of color? Has that changed things, too?

DC: That's more complicated.

JP: How so?

DC: Well, you have to be *careful* about what you say around some people. [emphasis in original]

JP: Be careful about saying what?

DC: I think that's *obvious*. You can no longer say *certain* things. [emphasis in original]

JP: Okay, but it's not obvious to me. I don't work here. So, I don't know what you can say and what you can't say.

DC: [mimics my statement in an exaggerated falsetto voice] "But, it's not obvious to me. I don't work here." [then, in a loud voice] Okay, I will spell it out for you. In San Francisco, you can't say faggot, nigger, or spic. Is that clear enough for you?

Dumbfounded in the moment, I finally found my voice and argued with him about his comments. He glared angrily at me through our heated discussion, and, finally, I rose and gathered my things in preparation to leave. Given his great love of courtroom theatrics, I felt sure that he was baiting me for the sport of it. So, as I began to walk out the door, I turned to face him to make a parting shot. "And, as a lesbian, I find what you said particularly offensive. You, no doubt, intended to personally offend me."

Later, when I discussed my obvious failure of my composure in the interview with some of my colleagues, they reminded me that most of my interviews had gone fairly well—I had done over twenty interviews at this point—and no one else had responded in such a vitriolic way. As mentioned above, the majority of white men I interviewed were seemingly reluctant to talk about affirmative action or discrimination candidly. Only Jason was willing to talk more openly about these issues.

In David's case, I suspect that he was straightforward in his scathing critique of affirmative action and about the presence of women in the Legal Department, but I also felt sure that he was purposefully baiting me with the racial and homophobic slurs for shock value. I doubted that he used these slurs with great regularity in professional conversations or even at home with his spouse and close friends. Perhaps he read my tailored but slightly hip pantsuit, my short, spiky haircut, and very little makeup as signifiers for a lesbian before I self-identified as such and knew that I would find his language offensive.

The fact that the first word on his list of epithets was "faggot" suggests that he hoped to personalize his attack. Of course, it also possible that he resented the questions I was asking. Mimicking my comment in a high falsetto voice, "but it's not obvious to me, I don't work here," was not only rude, but also indicated his irritation with my queries about people of color in the workplace. Here, he may have hoped to discipline me for raising topics he found distasteful or uncomfortable.

As the same time, David's angry tone also signaled that my questions threatened something he valued, something he perceived as having lost. His first sign of irritation appeared in his comment about "some idiot judge" who got to tell him whom he is supposed to hire. His reference to his twenty-five-year legal career, as well as his being forced "to hire unqualified individuals" suggest he no longer felt that his professional authority counted in making hiring decisions. As I persisted in asking questions about the experiences of white women and people of color, he compared his previous experiences to the present. In 1972, he didn't have to listen to women complaining about the difficulties of childcare; now he did. Further, his reference to having "to be *careful* about what you say around some people" suggests discomfort with new norms for social etiquette in an interracial workplace. David's frequent references to the past and, in his view, the more problematic present, as well as his bitter tone, suggest he has lost what he most prized: the privileges he had as an autonomous professional and as a white man who didn't have to take feminist concerns seriously or to censor racially derogative remarks. Here, too, both neoconservative and neoliberal elements of anti-affirmative-action rhetoric emerged. His use of the term "unqualified" suggests he saw people of color as morally undeserving, while his critique of "regulations" resonated with the logic of free-market advocates. Finally, he blamed judges, regulations, white women, and people of color for his discontent. He didn't see himself as responsible for discrimination; he was innocent.

The Costs of Navigating a "Colorblind" Workplace for Men of Color

In contrast to the majority of white men's indirect references to racial issues, Randall Kingsley and Tyrone Lewis, the two male African American litigators I interviewed, talked frankly about race and racism at work. (There was also a third African American, a woman, whom I discuss in Chapter 4.) Moreover, unlike the white lawyers' narratives of hard work and professional success, the

African American lawyers who left the Legal Department both told stories of marginalization, alienation, and then exit from the department. In what follows I draw at length from Randall Kingsley's narrative as a representative of these stories.

When I interviewed Randall in 1998, he described himself as "a sort of jack of all trades." Most of his cases were employment disputes, but he also did the occasional personal injury case, drew up a simple will for a friend, or provided advice about getting a divorce. Though he enjoyed his independence as a solo practitioner and found his work interesting, he complained that it was "often difficult to make ends meet." In 1989, when I first interviewed Randall in the Legal Department, he was making $45,000 a year. His annual salary in 1998 was $47,000. Ten years had passed and he was making only $2,000 more a year than when he first left law school. Although it would be inaccurate to describe him as downwardly mobile, he still practiced law and considered himself to be "solidly middle-class." Within the stratification of the legal profession, he had moved from the top tier of highly paid corporate law to the lower-paying practice of the solo professional.[13]

Randall's work history narrative, like those of many other black professionals, began with the opportunities opened up by affirmative action programs and policies in the early 1970s.[14] In 1985, after he finished law school, he applied for jobs in several big firms in employment law, and he ended up getting offered one position in a local District Attorney's office and another in the litigation section within BC's Legal Department. Both were known for hiring minorities and for their affirmative action recruitment policies. He decided to take the position in the Legal Department, because "the salary was better and the opportunities seemed greater." Four years later, when he left, his initial move was not up but rather lateral, to a legal department in another large corporation in the Bay Area with the same salary, $45,000 a year. "It had a good reputation as a kind of progressive place, but it turned out to be very conservative," he said. In 1993, he decided that he had "had it" with the corporate environment and opened his own practice with an African American friend from law school. Randall's reasons for leaving the Legal Department were, in his words, "a long story."

> RK: Part of it has to do with how they hype their affirmative action program there. [adopts a booming announcer voice] We have the best affirmative action program and we are all one happy family. Diversity is excellence. Rah, rah, rah . . . [returns to regular voice] But, they don't really believe that. It's just assumed that if you are black then you can't possibly be qualified for the job.

JP: So, did you feel like affirmative action was a kind of stigma there?

RK: Yeah. In their heads, it went something like: "minority" equals "affirmative action hire" equals "unqualified." I don't mean everyone thought this way, but enough people did to make it matter . . . So, yeah, it was disappointing. I mean, part of the reason I went there was because they have a reputation for having a good [affirmative action] program. You know, it's like they made mistakes in the past, but they did something about it . . . And, uh, to be completely fair, they did improve a lot some areas like clerical, sales, and craft [factory]. But there still aren't a lot of women and minorities in management-level positions. In litigation, I was one of three African Americans in the entire department . . .

JP: So, why did you leave?

RK: It started with a lot of small stuff, and the small stuff just added up . . .

The small stuff began when Sam Nelson, the head of department, whom Randall described sardonically as "pretty liberal for a white guy," gave him his first assignment: legal research in an area that lay outside Randall's area of expertise. Randall expressed some concern, but Sam told Randall not to worry about his inexperience in this area, saying, "There's a whole department here of folks to help you out."

"So, I decided against my better judgment to take it on and get some help from some of the other litigators in the department," said Randall. When he first approached one of the white lawyers, Bill Fischer, Fischer was cool and brusque and told Randall that he was "too busy." In the meantime, Randall, who felt he was "being brushed off," decided to approach other senior litigators in the department for advice.

Randall felt that these men reacted indifferently or even negatively to him and heard from some of the secretaries and paralegals that they joked among themselves about his style of dress and personal manner. He experienced this undercurrent of resistance in different ways. One attorney lost a key memo that Randall had spent days researching, another made jokes whenever Randall came into his office, still another ignored his remarks in meetings, and another "forgot" a lunch date he made with him. He began to see these multiple interactions as many small acts of discrimination. Moreover, it is clear to him that the other new junior associate, who was white, was not treated in the same way. He began to feel alienated from his colleagues, isolated, and angry. His story of leave-taking continued:

RK: So, I finally decided to call them on it. First, I went back to Sam and asked him why he had given me this assignment at the beginning. I wanted to know why my first project was outside my area. I mean, I had been hired to do labor law and they had me working on a patent case? He got really defensive and he had all these excuses. Then I said that I felt like no one was really mentoring me, you know, that they weren't helping me. And, I knew that Todd [a new white male attorney] was getting all kinds of help. [Sam] made more excuses. I said that I wanted to know what was going on. You know, because this was an incident of differential treatment. I used those words, 'differential treatment,' very carefully. Oh, he got so mad. He started yelling, "Are you calling me a racist?"

And then [later] he tells everyone else in litigation that I said he was a racist and they all start acting weird, really nice, but really defensive . . . Suddenly, Bill, who is like, you know, a cold fish, is like, saying hello all the time and telling me how he was really busy when I stopped by asking for advice. And, how he was really sorry if there was any misunderstanding. And by the way, did I know that he belongs to the ACLU? . . . And Ralph kept saying over and over that he really forgot that lunch date with me, "it doesn't have anything to do with [pause], you know . . ."

JP: It doesn't have to do with the fact that you are African American?

RK: Yeah, that's what he meant, but he wouldn't say it. So after that they all started doing it. It's like they were just racing for innocence. . . . And things just got weird. It seemed like either I did the wrong thing or people just reacted weirdly to me. . . . And so I decided to move on.

The stories these white attorneys told me about Randall's career trajectory since he left the company were quite different from his own. Recall that Sam Nelson, his former supervisor, said, "he's done very well for himself." Another lawyer, Bill Fisher, described Randall in less flattering terms, telling me that he had "cashed in on all the opportunities available for minorities" and had landed a much-higher-paying job at another firm. He also confided that he found Randall "demanding" and "abrasive" and doubted Randall's "qualifications from the beginning," but hastened to add that "this assessment has nothing to do with the fact that Randall is African American." Other attorneys told me that Randall had taken a much better job somewhere else, though they could not recall the name of the firm. One remarked that he knew Randall must be doing well because "he's driving one of those BMW convertibles now." (Randall actually owned a Japanese economy car.) Although they all agreed that Randall was a "go-getter," they made disparaging comments about the way he dressed—"he's too flashy"—and complained about his requests for help—"he's too demanding." For these white men, each of whom had had two, maybe three interactions with Randall, the issue was reduced to one of style and personality; and Randall, as one attorney put it, just didn't "fit in." (Given the racially skewed proportion of lawyers in this workplace, white lawyers were likely to have had only a very small number of daily interactions with Randall.) He wore the wrong clothes (a pink rather than light blue button-down shirt), he said the wrong things, and he was much too obvious as a go-getter. For them, Randall's complaints were simply isolated incidents.

Looking at his leave-taking from the standpoint of the two groups—the perspective of the white male attorneys and Randall's perspective as one of two African American men—demonstrates that what looks "individual" to members of a dominant group is often "experienced as systematic bias by nondominant group members."[15] This helps to explain, in part, why many of the white men I interviewed claimed to be innocent of racism. They are innocent in the sense that they are oblivious to the consequences of their actions. They simply do not experience the sum total of their actions toward Randall or their statements about him. Because they can treat each meeting as an isolated incident, it is difficult for them to see how making jokes or comments about Randall's style of dress can be construed as racist. They simply act out of a sense of their right to act. As a consequence, they fail to see how they participate collectively in constructing what Randall experiences as an unfriendly work environment.

Their narrative of Randall's experiences fits neatly within the framework of meritocratic and individualist thinking. They look at everything Randall did as an individual action, a product of free choice, individual will, and hard work. On one hand, Randall left because he either chose not to "fit in," as one lawyer contended, or lacked the right qualifications to begin with, as another suggested. On the other hand, Randall, for whom the majority of interactions had been with these white men, saw a pattern in their behavior, a practice and disavowal of everyday racism. What he experienced as systematic and unrelenting forms of indifference, derision, and exclusion, the white lawyers insisted were isolated events. Analytically, Randall's story is a structural one about the reiteration of whiteness through practice, a doing that is often unwitting in its reproduction of power and privilege, while theirs is a liberal individualist one, invoking Randall's failure to live up to its ideals.

In explaining the divergence in perspective between these two groups, my analysis in the last two paragraphs treats these narratives as equivalent accounts. However, there is additional evidence from my 1989 field notes to corroborate Randall's story. As discussed in the Introduction, the unfriendly joking by white attorneys about the affirmative action program and its "unqualified minorities" occurred frequently behind closed doors. In addition, I have detailed notes about lawyers making fun of his style of dress, about the day the memo he wrote was lost by another attorney, and counts of the number of times his comments were ignored in meetings. I was also able to verify his employment record and salary after he left the Legal Department. By contrast, there are many inconsistencies in the white lawyers' narratives about Randall. They misrepresented (to me or, perhaps, to themselves) the kind of position and salary that Randall had after he left the company. And most, like Sam, were unwilling to discuss the specifics of Randall's departure from the company. Their inconsistent accounts, their reluctance to discuss why he left, and the defensive tone running through their interviews all suggest more complicated circumstances surrounding Randall's departure from the firm than the content of their narratives reveal.

"Racing for Innocence"

The white male lawyers' discursive strategy which maintained everyday racism while denying white accountability for that racism is what I term "racing for innocence." This "race" surfaces in the defensive narratives the white men constructed in their interviews, such as Sam Nelson's insistence that "things are better" when in fact the number of lawyers of color in his department continued to be quite small, or in the white lawyers' collective insistence that Randall had left for a better job opportunity, when by his own account he had left because he faced an unfriendly working environment. From all indicators, his new job was a lateral move, not an advance. This "race" also appeared in Tyrone's depictions of the white male lawyers' behavior toward the African American lawyers. (Tyrone was the only other male African American lawyer in the department, and he too eventually left for another job, though under less dramatic circumstances.) Tyrone also provided accounts of being "brushed off" by white men who were too busy to advise them, but not too busy to assist white junior colleagues, and who became defensive when asked to explain their lack of interest. He also shared stories about forgotten professional engagements with white colleagues, who, when asked about these missed appointments, recited their credentials as "good" white people who belonged to the ACLU, told him about having a black friend, or even a distant relative "who is married to one," as one lawyer told him. Because these systematic and routine practices of exclusion and denial typically remained unchallenged, whiteness continued to be maintained and reproduced as a structural relationship of inequality in this workplace.

Interestingly, these stories about Randall's departure function here, as anthropologists have argued, as gossip does in other social situations: as a mode of social sanction.[16] By telling these stories about Randall, they reproached his behavior for falling outside of normative parameters. If Randall complained about his treatment, he wasn't working hard or doing a good job as professional meritocratic ideals demanded, but rather fulfilling a role as a person of color who was "overly sensitive" about racial issues. In this way, their stories about him, much like the narratives about black politicians in Hollywood films discussed in the last chapter, became part of the office's folklore about people of color who "make trouble" in the workplace. These stories circulated both in the white lawyers' personal narratives and in my field notes where I recorded negative comments made to me privately about the problems "unqualified minorities" created for BC Corporation. Here I argue that these stories become "screen memories" that supplant others and fill in as memories for events that never actually happened. Recall that the first job Randall took after leaving BC's Legal Department was a lateral move, that it was not a better position, that he left because he found the workplace inhospitable and not because he "cashed in on all the opportunities for minorities," and that he did not own a BMW convertible. Further, as suggested by my observations from field notes, the white lawyers' personal memories became not only collective ways of remembering Randall, but also of thinking about people of color more generally in this workplace.

In addition to their function as department gossip, the narratives white lawyers told about affirmative action bear many similarities to media narratives about white male innocence and injury: Affirmative action isn't necessary because discrimination is no longer a problem; people of color are "unqualified," and hence, undeserving of the jobs they receive; and government regulations are burdensome forms of "social engineering." Furthermore, their personal narratives are also similar to those of white working-class men in other studies who view affirmative action as a threat because they see their jobs being "taken away by people of color."[17] While the professional men I interviewed were rarely this explicit—they were more likely to launch a general critique about the alleged unfairness of the program, to invoke the problems of bureaucratic inefficiency, or to point to a seemingly ambiguous shift in the etiquette of workplace interactions—they arrived at a similar conclusion. For them, affirmative action was not necessary because attorneys who worked hard would reap the benefits of their own initiative and talents.

Here, we can see how racing for innocence draws from the larger cultural discourse of liberal individualism. By defining social life as the sum total of conscious and deliberate individual activities, these white lawyers were able to ignore the very systematic practices they themselves deployed, practices that excluded and marginalized African American lawyers. Despite their insistent denial of responsibility for the small number of people of color in the Legal Department, a hostile work environment, or Randall's departure, these narratives are not entirely seamless. The emotional tone of embarrassment and defensiveness running through them suggests something is unsettling their stories, "a seething presence, acting on, and often meddling with taken-for-granted realities."[18] What is it that, in sociologist Avery Gordon's sense of the term, "haunts" and upsets their accounts?

Indeed, one might ask, how, in the face of evidence to the contrary, do these white men continue to race for innocence? Why is it so important to them to deny accountability for racist acts, however small or subtle? Here, feminist scholar Aida Hurtado's article, "The Trickster's Play: Whiteness in the Subordination and Liberation Process," provides some insight. In her argument, white Americans "lack an elaborate language to speak about those who oppress—how we feel about, think about [it]. . . . Missing in the puzzle of domination is a reflexive mechanism for understanding how we are all involved in the dirty process of racializing and gendering others, limiting who they are and who they can become."[19] Given our nation's ideological emphasis on democracy and equality, it is not surprising that the white male attorneys I interviewed had a difficult time talking about power. Americans assume that we live in a classless society; we presume we are all equal under the law. In this respect, Americans are innocent of power.

As I pointed out in Chapter 1, stories of innocence have long been a part of the mythology about America's history and heritage.[20] And, stories about racism and genocide are profoundly shocking, as cultural critic Coco Fusco reminds us, because they deeply upset white Americans' notion of self as a good and tolerant people.[21] In this light, we can see that the white male lawyers' collective story about innocence not only served to deny responsibility for racially exclusionary behavior, but also is tied to a broader discourse about morality and national identity. Good people, like good Americans, are benevolent and tolerant of people unlike themselves.[22]

Just as print news media narratives and Hollywood film stories about antiracist white heroes were effective in promoting the notion of white male innocence, and ultimately the end of affirmative action in California, in BC's Legal

Department "racing for innocence," as a practice, effectively served to isolate, marginalize, and even vilify the only two men of color who worked there. In this light, it's not surprising they left. Their stories of institutionalized exclusion were dismissed, and when they left, the gossip that circulated about them focused on their "individual failings." In this professional milieu, like many others, the ideology of meritocracy is the central frame of reference for explaining success and disparaging failure. Importantly, stories about discrimination have little currency in American professional worlds. Within these meritocratic workplace cultures, there is no acceptable language for stories about structural inequality, such as institutionalized racism. Nonetheless, as sociologist Susan Chase finds in her research, there is a tension in broader American culture between "the emphasis on individual achievement and success on the one hand, and the persistent debates over the causes and meanings of inequality on the other."[23] One manifestation of that tension is the disjuncture between race-neutral narratives about professional work and racialized talk about inequality. While Randall and Tyrone as African American men stood at the center of this tension, the white men they worked with struggled morally to find ways to make themselves "good" non-racist people at the same time that they practiced exclusion.

These themes of marginalization and exclusion are certainly not unique to the experience of professional men of color. As the next chapter shows, both white women and women of color described similar dynamics and problems. In 1989, there were nine women working in the BC Corporation Legal Department. Though their numbers were larger, they, like Randall and Tyrone, were still "tokens" or the numerical minority in this workplace.[24] Further, though often ignored in media accounts, women too are beneficiaries of affirmative action. What were their experiences with discrimination? What did they think about affirmative action? What role, if any, do they play in this debate? These questions will be taken up in the following chapter.

4

Stand by Your Man

Women Lawyers and Affirmative Action

But, affirmative action is about women too!
—*Mary Brown, white attorney*

In 1995, the same year that the University of California Regents voted to do away with affirmative action in the UC system, the conservative group the Independent Women's Forum (IWF) deployed country-and-western singer Patsy Cline's anthem in their political work. In their view, conservative women should "stand by their men" in calling for the end of affirmative action. In asking that women defend their husbands and sons from the "injuries" of this policy, the IWF hoped to defeat it at the polls. In an editorial titled, "That's No White Male, That's My Husband," IWF member Ellen Ladowsky argued:

> The final undoing of affirmative action in women's minds, however, may not stem from consideration of their own careers. Women know the men who have been victims of affirmative action's reverse discrimination or men who consider themselves to be victims. They are the husbands, brothers, or sons. Non-working women—or women temporarily out of the workforce to raise the children—count on their husbands' salaries and promotions to support their families. . . . This "stand by your man" factor may turn out to be the force that causes female voters to reject affirmative action—first in California, and then across the nation.[1]

Though published in *The Wall Street Journal*, this "stand by your man" argument made few other appearances in the print news media. As we saw in Chapter 1, the news media constructed the debate as a racial conflict, and women were not a central issue in the affirmative action debate. Only a handful of newspaper articles mentioned women in the debate between 1990 and 2000. Furthermore, even in those articles that raised the issue of gender, little was said about women workers themselves as beneficiaries of affirmative action policy or about how they define it or understand it as influencing their daily lives in the workplace. This chapter renders visible this "stand by your man" argument by focusing on the rhetoric deployed by the IWF and examining the role it played—often implicitly—in the workplace lives of the women lawyers I interviewed 1989 and again in 1999.

It begins by reviewing some of the major political and legal changes that took place during the decade that elapsed between my initial fieldwork and interviews with women attorneys in the Legal Department in 1989, and the work life histories I collected ten years later in 1998 and 1999. Certainly, one of the most important events in California in the intervening period was the abolishment of affirmative action in state employment and education in 1996, but there were a number of other changes as well. I then critically assess what the media wrote about these changes and how it characterized women in the affirmative action debate in the small number of articles that attended to the issue.

The next section turns to women attorneys in BC's Legal Department. Affirmative action prompted many changes for women nationally as well as in this particular workplace—these women lawyers all benefited from changes in law school admissions that began in the 1970s and were hired after BC's consent decree went into effect.[2] Moreover, as part of the consent decree, the Legal Department also had a formal family leave policy long before many other firms did in the San Francisco Bay area. Despite these important changes, many of the women discussed subtle and not-so-subtle forms of discrimination in their legal careers in both their 1989 and 1999 interviews. Their most common complaint lay in their difficulty in getting additional family leaves from work and their mostly male colleagues' perception that women are "less committed" than men to professional obligations. As I show, this same group of women also supported affirmative action, though not without ambivalence. The final section turns to the personal narratives of the smallest group of women: those who denied that discrimination was a serious problem and opposed affirmative action. As I argue, neoconservative and neoliberal assumptions about unconstrained "choice" infused their responses both for and against affirmative action.

Women in the Media Construction
of the Affirmative Action Debate

Between 1989 and 1999, there were a number of important policy changes, legal findings, and government reports highlighting the problematic status of women's employment across the United States. In 1993, the Clinton Administration secured passage of the Family and Medical Leave Act, which provides workers with twelve weeks of unpaid family leave from work for the birth of a new baby or a serious illness in the family.[3] At the same time, a number of sex discrimination lawsuits involving the Federal Reserve Bank, the grocery store chains Lucky's and Safeway, Princeton University, and many others were either filed or settled, bringing national attention to continuing gender inequities in salary and promotion for women.[4] The findings in these court cases were supported empirically in a national study in 1995, when the Federal Glass Ceiling Commission released a report showing that white women and people of color continued to lag far behind white men in salary levels and rates of promotion.[5] Citing a pattern of discrimination rooted in "the perception of many white males that as a group they are losing—losing the corporate game, losing control and losing opportunity," the Commission found that "[m]any middle and upper-level white male managers view the inclusion of minorities and women in management as a direct threat to their own chances for advancement" and as a result, "they thwart the progress of others."[6] The report concluded by recommending the continued use of affirmative action policies to "select, promote, and retain qualified individuals."[7] In the same year, another government study conducted by the U.S. Labor Department revealed that actual cases of reverse discrimination against white men were quite rare. As mentioned in Chapter 1, of the 300 cases filed with the Equal Employment Opportunity Commission, "Reverse discrimination was established in six cases, and the courts provided appropriate relief in those cases." The study concluded that many of these cases were "the result of a disappointed applicant failing to examine his or her own qualifications and erroneously assuming that when a women or minority got a job, it was because of their race or sex, not qualifications."[8]

In addition to the empirical findings of these important federal government reports, by 1997 more class action lawsuits alleging sex discrimination in pay, promotion, and harassment were pending across the United States against companies such as The Home Depot, Publix Super Markets, Glorious Food, Motel 6, Dun & Bradstreet, Smith Barney, and Mitsubishi. The majority of these cases settled with significant payouts to women employees—a tacit, if not explicit, admission of sex discrimination.[9] Home Depot, for example, ended up paying $87.5 million to more than 20,000 female employees who claimed discrimination, while Publix paid out $81.5 million.[10] And, three years after Proposition 209 was passed in California, two settlements—both described as the largest ever made "under Labor Department affirmative action compliance programs"—were made in the favor of women. In the first case, Texaco agreed to settle a class action lawsuit filed against them for sex discrimination by agreeing to compensate women in midlevel management positions who had been underpaid for many years. The company, though not admitting wrongdoing, paid out $3.1 million to 186 midlevel female employees. In the second case, Boeing Company agreed to pay $4.5 million to women and racial or ethnic minority employees who had been paid less than their white male counterparts.[11]

These lawsuits and research findings suggest that while affirmative action had made a difference for white women in professional education and employment, discrimination continued to affect them in a wide variety of industries and occupations. Though some white women were able to file lawsuits and win judgments against discriminating employers, those who did not have the economic or political resources to do so had little recourse in ending either sexual harassment or discrimination. This suggests that women with significant financial or political resources fared differently from those who did not have access to them.

Interestingly, despite the fact that white women have been one of the beneficiaries of affirmative action programs and that government reports and class action lawsuits during this time period underscore continuing discrimination against women in the labor market, the *New York Times* and the *San Francisco Chronicle* devoted very little attention to women in the affirmative action debate during the 1990s. Approximately 1 percent of articles in each year mentioned women or gender. Moreover, the predominant focus of the debate remained centered on race, even in the few cases when affirmative action appeared to disadvantage women.[12] For example, media coverage of the 1994 *Hopwood* Federal Court of Appeals for the Fifth Circuit decision—a reverse discrimination suit filed and won by Cheryl Hopwood against the University of Texas Law School—focuses solely on race even though Hopwood was a woman. As the opening paragraph of a *New York Times* article states:

> From Cheryl J. Hopwood's point of view, if overcoming past hardship was counted as a plus when applying to the University of Texas Law School, she should have been among the more qualified candidates. . . . "Hopwood is the epitome of who is harmed by affirmative action," said Mr. Smith, a former state

legislator. "If she had been black, she would have been admitted. Every black applicant that had her credentials got a $7,000 scholarship and free tuition."[13]

According to the article, the central issue in the case revolved around "a value judgment about *what price it is fair and legal to ask whites to pay to provide opportunities* to previously denied nonwhites" (emphasis added).[14] Strikingly, nothing was said about the fact that a woman was now claiming to be discriminated against by the very policy that had long protected white women in employment and education. Nor was anything said about men who might resent Hopwood's admission to law school. Furthermore, such a framing rendered white privilege invisible. This article was not about African Americans who had *not* had the kind of class mobility advantages that the New Deal accorded to white Americans in the mid-twentieth century.[15] Rather, it was framed as unfair to ask whites who believed they had single-handedly earned their status to sacrifice their own desires in order redress the injuries of racism.

Despite the media's limited attention to women in the debate, women were actively involved in the struggle over affirmative action. In California and across the country, a number of women's organizations, such as the IWF and feminist groups such as the National Organization for Women (NOW), joined efforts either to abolish or support the policy. As American Studies scholar Barbara Spindel found in her research on the IWF, in 1995 this organization began an anti-affirmative-action campaign by testifying against affirmative action before Congress and publishing a series of opinion pieces in local and national publications with sensationalist headlines such as, "That's No White Male, That's My Husband," "Shattering the Myth of the Glass Ceiling," and "The Big Lie About Discrimination."[16] One penned by conservative political pundit Laura Ingraham in *The New York Times* in April 1995 urged feminists to abandon their defense of affirmative action. According to Ingraham:

> Aside from being patronizing and simplistic, the idea that women are constantly thwarted by invisible barriers of sexism relegates them to permanent victim status. It also stands on its head the cause that true feminists originally championed—equal opportunity for women . . . Instead of whining about an imaginary glass ceiling, why don't feminists celebrate the fact that women in the work force are at long last pushing against a wide open door?[17]

While Ingraham denounced the glass ceiling as a myth, the opinion piece published in *The Wall Street Journal*, titled "That's No White Male, That's My Husband," called for women to stand by their husbands, sons, and brothers who could be potential victims of affirmative action.[18] And still another penned by Elizabeth Larson argued that it was patronizing for feminists to suggest that women need special accommodations in education and the workforce, as her title boldly declared, "Women Don't Need Extra Help."[19]

As Lydia Chávez finds in her book, *The Color Bind: California's Battle to End Affirmative Action*, conservative groups poured money into the campaign to support the California Civil Rights Initiative; the California Republican Party raised nearly $1 million, the Republican National Party donors provided another million, and state Republicans paid for many expensive and deceptive television commercials.[20] In one 1996 commercial used by congressional and assembly candidates that clearly echoed IWF concerns, a white husband walked dejectedly into his kitchen telling his wife he did not get a job "because of quotas." "Her face lined with sympathy and frustration, the wife turns to face the camera and declares, 'It's just not right.'"[21]

While Republicans were airing television commercials designed to stoke fears about white men as innocent victims of quotas, NOW and the Feminist Majority Foundation organized to marshal support for affirmative action. In March 1995, Patricia Ireland, the president of NOW, and Eleanor Smeal, the president of the Feminist Majority, met with President Clinton's senior advisers to discuss the importance of affirmative action to American women and rallied for his support. "The President, they warned, risked a backlash if he failed to fully support affirmative action."[22] As Lydia Chávez found, in the following year when Proposition 209 was on the ballot in California, the Feminist Majority also worked with the Democratic Party, the Mexican American Legal Defense and Education Fund (MALDEF), and student groups such as El Movimiento Estudiantil Chicano de Aztlán (MEChA) to mobilize support for affirmative action across the state and to raise money for advertising against the Proposition.[23]

Although these activities received almost no attention in either the *Chronicle* or the *Times*, the dominant framing of the debate around race did not go completely unnoticed by the media.[24] In early March 1995, the same year that Ward Connerly began his campaign to abolish affirmative action in the UC system, *The New York Times* published an article titled, "Defending Affirmative Action, Liberals Try to Place Debate's Focus on Women" that detailed a news conference with a number of affirmative action advocates including the Reverend Jesse Jackson, members of the Feminist Majority, and leaders from the Congressional Black Caucus who "were trying to recast the debate over the issue so that it focused on the way programs benefit women." The article goes on to say:

The more that affirmative action is described as an effort intended primarily to help blacks, they fear, the worse its political prospects. . . . Polls seem to confirm that the public is more accepting of programs that give women preferences in hiring or college admissions than of programs that do the same for blacks or other minorities. A New York Times/CBS News Poll conducted last week found 43 percent agreeing that women should receive preferences in hiring and promotion where there had been bias against women in the past. But when asked whether preference should be given to blacks in cases where they had been racial discrimination, only 33 percent said yes.[25]

Several weeks later, in a *New York Times* letter to the editor responding to this article, titled, "What Feminism Has Done to the Workplace; Welcome to the Battle," Loyle Hairston writes

affirmative action, which has been deliberately misrepresented as an economic sop for less qualified black men. Though virtually ignored in the debate, white women have benefited far more than black men. . . . white women have finally raised their voices. I hope they haven't waited too late to joined the battle.[26]

And, another letter-to-the-editor writer in April of the same year said:

The arguments against affirmative action are almost always crafted in racial terms because the demagogues know that race is the way to get the emotional flames roaring. In fact, the primary beneficiaries of affirmative action are women.[27]

Despite these criticisms of anti-affirmative-action rhetoric and public calls by national and local organizations and activists to "recast" the terms of the debate, media coverage continued to focus on racial preferences throughout the 1990s.

In 1995, the only other reporting on women came in a handful of articles in the *San Francisco Chronicle* that focused on affirmative action and polling data. One article, titled, "Generation Gap, Color Gap, Women Split on Affirmative Action," emphasized the division in polling data between women of color who opposed Proposition 209 and white women who favored it. The issue was "so *deeply divided*," opined one article, "As women go, *so may go the war*" (emphasis added).

"The fact is, women have benefited from affirmative action, particularly starting in the late 1970s up until the present," says Martin Carnoy, a Stanford University economist who has studied the changing patterns of race and gender

discrimination. "The question is whether they will perceive that they have benefited and whether they perceive there is still a major amount of discrimination
in the labor market."[28]

Another *Chronicle* article on the same day, titled, "Family Ties Help Explain
Why Women are Split; Many Worried about Husbands' Jobs," reports that
"some students of public opinion say that white women are afraid that it could
put their husbands—and their families—at risk. . . . The white woman who
may have benefited from affirmative action also has a conflict because she may
be worried that her husband could be denied a job because of affirmative action."[29] And a May 10 article, "Perceptions: Minority Women's Views Opposite
of White Men's," reports:

> The new Chronicle/KRON-TV poll reveals stark differences in opinions on
> affirmative action between whites and minorities, and nowhere is that gulf
> wider than between minority women and white men. Although 55 percent of
> white men support an initiative to end preferences based on race and gender,
> only 31 percent of minority women favor it . . .[30]

Although these three articles do focus on women, like the broader theme of
racial conflict discussed in Chapter 1, they reinforce the notion that opinion on
affirmative action was sharply divided—either between *white women* and *women
of color*, on the one hand, or between *white men* and *women of color* on the other.
However, as other polling and survey data conducted during this time period
demonstrated, the way questions were posed—either as "affirmative action" or
as "preferential treatment"—often influenced the way people responded. Asking about racial preferences tended to evoke negative responses, while asking
about affirmative action yielded positive ones.[31]

As we saw in Chapter 1, the broader focus of the media worked to create a
cultural memory of "white male innocence and injury." While the more limited focus on women in the news occluded the fact that women were involved
in this debate at all, even this very small subset of articles operated to reinforce
the broader cultural narrative. As these television ads and articles suggested,
if white women played a role in the debate about affirmative action, it was
to stand by their husbands and sons, and protect them from discrimination,
by helping defeat affirmative action. As communications studies scholar Roopali Mukherjee suggests in her analysis of anti-affirmative-action television
ads, "Constituted within traditional heterosexist and gendered roles—wives,
mothers, daughters—women, and particularly white women, are strategically

positioned on the same side of the debate as white males. Such solidarities have served strategic and reactionary ends at other moments in time as well, suggesting that white women have historically served a critical role in the history of whiteness, recruited as allied during episodic turns from crisis to recuperation."[32] What we know less about, however, is how actual women understood this debate and where their loyalties lay.

Family Politics in a Changing Workplace

Before the Family and Medical Leave Act became federal law in 1993, maternity leaves, or the more gender-neutral term parental leaves, were not an option in most American workplaces.[33] With the advent of the Family and Medical Leave Act, workplaces are now required to provide women and men twelve weeks of *unpaid* family leave from work for the birth of a new baby or a serious illness in the family. Furthermore, the Act guarantees that their job will be there when employees return from their leave. While this policy is far less generous than those afforded in Europe and Scandinavia, for many American women it represented a significant improvement over existing leave policies in large corporations, because it meant they could count on coming back to their jobs after their leave ended.[34]

Like corporate America, the majority of large law firms in the Bay Area did not have formal maternity leave policies in the late 1980s.[35] By contrast, and as a result of its court-ordered affirmative action plan, BC did have a maternity leave policy, which gave women eight weeks off work after having a baby. Further, with the advent of the consent decree, the numbers of women lawyers in the Legal Department increased from 3 percent in 1974 to 18 percent in 1989. In this way, BC was more like many unionized American workplaces that adopted affirmative action programs in the 1970s and 1980s; it sought not only to hire more women and people of color, but also to create more flexible, family-friendly policies.[36]

In the BC Legal Department, some of the changes brought about by affirmative action met with resistance. As discussed in the last chapter, some white men resented the practice of family leaves, while others were uncomfortable with the shift in social etiquette in the workplace prompted by the presence of women and people of color. BC's women lawyers were not unaware of this undercurrent of resistance. In my 1989 interviews, many complained about the Department's implementation of family leaves and their requests for part-time work beyond the eight-week time period. Some observed that while men were able to obtain part-time work assignments for "health reasons," they were unable to work part-time after having their first baby. Mary Brown, a white woman, and, at the time, a divorced single mother, confronted the managing partner with this double-standard. He told her that "the men had families to support." "And women don't?" she angrily replied.[37]

Like Mary, another white woman lawyer, Susan Carlson, was also dissatisfied with the way the leave policy was implemented. She too eventually left the firm after having her first baby, and when reinterviewed almost ten years later, she was working, like many other women lawyers across the country, as an attorney in the public sector. She described her reasons for leaving her corporate position in litigation:

I moved because the hours were just insane. There was incredible pressure to put in those hours, like, you know, 60 hours a week. I was never home. I was always working. I mean, what kind of life is that? And, so few women made partner then . . . What did that mean for me? Then, when I got pregnant, I started to seriously reevaluate my life. What's really important, you know? . . . And, I could see how hard it would be to work full-time after my daughter was born because, you know, the firm didn't have much of maternity leave policy . . . And, anyway, I realized that I wasn't happy. I wanted to work and I wanted a family, but that just wasn't doable there . . . So, I came here. The work isn't all that interesting and I still work a lot. Sometimes, I work weekends, but I don't work sixty-hour weeks anymore. The most is fifty, and really that's pretty unusual. It's probably more like forty or forty-five. It's just a more humane kind of work schedule. So, I have time to spend with my daughter and with my husband. I have a more balanced life.

Later in her interview, I asked her how she characterized the policies for women and minorities in her current workplace. She replied:

Well, I work for a federal agency, so affirmative action is the policy here for recruitment, hiring, and promotion. And, there's just a lot more women and minorities here. . . . In fact, my former boss [in the federal agency] who I really liked was a woman. And that really makes a difference for things like mentoring . . . I mean, it's not perfect. I still feel sometimes like there's pressure not to talk too much about my family at the office. Like if I need to leave early to take my daughter to the doctor or something like that, I usually say I have an appointment because there's still this idea that women put family before career, you know, women aren't *committed* to their jobs. So, yeah, I still worry about things

like that. But, really that's more from the old guard, you know these older guys
with the wives at home, they just don't get it. [emphasis added]

In Susan's case, the long hours and the limited prospects for women in partnership eventually drove her to seek employment elsewhere. She found work in
the public sector, which by her own admission was much less well paid, but she
felt she was better able to balance her career with her family life. Nevertheless,
her worries about appearing to be committed to her job continued. In her
earlier 1989 interview, she talked about how putting in long hours at the office
was a way to demonstrate commitment.

> It's really a macho thing, you know, all the guys sit around and brag about how
> many hours they put in, about their late nights and weekends in the office, pull-
> ing all-nighters, and how many billable hours they have on their monthly time
> sheets, who had the most billable hours last month. So, there's like a culture of
> lots and lots of billable hours—long hours in the office . . . It's like there's is
> always this suspicion that you aren't working hard enough, that you aren't really
> committed. And, I think that's especially something that women have to face
> because I mean, here I am six months pregnant and I know if I talk about taking
> maternity leave or getting part-time work schedule or anything like that, the
> first thing the managing partner will say to me is, "Susan, are you committed to
> this job, because you know what we value is commitment."[38]

Susan had more to say about the meaning of commitment at work in 1999:

> We were interviewing several people for the job, and one of them was a woman.
> They [the hiring committee] kept asking about her over and over, "But do you
> think she's really committed?" I finally said "What about these guys [who were
> being interviewed], what about them, do you think they're really committed?"
> Everyone got real quiet. And, I think they got my point that, you know, that
> they were assuming that women are less committed than men. So, yeah, it's still
> there. It's still there all the time.

Though questioning commitment remained an issue for women lawyers in
Susan's new workplace in 1999, she felt more confident about effectively challenging the assumption when it arose.

Like Susan, Mary Brown also left the firm in the early 1990s after she re-
married. Because her husband has a professional job with a benefits package
for the entire family, Mary initially thought she would have more flexibility in
finding legal work that would complement her decision to spend more time
with her young daughter. Consequently, she decided to look for a part-time

legal position that would allow her to do most of her work from home. As she discovered, most legal positions in either large corporate firms or in the public sector did not take on part-time attorneys. By chance, she ran into a colleague who had graduated from the same law school and was working on a contract basis for a big firm in San Francisco. The friend made some introductions, and Mary also began working on a contract basis. As she put it, they "are happy to pay me well—though without health insurance—for several weeks or months of work at a time." Although she regrets feeling that she no longer has a "real career"—attorneys who work on a contract basis are not regarded as "real employees of the firm and don't have the same opportunities for advancement"— she enjoys spending time with her daughter and keeping her "hand in the legal profession."

In this part of her narrative, Mary describes her move from the Legal Department to her current part-time work as a contract employee as a partial success story. Although she is not working in a high-powered position, she is able, given her husband's financial cushion and the employment options available to her, to devise a solution that allows her to continue working and to spend time with her family. Her pragmatic, upbeat tone shifts later in the interview, when she recalls her previous vulnerability as a single mother and her anger at her previous boss.

> I can still remember how mad I was when I talked to the head of the department [in BC's Litigation Department] about working part-time. He was so matter-of-fact about saying that men have families to support—and here I am, a recently divorced single parent. Like women don't have these problems, too? These "good ole boys"—they're just dinosaurs, every one of them. . . . I don't regret the decisions I've made since then, and I love my family, but I will never forget what it's like to have all the worries that go with being the sole bread-winner. . . . And, then, well, do you know how hard it would be for me now to get a full-time job after having worked for so many years as a contractor? These big firms do not care that I am good at what I do or that I have been working for all these places—it's all part-time to them. My commitment to the profession would be in question.

Like Susan, Mary also recognized that her presumed commitment to the profession was jeopardized by family responsibilities—first, when she requested a part-time leave at BC to continue taking care of her new baby, and again in 1999, as an attorney who worked on a part-time contract basis to accommodate her desire to spend more time with her daughter.

Unlike Mary and Susan, neither Peggy Berkowitz nor Gail Johnson had children when I first interviewed them in 1989. Nevertheless, both white women also understood how the notion of commitment affected others' perceptions of them at work. As Peggy told me:

> PB: This question of commitment always seems creep into conversations about maternity leave. I don't know how many times I have I heard men say, "You just have to wonder about her!" "Do you think she will really come back to work after she has her baby?" "Do you think she is really committed?"
>
> JP: How does it affect you personally?
>
> PB: The assumption that because I am a woman, I will be the same way. That I won't work hard enough or long enough. That I am not committed to the profession because I might go off and have a baby.
>
> JP: And, you don't have kids.
>
> PB: I don't have kids.

On the other hand, in her most recent interview, Peggy said that she could also understand why employers sometimes raised these concerns.

> I guess for them, the problem is: Who is going to do the work when someone is on leave? Who interviews the client, who does the legal research, who writes the briefs, who goes to court? With budget cuts, they're not going to hire a temporary replacement. They just divvy up the work load and give everyone another assignment. So, one person's leave means more work for everyone else. [sighs] But, on the other hand, I know how hard it is for my friends with children. There's always something going on with the kids and there's never much leeway at work. So, I guess there has to be a better way to do all of this. [sighs] But, I don't know what it is.

In contrast to Peggy, Susan, and Mary who all described feeling that their commitment to the profession was suspect, Gail was one of the few women associates who felt pushed onto the "fast track" upon arrival in the Legal Department. When she interviewed for the position, as a UCLA Law School graduate who served on law review, she had already received a number of competitive offers from some of the large Bay Area firms; and, as a result, she was able to negotiate a much higher salary than her colleagues with the same years of experience. (She was also single at the time.) However, as time went on, her feelings about being on the fast track changed. In her 1989 interview, she told me:

When I first came to the Legal Department, [senior counsel] made it clear that I was on the fast track. After a couple of years under a supervisor who gave me complete autonomy without any kind of psychic reward, I felt burned out. I wasn't contributing to society, plus all the stress and long hours. I decided at that point to find personal satisfaction. I got off the sixty-hour-week fast track. I took a three-month leave of absence. I came back to work part-time. I work [here] four days a week and do pro bono work on Fridays. I work for legal services for kids—I need to do it.[39]

By working part-time—clearly an exceptional arrangement in 1989—and doing pro bono work, Gail found a way to satisfy her interests in the human side of the job: "When I go to work on Fridays, I feel like I am doing real work for real people with real problems. I don't have to pull myself up or put other people down. It's about real life."[40]

Ten years later when I reinterviewed Gail, she was practicing law for a public interest organization. When I asked why she had left BC, she told me that after working part-time for a year and half, the management committee told her they could no longer afford to let her continue the arrangement and asked her to come back full-time. Gail explained the situation:

GJ: At the time, I had no interest in going back to work full-time, and I think that was part of the problem. They knew I didn't want to be on the fast track anymore. They knew I liked the doing my work with homeless youth, and so they began to wonder about me.

JP: Wonder what?

GJ: Whether I had the commitment, the drive, the killer instinct to be a star litigator. Plus, I liked working with kids. That's not exactly the kind of work your typical aggressive litigator type likes to do . . . So, I had a decision to make—go back to the long hours or do something else.

Although Gail too mentioned commitment, it had a slightly different meaning for her than for the other women. It was not tied to an understanding of a suspect preference for family over work, but rather a desire to get off the fast track and practice a different kind of law, one that involved a domain understood as a traditionally female one—working with children.

As other studies reveal, organizations with an "overtime work culture" place a high value on commitment at work.[41] In such workplaces, commitment not only signals one's professional obligation to do the best possible work, but also means putting in long hours at the office.[42] In sociologist Mindy Fried's study of a large corporation in Boston with family-friendly policies, she found that employees were expected to put in long hours at the office and those who did not adhere to this norm were viewed as "less committed" to their jobs. Despite the fact that policies were specifically designed to be flexible to the needs of families, most women and men in upper management did not take advantage of flexible hours, part-time work options, or family leaves because they knew they would appear to be less committed, which in turn might jeopardize salary increases, promotions, and, with downsizing, possibly their jobs. As one mother and middle manager said: "It's always the women who take off . . . so just going out to have the baby, people think [that] takes away from your job, [and they think] the commitment you have to give to your family also takes you away from your job."[43] Such a workplace culture and its consequences are not unique. In another study, an employee of a large corporation reported:

> The culture is that you get credit for long hours . . . There is no forty-hour week; if you are not doing at least fifty, you are not a team player. It's a sign of dedication, [and it] doesn't matter if there's work to do . . . If there are two people of equal performance, the promotion will go to the one who has put in the overtime.[44]

Like Fried's study, this one also found that employees felt pressured not to work shorter hours or to take parental leaves. In her influential book *The Time Bind*, sociologist Arlie Hochschild uncovered a similar problem for employees, particularly women, who want to take time off from work in her research on a large New York–based corporation. And sociologist Cynthia Fuchs Epstein and her colleagues' research on women lawyers who work part-time in order to better balance family and career found that these women are taken less seriously in their professional lives because they are seen as less committed than their male counterparts.[45]

What these studies suggest is that the meanings attached to gender play a significant role in shaping how women are viewed by their employers. For many employers, women are regarded as mothers—whether they are actually mothers or not—and mothers, they assume, will put family before career.[46] For such employers, "not committed" becomes a shorthand expression for their gendered assumptions about the relationship between women, work, and family. It is the woman lawyer interviewed for the job whose commitment is questioned, as Susan reminds us, not the men's. In Gail's case, her commitment to being a high-powered, competitive litigator was also cast into doubt *not* because she wanted to have a family, but because she worked part-time, enjoyed doing so, and preferred to practice a different kind of law. Here, her rejection of long hours was regarded as lack of commitment, and her choice to practice law involving children's rights was understood as an implicitly female area of specialization—it wasn't something a "typical aggressive litigator type would like to do."

These seemingly gendered assumptions about the relationship between women, work, and family did not affect all women, however. Unlike her white female colleagues, Yolanda Jones, who was the only African American woman in the department in 1989, did not feel that her commitment to the profession was called into question. Before she came to the Legal Department, she had worked a number of years for the District Attorney's office and consequently had extensive trial experience. Given this background, as well as her considerable success as counsel for BC, she was regarded by most of her colleagues as one of the best trial attorneys in the department. At the same time, however, Yolanda often found that her success met with some resentment, though often disguised as a form of bantering. For example, as I noted in my fieldwork from 1989, in a meeting with the entire litigation group, Sam Nelson, the head of the department, jokingly dubbed Yolanda the "queen of sanctions" for her persistence in castigating opposing counsel for their failure to comply with discovery requests, arguing with the judge for appropriate sanctions and successfully obtaining them.[47] At the same meeting, she was also selected by the department head to find a new coffee machine for the department. "You'll be our litigation hostess," he said with a smile. The banter continued, and Allen Broadbent, a white male associate, corrected him. "You mean she will be our hostess czarina. Let's see, we have Yolanda the hostess czarina, Yolanda the queen of sanctions, what's next?"[48]

While the banter about Yolanda's reputation appeared to be friendly, beneath the teasing and joking lay assumptions about a raced and gendered division of labor. Yolanda, the *only* African American woman in the department and one of its most successful litigators, was relegated by the head of the department to the role of finding a new coffee machine. Thus, Yolanda was not only put in her place as a woman—none of the white men asked to take on this task—but she was also relegated to a domestic arrangement that has been the historic lot of black women.[49] (None of the white women attorneys were asked to do so.) Yolanda shared this interpretation; she said in her 1989 interview, "When I walked out of that meeting, I just could *not* believe that they were asking me to find a new coffee machine! What do they think I am—their house servant?" [emphasis in original]

Later in the same interview, Yolanda described the double-edged sword of her success. On one hand, she felt there were instances when she was given a hard time for being so good at her job: "Sometimes I think that being a smart black woman just scares them to death. It drives them crazy that I am so good at what I do." On the other hand, when she was recognized as the one of the best litigators in the department, she felt her success was used as a yardstick against which the two other African American male attorneys—Randall Kingsley and Tryone Lewis discussed in Chapter 3, who had much less trial experience than she did—were compared. In other words, she felt that her success was used to their detriment. As she put it:

> Okay, so they did affirmative action and they hired me, and they say to me, "Yolanda, you are the greatest." But they are thinking, "She's kind of scary smart. Do we really have to hire anyone else? I mean isn't one enough . . ." So, when they do hire someone else, they hire Randall and Tyrone [both of whom are African American] practically fresh out of law school, and they constantly compare the two of them to me. And, how can they ever measure up—I was in the DA's office for six years before I even got here. I mean, in six years, sure, they'll both be good litigators, but it takes time. . . . In the meantime, all these comparisons create bad feelings . . . I don't like the fact that my success is being used against the only other black attorneys in the Department.

As I learned when I reinterviewed Yolanda in 1999, this divide-and-conquer strategy, among other reasons, eventually led her to seek employment in a medium-sized firm that specialized in labor law, where she is now a partner. (The firm worked for unions.) Here again, she had mixed things to say about her success:

> YJ: They know I am good at what I do. And, quite frankly, I have to be good, *very* good at what I do. If you're black and you are a litigator, you *cannot* be just average. You have to be a star. Otherwise, they just won't take you seriously . . . [emphasis in original]
>
> JP: So, do you feel like you're taken seriously as a professional?
>
> YJ: I do, I do. But, I have to do a lot more work to be taken seriously. There's just more I have to do to prove myself. Because, you know, white people are *still* surprised if black people are smart . . . So, I'm always working against that, that assumption. Plus, when I first came to BC, I had to get used to the feeling that I was always under a microscope—when you're the only black woman, people watch your every step. And, if you make a mistake, *everyone* notices. So it's a lot of pressure. [emphasis in original]

JP: And, do you think it's the same thing where you're working now?

YJ: It is, but I guess what it is different is that I am not the only one. In fact, for a while, we got some attention in the press because we had hired more people of color than some of the other firms in the area. Plus, I am a partner now, which gives me some influence. But it's certainly not like I run the place. . . . But, I have to say, I have always liked my work—I like making arguments, I'm quick on my feet, and, of course, I really like to win. And, I usually do.

In contrast to her white female colleagues who work against the assumption that they are not as committed to the profession as men are, Yolanda, as a black woman, felt that she worked against the racial stereotype that she was less professionally competent than her white colleagues. Consequently, she felt that she must prove herself to be exceptional in order to be taken seriously. Though now a partner at another law firm where she has some influence and authority, she is still troubled by this perception.

Yolanda's personal narrative is not unique; it corroborates findings in other social science research on the experiences of African Americans in predominantly white professional workplaces.[50] As some of these studies demonstrate, blacks are often required to have far more impressive credentials than whites, even when competing for the same jobs. As journalist, psychologist, and author Brent Staples argues:

> For whites, elite university degrees are a nice enhancement, but for African-Americans, those same degrees are required just to get in the door. . . . These inequities are rooted in the logic of slavery and are based on the myth that blacks are intellectually inferior. As a consequence of this myth, black people face substantially higher barriers to employment than whites—especially in elite professions where whiteness has historically served as an unstated job requirement.[51]

Legal scholar David Wilkins draws similar conclusions in his research, which finds that African American applicants to law firms with average grades are less likely to be hired than their white counterparts with the same transcripts. In addition, he finds that African Americans who made partner were far more likely than white partners to have attended prestigious, elite law schools such as Yale and Harvard.[52]

These studies, as well as the work life stories I collected, draw attention to the divergent raced and gendered assumptions, meanings, and practices that women professionals confront in the workplace. Of the women discussed thus far, all worried that their work performance might be evaluated in negative ways, but as a comparison of their accounts reveals, the assumptions underlying such assessments were raced and gendered in distinctive ways. Whereas Susan struggled as a white woman with the challenge of being seen as not committed, Yolanda felt that she was constantly working against the notion that blacks are less intelligent than whites. Interestingly, none of the white women interviewed described feeling that their intelligence or qualifications were in doubt.[53] In fact, most of their male colleagues told me that Susan, for instance, was a very good lawyer. If anything, she was regarded by many in her office as highly qualified because she received her law degree from Stanford, an elite private university, whereas most of the lawyers in her office got their degrees from less prestigious, local night schools. Here, whiteness shielded Susan against assumptions of intellectual inferiority because in the United States whiteness is associated with a multitude of personal and social privileges, including entitlement to respectful treatment in social interactions, a good education, a good standard of living, and private property.[54] As this comparison suggests, the phrase "not committed," then, is more accurately described as a shorthand expression for a raced *and* gendered cultural logic about the relationship between *white* women, work, and family in this workplace. White middle-class women are presumed to be potential mothers—whether they are actually mothers or not—and motherhood is assumed to take precedence over professional work. By contrast, as an African American woman, Yolanda did not fit into this notion of white female domesticity.[55] Instead, she had to contend racialized assumptions about intellectual inferiority.

Regardless of race, these women lawyers all felt that they operated under a cloud of suspicion in the workplace. They were working against what I term the "rhetoric of the imaginary glass ceiling." In using the term "rhetoric," my point is to draw attention to the distinction between the sociological concept of the glass ceiling as a structural obstacle to professional mobility and the individualistic language deployed in professional discourses about the means for achieving success. Within this discursive realm, professional success or failure is typically attributed to one's "individual competence, efforts, and ambition."[56] For white women, this rhetoric suggests that if they were truly committed to their jobs, that is, if they put in long hours in the office, they will be rewarded through raises and promotions. Those who do not, as members of the IWF contend, are "whining" about an "imaginary glass ceiling."[57] For women of color (and for men of color as indicated in Chapter 3), this rhetoric suggests that professionals of color with exceptional intelligence and qualifications will succeed. Those who do not and complain are viewed as "crying racism" in an effort to blame others for their failure. Although this rhetoric operates in distinctive ways for white women and people of color, its underlying assumptions about individual effort and accountability resonate within the broader cultural logic of liberal individualism.

Ambivalence and Affirmative Action

As I found in my interviews, the women who talked about the discrimination they felt they faced in their legal careers also tended to support affirmative action. Given that one of the central assumptions of the pro-affirmative-action stance is that discrimination continues to exist, this finding is not surprising. However, their thinking about this issue is typically more conflicted than the media's simplistic depiction of the debate, and their feelings about affirmative action are often ambivalent. In Mary's work life history, for example, after spending almost an hour talking about the ways that she and other women continued to confront sexism in the workplace, I shifted topics by asking her about "issues that may have to do with racial discrimination or with other kinds of categories covered by affirmative action policy." She said:

> Yes, yes, I know, the consent decree covered both race and gender. And, it's interesting that you bring this up because now that I think back then when people talked about affirmative action, they always talked about race. I mean, they always assumed that it was about race. But, affirmative action is about women too!

When I asked Mary to describe her position on affirmative action was, she told me:

> MB: Oh, I definitely support it. I think it's made a big difference for women and minorities—especially at BC. And, just think about it, about how much it has changed workplaces all over the country. In the '50s and '60s, women with law degrees like Sandra Day O'Connor were told flat out "we don't hire women." That kind of thing just doesn't happen anymore.

> JP: But what about Proposition 209? Didn't that bring about some changes, at least in California?

> MB: You mean the backlash? [JP nods] Yeah, that's very depressing. I remember reading somewhere that Boalt Hall [the Law School at the University of California at Berkeley] admitted only one minority after [Proposition] 209 went into effect . . . But, you know, I have to say, the opposition was effective, very

effective. They worked hard to mobilize resentment. You know the arguments. It's unfair to white men, etc., etc. And, it really seemed to work. I think they tapped into something there.

JP: What?

MB: Resentment. Resentment about fairness. That it's not fair to some individuals. I mean, I know why affirmative action is absolutely essential— discrimination did not magically disappear overnight. Believe me, I know that. It may be subtle at times, but it's still there . . . But then, you hear these stories about some kid with a 4.0 who didn't get into Berkeley and he's white. And, then you have to wonder, is that fair? You know, is that really fair?

JP: But, what do you think? Is it fair?

MB: I guess what I'm saying is that the opposition raised an important point. [pauses] And, I have to say, I don't know whether it's fair or not. I don't know. On the one hand, I know why we need it, I think it's important, and I do think we need it. But on the other, I can see how it isn't always fair.

Mary at once draws from the broader proponent's media narrative insisting that discrimination continues to exist and that affirmative action is necessary to combat it, but is also troubled by the assumption of individual fairness in the opposition's account. Interestingly, the very anecdote she selected to make her point about fairness—"some kid with a 4.0 who didn't get into Berkeley and he's white"—appears in many of the news stories about affirmative action and college admissions. Yet, compared to the media's depiction of two opposing and seemingly irreconcilable positions in the debate, Mary's position was conflicted: She supported affirmative action, yet she was ambivalent about its possible effects on individuals.

This tension between the plight of the individual and broader societal fairness emerged in other interviews as well. Like Susan, both Peggy and Mary also supported affirmative action policy. At the same time, they expressed ambivalence. As Peggy said:

PB: On the one hand, there is still disadvantage. No question about that, there is still disadvantage. Just look at our public school system in the Bay Area. You can't tell me that kids here all get the same kind education and then they are supposed to go on compete on an even playing field to get into college [after Proposition 209 passed]. . . . But, on the other, there's the issue of fairness. Is it fair, you know, to give a slot to a person of one race, so that another person of a different race doesn't get in? So, I guess that's the conflict for me.

JP: But you still support affirmative action?

PB: I guess I must sound like I don't, but I do. I really do. I'm just conflicted sometimes about this issue of fairness.

Like Susan, Peggy recognized that there are structural obstacles that disadvantage particular groups, but when considering the moral dilemma of the individual, she momentarily lost sight of this broader context and expressed ambivalence.

Gail also talked about fairness, though she framed it in broader terms:

GJ: In the end, it comes down to different ways of thinking about what's fair. Do we want to do something that would bring about more fairness to society in general, or do we want to focus on one individual at a time? The kind of work I do in [public interest organization] is about bringing fairness to society in general. . . . [she provides several examples from her work to illustrate this point] At the same time, I can see it from the opposition's viewpoint. If I were the one who didn't get into college and someone else did get in through affirmative action, I would probably feel like it wasn't fair to me.

JP: Has anything like that ever happened to you?

GJ: No, no. And if I did, I hope I could hold onto the broader notion of fairness.

While these white women expressed ambivalence about the fairness of affirmative action policy, Yolanda's concerns about the policy reflected ambivalence about a different issue.

Like I said, I demand to be recognized as an intelligent, capable litigator. And, what's hard is that there is this idea that if you were an affirmative action hire, then you probably aren't all that good. And that's where the stigma argument comes in, that affirmative action, is, you know, a stigma . . . What's interesting to me is that if you think about this historically, affirmative action was initially understood, at least by black people, it was understood as a reaction against racist institutions. Historically, highly intelligent, capable black Americans have always applied to law school and medical school, but they couldn't get in. What affirmative action did was force these institutions to look at their practices and to change them. And, what's interesting to me is that no one thinks about it that way now. Now, it's regarded as some sort of government hand-out . . . And that's just maddening, because I want to be recognized as a highly qualified professional, and at the same time, I know some people, some white people, think I am just another affirmative action hire . . .

For Yolanda, whose central concern was being recognized as a competent professional, she recognized that the misperception of affirmative action beneficiaries as less qualified had consequences not only for her personally, but also for other people of color. Though she was troubled by this perception and its potentially harmful effects, she also supported the policy. At the same time, she provided a historical context for understanding the rise of affirmative action, its original objectives, and how public understanding of the policy has shifted over time. From her vantage point as a black professional who received her law degree in 1979, she had witnessed the debate around affirmative action as it evolved over a twenty-year period and recognized what I described in Chapter 1 as the emergence of a neoconservative discourse. In their view, affirmative action and many of the Great Society initiatives constituted government interventions that undermine the importance of individual achievement, responsibility, and hard work.[58]

Like Yolanda, Susan also told me that she supported affirmative action. In fact, she described herself as a beneficiary of the policy: "I'm sure it's why I got into law school when I did [in 1982]. Suddenly classes had all these women, and I know BC was still operating under the consent decree when I was hired." When I asked her about other beneficiaries of the program, particularly minorities, she emphasized its importance, but also noted as Yolanda did that affirmative action carried a "stigma."

SC: It's like they think because a minority got hired, it must be because of affirmative action. And, so, there's this stigma—that minorities aren't as good, or as smart, or as qualified. You know, it's like they think you only got in because you were black or Latino or whatever.

JP: Some people might argue that simply being person of color in this country has always been a stigma, regardless of affirmative action.

SC: Of course, that's true. I mean that's why the policy got created in the first place, to force employers to take these issues seriously, especially in recruiting and hiring. . . . But, it's also true, that's how conservatives, and sometimes even liberals, use it against minorities. And, you know, you hear it all the time about it being a stigma. And so I think that perception can be harmful to minorities.

JP: Do you think it's the same perception for white women? You know, because women are beneficiaries, too?

SC: Good question, good question. I never really thought about that before. [pauses] You know, I don't think it does. I mean, I do think other things happen to women, that there are other perceptions that are harmful to women. [she revisits the issue of perceptions about women's commitment to the legal profession] . . . So, for women, I don't think it's about affirmative action.

What's interesting here is that Susan had to think about the fact that affirmative action applies to women, too. It suggests that the media's framing of this issue as a racial one had been successful. At the same time, Susan struggled both with the need for affirmative action and the ways this policy seemed to harm minorities. Lisa Voedisch framed the issue a different way:

> LV: Affirmative action was designed to address a social problem: racial inequality in American society. Remember LBJ's famous speech about racial inequality in America and the metaphor of a race where we find one person hobbled at the starting line and the other is not? He recognized that, given our history, we don't all start on an even playing field. And, in his vision, his vision of the Great Society, affirmative action was a remedy—a means for addressing the problem of inequality. So, affirmative action was purposefully designed to remedy a social problem. . . . What we have now from the opposition are arguments about fairness *as they apply to individuals*. But, affirmative action was never about an individual. It was a policy designed to protect groups of people, groups of people who encounter discrimination. [emphasis added]
>
> JP: I like the distinction you're making, the distinction between the two sides. That makes sense. But, can you say more about your own position? Do you support affirmative action or—
>
> LV: [interrupts] Oh, I definitely support it. The point I was trying to make is not so much about my own position, but about the ways that affirmative action as a policy has been misconstrued. It was designed through the Great Society programs to combat a social problem—discrimination. The Republicans completely ignore that point and focus on unfairness to individuals.

Like Yolanda, Lisa historicized the objectives of affirmative action policy and highlighted the ways Republicans had reframed the issue as one of individual fairness. Later in the interview, she told me that the debate about affirmative action had been controversial because "race is such a loaded issue in this country." Though she did not describe herself as conflicted about the policy, she identified in other white Americans what a number of scholars have described as a "generalized ambivalence" toward black Americans.[59] As she put it, "There are white employers who say they love Michael Jordan [the former Chicago Bulls basketball star], but when it comes down to it, they still won't hire an

African American." In her view, this problem would not change "without the encouragement of affirmative action."

With the exception of Lisa and Yolanda, then, all these women lawyers supported affirmative action but were ambivalent. They at once supported its goals for protecting against discrimination, and thus contributing to a "good society," but they remained troubled by the potential moral dilemma of unfairness to individuals.

"But, Being a Woman Has Nothing to Do with It . . ."

There were a few white women who strongly rejected being seen as "women lawyers," denied that discrimination was a serious problem for them, and, as I found in their 1999 interviews, strongly opposed affirmative action. These two were the only women of the original nine who worked in the litigation department in 1989 and were still working there ten years later. For example, in 1989, when I first asked Kathryn Mortimer about the challenges she might face as a woman and an attorney, she said, "Being a woman is just not an issue. I never think that because I happen to be a woman, blah, blah, blah will happen." And, when I asked her in the same interview whether she had ever experienced discrimination, she replied:

> Discrimination? Sometimes clients will say that it's odd to have a woman on the case. But I don't pay attention to that. You just get in there, roll up sleeves and you do the work. I worked hard, I put in the hours, and I made partner. In fact, I was the first woman partner in the department. But being a woman had nothing to do with it.[60]

Ten years later, Kathryn's reflections about discrimination appeared, for the most part, to be unchanged.

> KM: You know, I've worked very hard to get where I am. And I am so tired of hearing other women talk about discrimination this and discrimination that. They all see themselves as victims. I absolutely refuse to think of myself as a victim and I don't need extra help. [in an angry voice] I've never needed extra help. Why should women need extra help? It's so paternalistic.
>
> JP: So, you don't feel you ever encountered discrimination?
>
> KM: No, I didn't say that. I just don't spend all my time thinking about it. I am an attorney. I know discrimination law. If someone does something, I will point it out to them in legal terms what they are doing wrong. I spell out the letter

of the law . . . [gives a number of examples] But these younger women seem to expect special treatment. They are always complaining that maternity leaves aren't long enough, that the company should do more. What makes them so special? We all have work to do. That's why we're here. No one ever said being a litigator was easy!

When I asked Kathryn in the same interview whether she thought affirmative action had anything to do with getting her position at BC in the early 1980s, she said:

KM: What I don't like about questions like that is the assumption that I got my job here because I am a woman. The assumption that I received special treatment. I have always worked hard and I do excellent work . . . My son was very young when I first started here, I didn't let that hold me back. I just kept working.

JP: How did you manage that?

KM: I've always had help. We've always had someone help with my son. And someone else to help with cooking, with cleaning, with the yard. It's all about choices. I made a choice to become an attorney and to have a family. I made a choice to get help. These women who complain about how hard it is think they're entitled to all this time off. They made a choice to be an attorney. They know what the workload is like. It's no secret that we work long hours.

Like Kathryn, Isabella Marini, the only other woman from the original cohort who still worked in the Legal Department in 1999, held similar views. In response to my question about whether she has ever faced discrimination in her career, she told me in her 1999 interview, "Crying discrimination is the easy way out." When I asked her to elaborate on this point, she replied:

IM: I mean that it's easier to point to discrimination than it is to realistically evaluate your own work ethic. Women who talk all the time about discrimination don't take responsibility for their own actions. They don't look hard at their own work. They complain that the men do this and this and this when what they really should be doing is taking advantage of the opportunities they have and doing good work.

JP: Do you mean women in general or are you referring to women attorneys here?

IM: [pauses] Here.

JP: Can you say more about that?

IM: Let me qualify that. I'm not referring to all women attorneys here or anywhere, but let's say a subset of women. This subset talks a lot about discrimination, the glass ceiling, chilly climate, and I think it's all a lot of bunk. I mean, what is the glass ceiling, anyway—some sort of invisible barrier that beats women down? That's so easy. If you don't get what you want it's because of this invisible glass ceiling. If you don't get what you want, it's because of discrimination. I just can't take that argument seriously.

JP: Why not?

IM: Because I worked hard and I made it. Why can't they?

JP: But, isn't it true that BC was sued for sex and race discrimination in the 1970s and that's why the consent decree was ordered by the court in the first place?

IM: *That* was a *very* long time ago. [emphasis in original]

JP: Okay. But what about balancing work and family? Some studies show that contemporary workplaces have been resistant to accommodating family and medical leaves to women who have childcare or eldercare responsibilities.

IM: That has nothing to do with discrimination. You're talking about *personal* choices that individuals make. If women decide they want to spend more time with their families, well, that's their choice. We're *not* responsible for accommodating personal decisions. [emphasis in original]

While Isabella denied that discrimination was a problem, though she did reluctantly admit that it had existed in the past, Kathryn recognized its existence but insisted, at least in her most recent interview, that there were legal means for addressing it. Nevertheless, following the cultural logic of individualist thinking, both women emphasized the importance of individual choice, effort, and hard work to explain their success. At this point in their careers and life-course trajectories, both women had achieved the equivalent of partnership and both lived in exclusive suburban areas in the Bay Area with their families, and each woman had a son. Moreover, both took a dim view of women attorneys who "complain about discrimination." Kathryn, for instance, contrasted herself to the "younger women" who seem to expect "special treatment," refusing to see herself as a "victim." Here, the very language Kathryn adopted to criticize women who think they should get "extra help" resonated with the arguments of affirmative action opponents who considered it an undeserved government handout. Like IWF advocates, she rejected such help as "paternalistic." Isabella too set herself apart from a "subset" of other women attorneys who complained about discrimination, calling them "whiners." Strikingly, her characterization of the "the glass ceiling" as "an invisible force" that beat "women down" also resonated with the language of conservative IWF publications.[61]

A number of feminist scholars have argued that the denial of discrimination by successful professional women—whether as academics, physicians, or scientists—reflects not their actual experiences, but rather their sense of marginality in a male-dominated workplace.[62] To become accepted as a competent professional, such a woman may feel she has to work against pejorative stereotypes of women, and in doing so distance herself "from the group *women* in order to identify herself with professionals in general" (emphasis in original).[63] While such an explanation is compelling, it does not explain why some of the white women I interviewed adopted this stance and others did not. Isabella's position on discrimination, for instance, contrasted sharply with those of the younger women she criticized. While Kathryn, conversely, told me in her first interview that she didn't "spend all my time thinking about it," in her second she acknowledged discrimination but argued that there were ways to address it through the law.

Part of the problem with this explanation about women's marginality in the professions is that fails to contextualize personal narratives historically and within distinct generations.[64] As sociologist Mary Blair-Loy's study of women executives demonstrates, professional women who first entered the workplace in the 1960s and 1970s had different expectations about balancing work and family than post-baby-boom cohorts had. Or, put another way, they had a different sense of entitlement than the later generation did. While earlier cohorts expected to focus singularly on their careers, later cohorts hoped to pursue their careers *and* have families. As Blair-Loy found, their divergent expectations stem, in part, from historical changes in cultural narratives about women and work, particularly those espoused by the women's movement which not only called for "equal pay for equal work," but also more family-friendly workplace policies.[65] Compared to her younger colleagues who were in the early stages of their careers when I first interviewed them in 1989, Kathryn, who had attended law school in the mid-1970s, was already senior counsel (or the equivalent of a partner in private firms). The majority of the women in question had graduated from law school in the early to mid-1980s, and few had practiced law for longer than five or six years (see Table 4.1). Although Kathryn had attended college and law school at a historical moment when feminist social-movement organizing was on the rise in the United States, she herself had not been involved in any political organizations; or, as she put it, "I am not

Table 4.1 Women lawyers interviewed, dates of law school graduation, and job in 1999

Name	Graduation year	Position in 1999
Peggy Berkowitz	1982	Federal government
Mary Brown	1985	Part-time contracting for law firms
Susan Carlson	1983	Federal government
Lisa Voedisch	1987	Civil rights organization
Gail Johnson	1983	Public interest organization
Yolanda Jones	1979	Medium-sized private firm
Isabella Marini	1972	BC's legal department
Kathryn Mortimer	1975	BC's legal department

a joiner." She attended law school when the numbers of women were certainly growing but still quite small, compared to the dramatic increase in numbers of women in the 1980s when they constituted 40 percent of incoming classes.[66] Kathryn, by her own admission, was much "more accustomed" to working in male-dominated settings, both in law school and in the BC Legal Department. And, like the earlier generation of corporate executives in Blair-Loy's study, she more closely adhered to a model of success that entailed a singular focus on her career. In addition to these generational differences, compared to her younger colleagues, Kathryn has now spent most of her life in a professional milieu and, as mentioned earlier, it is infused with the language of liberal individualism.

Certainly, the history of the civil rights and feminist movements have made stories about discrimination familiar by giving them some public currency, but compared to the dominance of liberal individualist thinking, such stories are now much less prominent in contemporary American culture.[67] Having entered her career at a time when professional women were rewarded for a singular focus on career, and spent twenty-five years of her life in a professional world that emphasizes individual merit and achievement, it not surprising that Kathryn would look back and justify her success in this way.[68] The "cultural tools" most readily available to her within her professional world are firmly ensconced within the language of liberal individualism.[69] Further, compared to the younger women who see themselves working against the "rhetoric of the imaginary glass ceiling," Kathryn, wittingly or not, is working to promote it.

At the same time, however, it is important to note that Kathryn's account of discrimination was not entirely seamless. There are a number of points in her 1999 interview when her tone of voice was defensive, even angry, when questions were raised about the issue. Recall her reply: "I've never needed any extra help!" Kathryn contradicted this statement later in the interview with a description of her privately paid help at home—the maids and gardeners who performed the domestic labor behind the scenes that enabled her to focus singularly on her career.[70] Moreover, when I ask her whether she had been hired when the consent decree was still in effect, she responded defensively that "being a woman may had nothing to do with it" despite the fact that the decree was in effect at the time. The contradictory assertions and the defensive tone running through her account all hint at something unsettling Kathryn's story. Much like the vitriolic exchange I had with David Cooperman, the white male lawyer discussed in Chapter 3, Kathryn's defensiveness suggested that she was protecting something she valued: her sense of self as an autonomous professional who had worked hard to overcome obstacles and achieve success.

As a number of scholars who study professional women in the workplace have found, there is a tendency for many to say that they do not see themselves as women but as scientists, physicians, managers, or academics.[71] For example, as Susan Chase found in her study of women school superintendents, many experienced sex or race discrimination in their professional lives, but were unable to convey what had happened to them within the cultural logic of individualist thinking except in very halting and awkward terms.[72] For Chase, this "halting language" reflects a larger tension in American cultural life between individualist ideals and the reality of material inequality and discrimination—a tension that also surfaced in Kathryn's account. Interestingly, this tension was also present among the other women lawyers I interviewed who, though not defensive, remained conflicted about the fairness of affirmative action.

Given both Kathryn's and Isabella's rejection of discrimination as a serious problem and their strongly individualistic accounts of their success, it is not surprising that both women also opposed affirmative action. As the media analysis in Chapter 1 demonstrates, opponents assume that discrimination is no longer a problem. For example, when I asked Isabella to tell what she thought were the strengths and weakness of affirmative action programs, she replied:

> IM: I can tell you a lot about its weaknesses. It begins with the assumption that women and minorities can't make it in the world of work and need special help. I find that demeaning. It also encourages the notion that discrimination is everywhere just waiting to be discovered. This is the '90s, not the Jim Crow South. Times have changed.
>
> JP: So, it sounds like you think that discrimination is an issue of the past?
>
> IM: Look, if you want to talk about discrimination, let's talk about the ways affirmative action discriminates. My son was a 3.9 student at one of the best

college prep schools in the Bay Area and did he get into Berkeley? No! I read
the papers. I know who gets in and who doesn't. Minorities have the edge today.

Here, Isabella opposed affirmative action on the grounds that women and minorities don't need "special help" and found the assumption that they might
to be "demeaning." In her view, because "times have changed," presumably
discrimination was no longer an issue. Strikingly, while she was quick to discount other women's claims of discrimination earlier in her interview, here
she blamed discrimination, or more accurately "reverse discrimination," for her
son's failure to be admitted to UC Berkeley. Interestingly, in going to an elite
private high school, her son did receive "special help," but rather than counting
against him, this fact entitled him to admission to a prestigious university. Here
again, strands of anti-affirmative-action rhetoric, specifically that of the IWF
about defending sons and husbands against the "injuries" of affirmative action,
emerged in Isabella's narrative.

Kathryn's objections to affirmative action differed somewhat from those of
Isabella. When I asked her to tell me what she thought about affirmative action,
she said:

> KM: Quotas and timetables, things like that?
>
> JP: Well, uh, yeah, if that's how you define it, but what I wondered is what you
> think about the policy itself?
>
> KM: A colossal waste of time. We don't need it. We have discrimination law. We
> are protected by anti-discrimination law. So, we don't need it.

While Kathryn objected to affirmative action because she thought anti-
discrimination law alone would take care of problems, Isabella opposed it
because she found the implicit assumption of "extra help" demeaning. Furthermore, she regarded affirmative action as a form of discrimination directed against
white men or, more specifically, her son. In addition, Kathryn appeared to define
affirmative action as "quotas and timetables." As discussed in the Introduction,
quotas are only legally permissible in the case of court-ordered consent decrees,
and these decrees are rare when compared to other forms of affirmative action,
such as voluntary programs that rely largely on a company's good-faith efforts
to recruit underrepresented groups or federal contracting programs that rely on
goals and timetables rather than quotas.[73] Although it not clear whether Kathryn
was referring here to affirmative action in general or to BC's consent decree in
particular, it is interesting to note that she did not distinguish between different
types of affirmative action and used the term "quotas" as a general referent.

In addition, Kathryn's assertion that anti-discrimination law alone can take care of these problems missed the fundamental distinction between equal opportunity law and affirmative action. As social psychologist Faye Crosby points out in her book, *Affirmative Action Is Dead, Long Live Affirmative Action*, equal opportunity law and affirmative action are two different mechanisms for combating discrimination. Under equal opportunity law, "individuals who have been victimized" are expected to come forward with an attorney who will file an anti-discrimination lawsuit on their behalf. (This, of course, assumes that the individual has the financial means to hire an attorney.) Affirmative action, on the other hand, requires organizations to take a proactive stance in preventing discrimination before it occurs.[74] While this particular distinction is seldom made in the news media, one might reasonably expect that a lawyer who is well-versed in anti-discrimination law would be aware of it. Recall that earlier in the interview Kathryn took great care to "spell out the letter of the law" to me. My point here is not to cast doubt on the accuracy of her account, but to highlight what is absent in her narrative. Rather than discussing a method for combating discrimination that relied on organizational or government intervention, she focused on the options available to an individual. In this way, her story about discrimination also fit neatly within neoliberal and conservative IWF rhetoric emphasizing individual choices within the free market.

Conclusion

In spite of the fact that white women are one of the main beneficiaries of affirmative action programs, and that government reports and class action lawsuits highlighted the continuing existence of discrimination against women in the labor market during the 1990s, the media paid little attention to women in its coverage of the affirmative action debate over this ten-year period. Even in the few articles that focused on women, little was said about how women defined affirmative action or whether they understood it as an influence on their day-to-day experiences in the workplace. As the women lawyers' personal narratives revealed, there was a range of opinions and beliefs about discrimination and about affirmative action. The most common complaint among white women concerned the difficulties in obtaining family leaves both before and after 1993 when the Family and Medical Leave Act became national policy. Even white women who did not have children felt they were working against the presumption that women were less committed to the profession than men.

By contrast, Yolanda, the one African American female attorney, felt she worked against a very different set of raced and gendered assumptions.

With respect to affirmative action, some of the women like Susan understood themselves as beneficiaries of BC's consent decree, while others such as Kathryn denied this fact. A few women, such as Yolanda and Lisa, understood the historical origins of the policy, its goals, and procedures, especially when compared to the information presented in the media, whereas Kathryn depicted it inaccurately as "quotas and timetables" and Isabella dismissed it as a form of reverse discrimination. Finally, with the exception of Kathryn and Isabella, the majority of white women, along with Yolanda, supported affirmative action.

While elements of the print news media's depiction of the affirmative action debate circulated in their accounts, they were rarely accepted wholesale. Some criticized the construction of the debate itself, others contradicted it, and still others accepted some elements and rejected others. For example, as Mary pointed out, the affirmative action program at BC was often understood in terms of racial preferences—just as the media constructed the debate—when actually it was intended to protect women from discrimination as well. Yolanda reminded us of the original goals of the policy as a means of combating the discrimination that excluded qualified African Americans from professional schools and criticized contemporary public discourse for its depiction of the policy as an undeserved "government handout." Lisa too reminded us of the original objectives of affirmative action within the historical context of Lyndon Johnson's Great Society programs and argued that Republicans had misconstrued its original intent. Moreover, in stark contrast to the media depiction of the debate as sharply divided between those who support the policy and those who do not, the majority of women in this study expressed feelings of ambivalence. Mary, for example, believed that discrimination continued to be a problem and supported affirmative action, but was also troubled by what she perceived as its potential unfairness to individuals. Gail also talked about fairness though she framed the debate in broader terms, explaining that each side of the debate thought about fairness in different ways and though she favored a notion of fairness based on the good of society, she recognized that it might feel unfair to individuals. Finally, Yolanda and Susan were also advocates but worried that the stigma of "an affirmative action hire" created an inaccurate and harmful perception about the qualifications of people of color.

By contrast, Kathryn and Isabella appeared to embrace that anti-affirmative rhetoric uncritically. But, even in their accounts some tensions emerged.

Kathryn's contradictory assertions about discrimination and the defensive tone running through her interview unsettled her seemingly neat description of career success. Despite the predominance of individualist thinking in American culture, these kinds of tensions and conflicts continued to haunt these two women's discussions about discrimination, affirmative action, race, and gender. Much like the white male lawyers in Chapter 3, defensiveness, discomfort, and silence disrupted the seemingly smooth trajectory of their work life histories. The short story in the next chapter explores what might lie behind these forms of "disrupted talk."[75]

At the same time, there are some important differences from the white male lawyers' personal narratives. First, most of the women interviewed were much more forthcoming about their views and experiences than were most of the men. As I suggest in my Reflections on Methodology (Appendix A), the fact that I too am a professional woman may have influenced their level of comfort in discussing these issues. In addition, given that many of these women experienced discrimination suggests that their professional lives were quite different from those of white men whose gendered and racial status garnered for them automatic acceptance and privilege. Indeed, much like the African American attorneys Randall and Tyrone, these women worked in a professional world where meritocratic ideals of success did not provide language for gendered and racialized forms of discrimination. Though black men and white women struggled with divergent raced and gendered assumptions as either "not qualified" or "not committed," respectively, the result was the same. Their experiences were not taken seriously, and most chose to leave.

Of course, not all of the women left. The two affirmative action critics, Isabella and Kathryn, both attained positions as senior counsel and remained in the BC Legal Department. Interestingly, in defending *against* affirmative action, they were simultaneously defending the life chances and livelihoods of men in their lives. They wanted their sons to get into the colleges of their choice and their husbands to obtain well-paying jobs without the impediment of government regulation; they were in the rhetoric of the IWF and Patsy Cline's anthem, standing by their men. If as Roopali Mukherjee provocatively suggests, the debate about affirmative action can be interpreted as "an episodic crisis" about whiteness, these two senior counsel women were working to recuperate privilege for the white men in their personal and professional lives. In doing so, they not only reproduced whiteness as a structure of inequality in this workplace, but also masculinity. Put another way, their beliefs and practices sustained a workplace organization that was predominantly white and male.

5

Small Talk

A Short Story

Robin Healy sits in the lobby of San Francisco's Hilton Hotel waiting for James McElroy, the managing partner from Diamond & Whitney. Despite an afternoon of grilling by a panel of top litigators in the interview, she feels alert and thoughtful. She loves taking apart the finer points of law and discussing her cases. What she is not looking forward to is the evening ahead. Social events, like this dinner, are supposed to continue the job interview in a more relaxed environment, but for Robin these events are never relaxed. She has never been interested in small talk, finding those kinds of conversations pointless and disingenuous, but she knows they are part of the game.

As she smooths her cream silk blouse and adjusts her light gray suit jacket, Robin overhears a couple talking nearby.

"Did you see the headlines? The Regents abolished affirmative action in the University of California system!" the woman says in an exasperated tone.

"But it wasn't a unanimous decision," he says. "And it would have been very different if faculty governance were taken seriously."

Robin thinks he is referring to the fact that many faculty members opposed the decision. A protest against the Regents at Berkeley had been on the evening news. She wonders why it matters that the decision was not a unanimous one.

A man with dark brown hair shot through with silver interrupts her thoughts. It's McElroy. "Robin, sorry, I am a few minutes late. Why don't we go into the dining room? Bill Mankowitz is already there." Mankowitz is another member of the hiring committee and the only partner from the litigation department that Robin has not yet met in the interview process. From the research she's done, she knows he made his reputation in a high-profile construction case years ago, but she has yet to discover anything about the work he has done recently.

She smiles a professional smile and follows McElroy into the dining room of the hotel. Lights in small chandeliers are low in the large, elegant room paneled in dark wood. Tables are covered with white linen tablecloths, elaborate silver place settings, and crystal water glasses. The few couples scattered across the room at small tables look up and see a black woman and a white man crossing the room. Robin feels as she sometimes does in situations like this one: as if she were on display.

They come to a table in a far corner of the room where a heavyset, balding man in a dark suit is seated. "You're Robin," he booms as he reaches out to shake her hand and quickly looks her up and down. "Bill Mankowitz."

In spite of the once-over, Robin prods herself to be polite and shake hands. He is one of those men who believe in making a good impression by squeezing the other person's hand as hard as he can. Accustomed to this, she squeezes back and watches as he grimaces ever so slightly. Her father, a retired steel mill foreman, schooled her in these masculine rituals; she is always amused when men don't anticipate her knowledge.

"So, where are you from?" asks Bill.

"Chicago," she replies.

"Really?" He smiles warmly, "Me too. Great city. But I can't say I miss the winters."

"I don't miss the winters, either."

"So, you must be a Bulls fan. What about that Michael Jordan?"

She manages a weary smile and says awkwardly, "What about that three-pointer he nailed at the end of the game against the Lakers?"

He grins and says, "Yeah, wasn't that something? Hey, did you ever make it to any of his games?"

"No. I'd already left Chicago by the time he was playing for the Bulls."

He and McElroy look at her expectantly. Robin falters, trying to imagine how to keep the conversation going without talking about sports. She has already exhausted her knowledge of basketball. She finally says, "Actually, when I lived in Chicago one of my favorite places to go was the Art Institute."

"You like the Art Institute, huh? Well . . ." he hesitates for a beat. "I mean, growing up in Chicago I always thought that the Art Institute was very la-di-dah. You know, upper-class snooty and all that."

McElroy quickly interjects, "My wife, Nancy, is also a big fan of the arts. You know, just this year—"

Bill continues, talking over McElroy, "I mean, I grew up in a Polish working-class neighborhood. Going to the Art Institute just wasn't something you did. I mean, no one ever talked about art where I grew up." McElroy flashes an ominous look his way, but it goes unnoticed. Robin thinks of a car she watched on one of San Francisco's hilly streets where someone had neglected to put on the parking brake and it started to roll faster and faster down the hill toward the intersection.

"When I was growing up in Chicago, there was lots of discrimination against Polish Americans. You wouldn't hear this kind of stuff today. 'Polack this' and 'Polack that.' You wouldn't believe how many Polack jokes I heard. Teachers never expected me to do well in school."

Bill takes a drink of his beer and looks directly at Robin. "I know what it's like to be discriminated against. Nobody ever thought I would go to college. And I did it. I was one of the few from the neighborhood who went. I put myself through working part-time—"

"Bill," McElroy interrupts firmly, "I doubt that Robin is interested in the details of your college career. We're here to find out if she has questions for us."

Robin thinks that in the courtroom McElroy would be the type of lawyer who slips in an objection before the other side has a chance to take a breath. At the same time, she has a sliver of sympathy for Bill. She worked her way through college, too, though she would never mention this fact to people she is meeting for the first time.

Red-faced for a moment, Bill frowns at McElroy. A male waiter with slicked-back blond hair and a gleaming white shirt appears. "Can I get you something to drink?"

"I'd like a Scotch on the rocks," says McElroy smoothly. "Robin?"

She considers ordering a glass of wine, but wants her mind to be clear. "Perrier with a twist of lime."

Bill raises his eyebrows at Robin's order, but says, "I'll take another beer—whatever you have on tap."

McElroy turns to Robin, "Maybe we should look at our menus. They have excellent seafood here."

There is a short silence as they each open their enormous red-leather menus with tiny gold lettering. Scallops in a white wine sauce, salmon topped with a mango salsa, fresh grilled swordfish, Chilean sea bass. Robin likes seafood, but nothing sounds good right now. She knows she should have a pithy remark to make about the menu items, the restaurant, or something, but her mind has become blank. She now wishes she had ordered a glass of wine to ease her growing anxiety.

"The management committee was very impressed with how you handled the questions today," McElroy says. "You know the Rules of Civil Procedure inside and out."

"Thank you."

"But we're not here tonight to grill you. This is a social occasion."

These are never *just* social occasions, Robin thinks as the waiter returns with the drinks. As he puts down each drink, he mixes up the last two orders and places the beer in front of Robin and the glass of Perrier in front of Bill.

"Hey, this isn't mine," he protests as he pushes it aside. Under his breath, he mutters, "Jesus Christ! What a fucking idiot!

Robin says nothing, but arches an eyebrow in his direction. Catching her look, Bill shifts uncomfortably in his seat.

McElroy, who also notices the look swiftly retrieves the subject. "Do you have any questions for us?"

"Yes, I do have a few," she says in a businesslike voice. "Given that I already have several years of trial experience in the District Attorney's Office, I'm wondering whether that might count toward partnership. I understand that if I were hired I wouldn't be considered for partnership right away, but would those years count? Or, would I technically be starting over like new associates just out of law school?" Robin feels a jolt of anxiety. She knows these questions will be perceived as too blunt. How many times have her colleagues pointed out that her direct, no-nonsense approach works well in the courtroom, but not in social situations?

In response to her questions, McElroy begins to explain the criteria for partnership—the number of years with the firm, the billable hours, and the importance of developing relationships with clients.

Once he says that some of her time in her current position would count, Robin begins to pay closer attention to the two men sitting at the table. McElroy is clearly the most at ease socially of the two. His expensive dark blue Brooks Brothers' suit with a crisply starched light blue shirt and red tie accentuates his standard good looks: blue eyes, dark hair, and an aquiline nose. He is affable with a pleasant speaking voice: authoritative, but not patronizing. Robin recognizes it as the superficial affability developed in expensive upper-middle-class East Coast prep schools: a pleasant, polished exterior that could easily mask displeasure or rage. Bill's charcoal gray suit also looks expensive, but his white shirt is rumpled and his gold tie has a small dark stain on it. He has deep frown lines in his forehead, bushy gray eyebrows above bleary brown eyes, and a bulbous red nose that looks as if it's been in the sun too long. From his mode of dress and the slim white line on his ring finger, she guesses he is divorced. During most of McElroy's soliloquy, Bill stares down into his beer mug. She suspects he's still irritated because McElroy interrupted his I-worked-my-way-through-college story.

As McElroy's explanation of partnership winds down, he says, "Of course, we imagine that you would sail through this process. You have an impeccable trial record. Everyone is very impressed. Especially with the Landers case."

He is referring, Robin knows, to a highly publicized rape case she successfully tried as a new assistant in the District Attorney's Office. Because Jim, the lead attorney she was working with on the case, had become ill the night before trial, Robin had taken his place and given the opening statement on the first day. Given that she was only two years out of law school at the time, what had surprised everyone was how easily Robin took command.

The Landers case led to many other court cases, and more victories. Then, a few of San Francisco's big firms, the very firms that declined to interview her when she first graduated from law school, began courting Robin. She appreciated that irony. A degree from a local night school typically did not secure consideration in elite firms. But she also enjoyed her job and held the public attorney's moral qualms about private firms and their clientele. Still, there were few prospects for mobility in the D.A.'s office for someone as talented and ambitious as Robin. If she wanted to make a move and advance her career, a position in litigation at a prestigious firm would be the perfect springboard. And if she were to make a move, it had to be now. Lawyers who stayed in the public sector for too long seldom left.

"Thank you. That is very kind of you to say," says Robin. "You know, the legal issues in the Landers case were not that complex. The problem lay in convincing the judge to admit evidence—"

Bill interrupts, "The Landers case—isn't that the one where the guy used a condom?

"Yes."

"It's a bizarre detail, all right. So, what's the story?"

Robin moves easily into her prosecutorial tone. "The victim intended to deter the rapist by telling him that she had AIDS. Unfortunately, that only made him angrier and more abusive and he started beating her until she finally told him that there were condoms on her nightstand."

"Jesus. How did he end up in her bedroom?" Bill asks.

"Bill," says McElroy.

"He broke in through her bedroom window."

"It used to be you didn't have to lock your windows at night, but nowadays . . ." His voice trails off.

"Bill, Robin already spent much of her interview earlier today discussing this case."

"Actually," says Robin, "I enjoy talking about my cases." Though I probably shouldn't mention that I threw up every morning during that trial, she thinks. At the time, one of her colleagues told her it was "rookie nerves."

Giving Bill a dark look, McElroy says, "As I said, this evening is an opportunity for Robin to ask us questions. And the question she asked about was about partnership. As I said, Robin, given your record, I think you would sail through—"

Bill interrupts, "But partnership is never a guarantee. You gotta' do the work, impress the clients, bring in those billables, and you have to be a team player. You know, you got to *fit in.*"

Robin wonders about his emphasis. Is the implication that she won't fit in? Or, is he suggesting that it's been hard for him to fit in?

"I think what Bill is trying to get at," McElroy says, "is that it's a highly competitive process. But we wouldn't be interested in hiring you unless we thought you were partnership material."

Bill drains the remainder of his beer, signals the waiter for another, and then turns to Robin with a wink, "That's what he says to all the new associates."

Robin is tempted to laugh, but maintains her best poker face. One minute Bill seems intent on insulting her, and the next on contradicting McElroy. She also sees the truth in his assessment of McElroy. She's not sure what lies beneath the managing partner's polished exterior, but she recognizes the determined attempts to manipulate and control.

McElroy says, "Since you so rarely work with associates, Bill, I doubt you would have any knowledge of what I may have said to any of them."

Bill ignores this remark, turns to Robin, and asks, "So, you got any more questions for us?"

McElroy continues to smile pleasantly. Robin guesses that McElroy would continue to smile pleasantly if an elephant stomped on his foot.

"I'm wondering what percentage of associates make partner," she says. "How many partners are women? How many partners are people of color?"

Robin knows she is being too blunt again. No one at big firms likes being called out by these questions. Another part of her feels there is no point to beating around the bush. How else is she going to find out whether she has a fair shot at partnership?

Bill shrugs his shoulders and looks over at McElroy as if to say, "This one's yours," and then begins to trace patterns with his fork on the white linen napkin. McElroy says easily, "Well, I don't have the precise numbers in front of me, but I believe about twenty percent of our associates make partner. Of course, some drop out along the way. So, if you look at who actually stays to be evaluated, the percentage is a bit higher."

"And women?"

"There are two women partners in the firm," McElroy says.

"And, there is one minority female," says Bill looking up from the patterns he is tracing on his napkin. "Her name is—"

"Elizabeth Roberts," McElroy says firmly.

"She's also a woman," Bill adds, "but not a partner."

"And there's Terrence Murphy and Keith Johnson, too," says McElroy.

"They aren't partners or women," says Bill with a smirk directed at McElroy. "But they are minorities."

"I see," says Robin thinking, that the numbers are small for a firm with over two hundred attorneys.

As if anticipating her criticism, McElroy says, "According to the 1995 American Bar Association's Report on the status of women and minorities in the profession, the numbers are low nationwide. Our numbers aren't that different. It's a pipeline problem," he adds.

Robin nods. She read the report when it came out.

Bill stares into the bottom of his beer stein with a faint, amused smile on his face. McElroy looks expectantly at Robin. She struggles again to think of something to say. A friend's advice comes to mind: When in doubt, ask about the other person.

"James, didn't you mention this afternoon that your daughter was in her last year of college?"

"That's right," he says with a pleased smile. "She'll be finishing up in economics at Cal this spring."

"That's great. Berkeley is a great school."

Okay, now what should I talk about? she thinks

Suddenly Bill pipes up, "My daughter goes to Cal, too."

"Really," says Robin, thinking, *You* have a daughter?

"I had forgotten that your daughter went to Berkeley," adds McElroy sounding surprised.

"I wouldn't expect you to remember," Bill says acidly to McElroy.

"Does she like Berkeley?" Robin finds herself asking. Her daughter, Sandra, still in high school, has expressed interest in going to college there.

Bill pauses, takes a drink of his beer, and says, "Oh, I think *she* likes it. I'm not so sure that I do. She's taking all these creative writing classes because she wants to be a poet. She even got a prize for one of her poems," he adds with a note of pride. "But I don't know where she thinks she's going to get a job writing poetry."

Reflecting on her own daughter's mercurial interests, Robin understands the difficulties of convincing teenagers to think seriously about the future, and nods.

Bill carries on, "I can't believe what teachers let students get away with these days. You should hear some of the stories she tells. In one of her classes, the professor asked them to write an essay about a place. And when they read their essays aloud in class, it turns out that one of these kids wrote an essay about having sex with a piano."

"Bill," McElroy says.

"What? He wrote about fucking a piano." He turns to Robin and says, "Can you believe it? I mean, what can you possibly learn from crap like that?"

After a moment Robin says, "It's not a place."

They both look at her. "What?" asks Bill.

"A piano is not a place. It's an inanimate object."

"You're right. It's not a place," says McElroy smiling.

"The student didn't follow the assignment."

"It's not a place," McElroy says again. He smiles at Robin. She smiles back and they laugh quietly together.

Bill looks puzzled and slightly annoyed. "I don't get it. Why's that so funny?"

As McElroy continues to laugh, the maître d' solemnly advances upon the table. "Excuse me, are you Ms. Healy?" he asks Robin.

"Yes."

"We have a phone call from your office. They said it's urgent."

"I'm very sorry," Robin says to McElroy. "I told the office I would be here if there were any emergencies."

"Go right ahead," he replies.

As Robin begins walking across the dining room, she thinks she hears Bill say something that sounds like "a real ball-buster." Did he really say "ball-buster"? she wonders. She reminds herself that this is a man who considers fucking a piano appropriate dinner conversation. Not someone to be taken seriously. What his role might be in the hiring process, she cannot fathom. McElroy clearly does not like him. She sighs deeply as she enters the hallway behind the maître d', following him to a small alcove with a black telephone in it. "Press line one," he instructs and strides off.

Robin picks up the phone and presses the blinking light. She waits to hear Melanie's voice apologizing for bothering her, but it's not her secretary.

"Robin, it's Barbara. Melanie just gave me your number. I am really sorry to bother you." Barbara is Robin's neighbor. Her daughter, Lisa, is one of Sandra's friends.

"What is it? What's wrong?"

"Lisa and Sandra were in a car accident. They're okay, but Sandra has been taken to the hospital."

Robin feels dizzy and puts her hand against the wall. Her face flushes; her stomach contracts. She prompts herself to inhale and exhale. She didn't throw up every morning during the Landers trial because she suffered from rookie nerves. Nor was it the fact that she had to watch Mary Landers sit through a cross-examination where she was treated as if she had invited the brutal ordeal. It was the fact that this could happen to her Sandra.

"Robin, are you still there?"

"Sorry, Barbara." She finally summons the calm to ask, "Is Sandra okay?"

"She broke her leg in several places and they need to do surgery to set the break. You need to come to Kaiser."

Robin exhales deeply and says, "Yes, okay, I understand."

As she turns to walk back into the dining room, she feels as if a kaleido-scope lens has turned; everything takes a new shape, a new prominence. The lighting of the elegant chandeliers now seems too bright and the dark paneled wood looks like a black wall. The few diners now appear as strange cardboard cutouts. Raised voices sound across the expansive room from the far corner table. Bill points his index finger in McElroy's face. McElroy pushes it away. Bill shakes his head. McElroy shakes his in turn. Robin feels like she is watching a play from a great distance. She wonders briefly what the actors are saying and realizes she doesn't care. As she nears the table, she can see McElroy's face set in a grim, disapproving frown. Bill, no longer speaking, glowers back at him.

"Unfortunately, an emergency has come up. I have to leave right away."

McElroy suggests they continue the conversation another evening. She agrees and murmurs her regrets.

"Hey, before you go, I wanted to ask you a quick question," says Bill.

"Bill," McElroy says in a warning tone.

Robin crosses her arms across her chest to hide her growing anxiety, gives Bill a stern look, and says, "I'm in a rush."

"I wanted to ask you about Ward Connerly."

She continues to look intently at him.

"The UC Regent," he adds.

She decides to force his hand. "Why do you ask?"

"Well," he spread his arms, "he's African American and he opposes affirmative action. I wondered what you could tell us about him." He smiles broadly.

"I'm not sure I understand," says Robin with her best poker face. "Why should I be the one to tell you about him?"

"Bill, leave it alone," McElroy says firmly.

"Well, you're African American and he's African American."

She sighs inwardly, looks directly at Bill, and says patiently as if speaking to the jury in her closing statement, "Now let me see if I can get this straight. Because I'm African American, I should be interested in Ward Connerly. Because I'm African American, I should be interested in Michael Jordan, but not in art. Because I'm African American, I need to be made aware of the historic discrimination against Polish Americans. You also want me to understand that you've worked hard for everything you've ever achieved and by implication because I'm African American, I have not. And, if I ask questions about partnership, it's only because I expect to be handed partnership on a platter without working for it. Anything else?" she pauses. "Oh yes. Because I'm African American, you don't feel the need to make polite conversation with me, but dredge up an offensive story about a piano."

She pauses for a beat. McElroy looks grimly satisfied. Bill's mouth hangs agape.

"In short," she says thinking of Elizabeth Bennet, her favorite Jane Austen character, "you, sir, are rude." She turns to McElroy, "Now, if you will excuse me."

As she sweeps out of the room, Robin hears McElroy, the managing partner, say to Bill, "Boy, does she ever have a chip on her shoulder. Like I said, what *you* would call a real ball-buster."

A few minutes later, Robin stands outside the front of the hotel on Union Square trying to hail a cab. A few taxis drive by, but none are empty.

She thinks, Thank God, it's only a broken leg. For the briefest of moments on the phone, I thought Barbara was going to tell me . . . But it's only a broken leg. Sandra will be fine. Oh, what a complete a complete fool I just made of myself! What was I thinking! It's always the ones who smile right in your face who are the worst. Where are all the cabs tonight? Maybe it would be faster to take the Muni. Oh, I thought I was being so clever. Elizabeth Bennet!

"Where are all the cabs tonight?" she says aloud.

One of the bellhops standing in front of the hotel asks, "Do you need some help, ma'am?"

"Yes. I need a cab to Kaiser."

"I'll see what I can do. It's been hard to get cabs today. There are a couple of big conventions in town." He walks out into the street with a big silver whistle in his hand.

"Thanks. And, it's Kaiser, the hospital," she adds in a loud voice.

"What are you going to Kaiser for?" a familiar voice asks.

She turns to find Bill standing right behind her.

"My daughter was in a car accident," she says icily and turns back toward the street.

He says with concern, "Jesus Christ. Why didn't you say something?"

Why can't you leave me alone? she thinks as she watches the traffic and Bill comes to stand next to her.

She says, "Are you kidding? If you talk about your children in a professional milieu, men don't take you seriously. They'll think you should be home baking cookies or something."

"In an emergency like this?" Bill asks.

"This was a job interview. Wouldn't you wonder whether something like this happened to me all the time?"

"But things like this don't happen all the time," Bill says

Why am I bothering to argue with him? she thinks.

She says, "No they don't, but that's not my point. My point is that when they happen to women people make different kinds of assumptions than when they happen to men. A man who rushes off to the hospital to take care of his daughter is an extra-special kind of man. A professional woman who rushes off is putting her family before career."

"That's not true."

"Maybe you should try reading one of the ABA's reports on the status women in the legal profession. You might learn something."

He shakes his head and says, "If you told us what was going on, we could have done something to help you out."

"Somehow I can't picture McElroy escorting me to the hospital. Wouldn't that defile his pedigree or something?"

Bill guffaws and says, "Now *that's* probably true."

Robin continues to watch the bellhop in the street as Bill stand next to her rubbing his hand over his bald pate.

He thrusts his hands into his pockets, and says "Sorry about your daughter, though. Is she going to be okay?"

Surprised, Robin examines him closely. Only five minutes ago she told this man he was rude to his face. Why is he being so nice?

She says, "The doctors think so, but she's having surgery."

"Jesus. That sounds serious."

Bill looks at the ground and shifts from one foot to the other.

"Hey, why don't you let me drive you to the hospital," he says.

"No, thanks. I'll get a cab."

"Look, it's the least I can do. And my car's right here."

Robin looks at him again, considering his offer; it feels genuine. She doesn't want to spend another minute with this man, but she also wants to get to the hospital.

"How fast do you think you could get me to Kaiser on Geary?" she asks.

"In this traffic? Maybe fifteen minutes."

"Then let's go."

She signals to the bellhop that she has a ride as Bill leads her across the street toward the parking garage beneath Union Square. On the Square, two tourists sit on a green wooden bench with Macy's shopping bags piled next to them. A gray pigeon flutters above an overflowing trash can. A yellow McDonald's wrapper blows across the grass. A young woman with long dark hair in blue jeans and an SFSU sweatshirt plays a mournful tune on her saxophone. As they pass by, Bill reaches into his pocket and drops some change into the open case lying on the grass.

"So, about before . . ." Bill begins. "Just so you know. I really do like Michael Jordan. I didn't just say that because, uh, you know. I was just looking for something we might have in common. You know, Chicago, the Bulls."

Robin hates these kinds of conversations; she especially hates the fact that it's partly her fault. Still, he's trying, but she's not going to let him off the hook entirely. "Right," she says, "I get it. But you think people who enjoy the Art Institute are snooty."

"Okay. That was a rude thing to say. I'm sorry. I'm no good in social situations. I always end up saying the wrong thing."

She sighs. "Actually, I'm the one who said the wrong thing. Usually I see right through people like McElroy. Anyway, I apologize."

"Hey, don't feel bad. Most people never figure out he's a prick."

They walk down the cement stairs leading into the underground lot. "By the way," he adds, "your closing argument was pretty impressive."

Robin smiles ruefully. "Yeah, well, too bad I didn't deliver it to the right person."

"Maybe you'll have another opportunity."

"I doubt it," Robin says as they weave through the maze of parked cars. "But I do have a question for you. Why in the world did you ask me about Ward Connerly?"

"Oh that." Bill's face reddens. "It's kind of a long story."

"Go on."

"Well, I don't know if you heard it, but when you left the table the first time McElroy said to me, 'Ms. Healy's what you would call a real ball-buster.' And I told him not to put words in my mouth. I don't use the term 'ball-buster,' the correct term is 'ball-breaker.'"

"You argued about the appropriate terminology for insulting me?"

"Uh."

"Right. Sorry I asked. Can you just get me to the hospital?"

"Hey wait, let me finish. He said Ms. Healy is, quote, busting his balls, unquote, with all these questions about minorities and partnership. And I said that I thought Ms. Healy was just asking about her professional opportunities. Why would an ambitious young lawyer wanna go to one of those firms where no one makes partner? Then, he said, quote, those people, unquote, think that affirmative action entitles them to everything. And I said that's not true, some blacks oppose affirmative action. He said that was b.s. And so I thought . . .'"

"You would ask me about Ward Connerly."

"Right."

"So you thought it would be a good idea to ask a black woman you just met about a controversial political figure the day after the University of California Regents voted to end affirmative action."

"Well, I guess I thought that it would give you the chance to talk about the fact that some blacks don't support affirmative action."

Robin shakes her head. "And, you thought that was a good idea?"

Bill stops in the back of a bright red Porsche convertible parked next to a silver Mercedes-Benz sedan. He fishes through his pockets for his car keys and pulls them out.

He says, "So, I guess you thought it was a dumb question?"

Robin ignores the question, nods at the convertible, and asks "This is your car?"

"Yeah."

She finds herself grinning. It has a bumper sticker that reads, "Competence is spelled W-O-M-A-N."

He unlocks the car doors. "What?"

"Nice bumper sticker."

They both get in.

"My daughter put it on the car. She has a highly developed sense of humor."

"Because she thinks women are competent?" Robin asks sharply.

"No. Because she put it on my car."

Robin shakes her head again.

"I think I might like your daughter," she finally says.

"Yeah? I bet she would like you, too."

Bill turns the key in the ignition and the car roars to life.

Commentary: Ambivalent Racism

As discussed in the Introduction, my short story, "Small Talk," is an attempt to apprehend the meaning behind the white male attorneys' silences and hesitations that I described in Chapter 3. It examines interracial and cross-gender dynamics during a dinner following a professional interview. The story is told from the perspective of a black woman, Robin Healy, a highly experienced and successful litigator who is being considered for a position at a large San Francisco law firm at the very political moment that affirmative action is being abolished in the University of California system. The two men in the story, a managing partner and another lawyer, are both white. My intent in writing this story was not only to move into a social situation that I did not have access to in my fieldwork, but also to encourage readers to think about the ways that fiction can reveal thoughts and feelings about affirmative action, race, and gender.

In "Small Talk," ambivalence and ambiguity are central elements of two of the main characters: Bill Mankowitz, a white lawyer who grew up in a Polish, working-class neighborhood in Chicago; and Robin Healy, an African American female job candidate, who is also from a working-class background. Robin appears professionally poised and articulate, though her thoughts reveal both doubts and misgivings about her performance in this social situation. By contrast, Bill is socially social awkward, almost always managing to say something inappropriate or rude. At the same time, because he wears his heart is on his sleeve, he is somewhat refreshing as a character (as some readers have suggested), because he says exactly what he thinks; and in this respect, he is completely unlike his polished, upper-middle-class colleague, James Mc-Elroy, the firm's managing partner. (Appendix A discusses how different readers have responded to the short story.) For instance, when Bill first meets Robin, who tells him that she enjoys Chicago's Art Institute, he not only tells her that people who go to the Art Institute are "snooty," but then launches into a story about his own experience of discrimination as a working-class Polish American growing up in Chicago in the 1950s. Further, he contradicts McElroy when he assures Robin about her prospects for partnership, telling her that in addition to all the work it entails, she has to "fit in."

Robin, on the other hand, is unsure whether this is intended as comment about himself as one who does not "fit in" or a commentary on her status as black female. Later, when Bill mentions his daughter, he reveals another side of his personality—a father's pride in his children's accomplishments. At the same time, he is disgusted (predictably at this point for some readers) by the description of her creative writing classes, where a student writes about "fucking a piano." Finally, when Robin announces that she has to leave to attend an emergency at work (though the emergency actually concerns her daughter), Bill cannot resist asking her opinion of Ward Connerly, the African American businessman and UC Regent who opposed affirmative action. This query combined with the stress of her daughter's accident prompts Robin to give a lawyerly closing statement summing up Bill's rude and seemingly racist and sexist behavior.

Once Robin leaves the restaurant to go to the hospital, she encounters Bill on the street while she is trying to hail a taxi. Here Bill displays concern about her daughter, but still manages to say all the wrong things. He argues with her reasons for not telling them about why she actually had to leave the dinner. He can't imagine that she would be judged differently because she is a woman. Surprisingly, he does offer to drive her to the hospital. Robin, who is conflicted about accepting a ride from him, finally agrees because she wants to get to her daughter as quickly as possible. But even here, Bill manages to add insult to injury. He lays the "ball-buster" insult at McElroy's feet, but we learn that he and McElroy were actually arguing about whether "ball-breaker" or "ball-buster" was the most appropriate term of derision. He also tries to explain why he asked her about Ward Connerly—an explanation Robin finds politically naïve. Finally, when Robin spots the feminist bumper sticker on Bill's car that reads "Competence is spelled W-O-M-A-N," we learn that Bill's daughter put it there. To his credit, Bill left it on the car, telling Robin that his daughter has a "highly developed sense of humor." When Robin asks whether he thinks it humorous because his daughter thinks women are competent, he disagrees. It is because *his daughter* put it on *his* car, suggesting that he has some sense of humor about his own lack of feminist convictions.

How does this story, and Bill's character in particular, complement my ethnographic work in epistemological terms? Bill, for the most part, comes across as an embarrassing oaf. Some readers described his behavior, particularly his assertion that people who go to the Art Institute are "snooty," as "just plain rude," while others interpreted it as a signifier of his working-class background. Still others regarded his discussion of his ethnicity and the African American basketball player Michael Jordan as clumsy social attempts to find something in common with Robin, while others understood these comments as coded remarks veiling Bill's racist assumptions. For some, his stated reason for asking Robin about Ward Connerly suggested a naïveté about racial politics, while others saw it as evidence of racist, passive-aggressive behavior in an interview situation.[1] Regardless of whether we understand Bill as a clumsy oaf or a racist, his pride in his daughter's accomplishments, his offer to drive Robin to the hospital, and the bumper sticker on his flashy, red Porsche convertible suggest a more complex person. He is socially awkward, rude, probably racist and sexist, but also at times thoughtful, generous, and even humorous about some of his foibles. In this way, the short story provides a nuanced portrait of one professional white man's racism. It also hints at what *might* lie behind the silences and hesitations of some of the white male lawyers I interviewed in my ethnographic research: ambivalence.

My fictional portrait of Bill not only counters Hollywood portrayals of evil white-working-class vigilantes—recall that he too comes from working-class background—but also serves to complicate sociological theories of racism. Queer-of-color theorist Roderick Ferguson, following the lead of Polish sociologist Zygmunt Bauman, has argued that in establishing discursive authority, sociologists typically create concepts with clear and sharply defined boundaries.[2] For instance, survey research on prejudice constructs categories for individuals as either racist or not racist.[3] Such a theory, on one hand, suppresses the ambivalent-subject position that someone like the character of Bill occupies. On the other hand, theories of institutional racism, like my own, focus on the consequences of collective practices.[4] In this framework, ambivalence is irrelevant: What matters are how systemic patterns of behavior create racialized exclusions. Here again a simple dichotomy is produced: Individuals who participate in these practices are construed as racist, while those who resist are not. Neither theoretical framework leaves room for ambiguity or nuance.

In Ferguson's argument, fiction can provide readings that counter sociological theory's hegemonic discourse. In a chapter titled, "The Specter of Woodridge: Canonical Formations and the Anticanonical in *The Invisible Man*," Ferguson reads an unpublished chapter from Ralph Ellison's *The Invisible Man* against the research of sociology's Chicago School. While early twentieth-century University of Chicago sociologists such as Robert Park theorized a "race relations cycle" that promised assimilation as an inevitable and desirable outcome, Woodridge, the fictional black college professor in Ellison's book, reveals the contradictions inherent in such a possibility. Though Woodridge achieves middle-class respectability as a college professor, among his white peers he is never completely accepted as black man; his status and accomplishments are always those of an outsider. He experiences acceptance and rejection simultaneously.

Following Ferguson's argument, I suggest that "Small Talk" presents a fictional story that at once *counters* and *complements* sociological theories of white racism by providing a distinct epistemological viewpoint: one of ambivalent racism. Ambivalence about race both counters sociological theories of racism that create conceptually distinct binaries and stands as a distinct way of knowing that neither sociological theory nor my ethnographic findings could fully elaborate. It suggests an ambivalent white masculine subjectivity: one that is simultaneously racist and not racist. This not only provides some insight into why some of the white men I interviewed might deny racism as they practiced exclusionary behavior—their ambivalent racism makes it difficult for them to fully elaborate their position—but also points to problems with American sociological theories that do not fully embrace contradiction and ambivalence within their theoretical frameworks.[5]

Conclusion

As noted in the Introduction, there are far more sociological studies focusing on white working-class people and racism than those studying white elites. Perhaps one reason for this fact is that working-class people are less likely to edit their accounts and are more willing to talk frankly about what they think about race—even in an era of colorblindness. For example, in her covert ethnography of interracial interactions in convenience stories in the Boston area and in Atlanta in the late 1990s, sociologist Monica McDermott finds strong evidence of anti-black sentiment among white working-class Americans, especially when the topics of crime or school segregation are discussed.[6] Similarly, in sociologist Deidre Royster's influential study on the networks that men from trade schools rely upon to find jobs, white working-class men candidly reported that their sons, and not blacks, deserved these blue-collar jobs. They thought "affirmative action was helping less qualified blacks and hurting more qualified whites like themselves."[7]

By contrast, the professional white men I interviewed were rarely this explicit in their discussions of affirmative action—they were more likely to launch a general critique about the unfairness of the policy, to invoke the problems of bureaucratic inefficiency, or to point to an uncomfortable shift in the etiquette of workplace interactions. Although many complained that affirmative action led to hiring people who were not qualified, when asked directly, most were reluctant in their interview to attach this label to people of color. As a number of scholars have found in their interviews with whites, there is often concern with maintaining civility in discussions about race, especially among middle-class and upper-middle-class Americans.[8] By contrast, white working-class people are more likely to see this kind of civility as phony or disingenuous. Here, I suggest that white working-class Americans and upper-middle-class Americans not only operate under different rules for social conduct, but also that elites have far more power to control the public presentation of their personae. They may write autobiographies or memoirs, give carefully tailored speeches, refuse to grant interviews to those whom they do not trust, or simply not cooperate fully in the interviews they do grant. Further, the lawyers in my study understood the significance of intentionality in proving discrimination under the law and may have wished to maintain a middle-class civility in their discussions of racial issues in light of this issue. Ironically, what this means is that despite mountains of documentary evidence, sociologists, anthropologists, and historians may not be able to fully access to the subjectivity of contemporary elites—at least in the area of racial prejudice.[9]

Interestingly, in the few studies where researchers found that racial issues are discussed openly in interracial situations, it is often debate rather than civility that brings about understanding between people of color and white Americans. As political scientist Katherine Walsh found in her study of community dialogues about race across the United States in the 1990s, when dialogue broke down and people debated one another's assumptions, they had the opportunity to scrutinize claims and, in the end, most clearly convey respect for one another.[10] Obviously, in my study, I was not able to move white male lawyers to that point; and, as I have argued, this is one of the epistemological limits of my ethnographic approach.

Of course, I am not suggesting that all ethnographic studies are limited in capturing the subjective dimensions of individual lives. That was the limitation of my research with elite white men. My choice to provide a fictionalized account stands as an effort to apprehend the subjectivity of those I was otherwise unable to understand. Certainly, fictionalizing goes beyond what many social scientists and historians regard as acceptable rhetorical modes. Still, my approach recalls some of the challenges associated with studying elites: the particular nature of the "truths" revealed through life story analysis and the acts of empathy or imagination they entail on the part of the analyst. Importantly, the "truths" that emerge from the analysis of the white male lawyers' personal narratives may be unknowable; but, as I have argued, fiction provides one way of moving behind their silence. It creates an epistemological vantage point that is complex, contingent, and subject to interpretation.

Conclusion

Still Racing for Innocence

Focusing on the backlash against affirmative action in California, this book began by asking how it is that white elites who proclaim the virtues of a "colorblind" society come to deny the role they play in reproducing racial inequality. As I have shown, part of the answer to this question resides in cultural memory, that is, the stories articulated and disseminated through the mainstream news media and Hollywood films. During the late 1980s and throughout the 1990s, each medium established a dominant narrative or genre. The trope in news stories, which I have termed "white male innocence and injury," not only created stories about white men as unfairly harmed by affirmative action policies, but also served to obscure the fact that very few white men actually experienced "reverse discrimination." Furthermore, despite extensive evidence from social scientists and government reports documenting discrimination against people of color in employment, hiring, housing, and education, these issues received little attention in newspaper stories, thereby reinforcing a cultural memory of white male disadvantage vis-à-vis people of color. The dominant trope of white male innocence took a slightly different form in Hollywood films. Here, in telling stories about race relations, the film genre of "white racial progress" remained fixed on white, elite, and predominantly male experiences and understandings. People of color became background figures, though their relationship to the white central character served to support and "anoint" the protagonist as a savior; and working-class whites were demonized as the "true" racists. While the news media proffered accounts of white men who unfairly lost promotions and jobs to African Americans, Hollywood films told stories about elite white men who, in undergoing a transformation from racial innocents to racial understanding, became advocates who fought for racial justice.

Despite differences in these accounts, they shared a number of important elements. First, both focused on white experiences and understandings of race relations, and both emphasized white male innocence of racism. In this way, they provided a cultural repertoire of pre-existing arguments tailored to the interests of white men. Second, just as print news media accounts worked to reinvigorate neoliberal and neoconservative assumptions about "personal responsibility" and "free markets" as good for society, as well as moralistic understandings of who is most "worthy" of federal assistance, films in the white racial progress genre hyped Horatio-Alger–like assumptions about heroic white men who struggled valiantly and, ultimately, triumphed over racism. Such a discursive move not only obscured the institutional exercise of power that funneled rewards, resources, and opportunities to white Americans, but also implicitly suggested that federal programs and policies such as affirmative action that aim to dismantle structural inequality were unnecessary. In this way, the "white racial progress" genre in film and dominant media narratives on "white innocence and injury" shared similar political goals; both operated as assaults on systematic analyses of institutionalized racism.

Moving from the broader national landscape of cultural memory in the late 1980s and 1990s to the work life histories of lawyers in BC's Legal Department, this book makes a number of significant connections between these cultural and personal forms of remembering. While most of the white male attorneys interviewed refrained from making overtly racist remarks and denied accountability for racism, many expressed discomfort or remained silent when asked about affirmative action, while others insisted that government regulations were no longer necessary. Their stories of benevolence resonated with the "white racial progress" genre in Hollywood films as well as anti-affirmative-action accounts in the print news media that emphasized the importance of "personal responsibility" and "free markets" in resolving societal problems. As I have shown, this broader cultural memory became the means through which these elite white men practiced modern racism. At the same time that they claimed to be innocent of racism, they resisted fully incorporating people of color and white women into their workplace through a discursive practice I have termed "racing for innocence." In doing so, they contributed—wittingly or not—to the backlash against affirmative action.

By contrast, the women lawyers I interviewed told, for the most part, a very different story about their workplace lives than did their male counterparts, one that highlighted opportunities that came through affirmative action, but also pointed to the exclusionary practices of the "good-old-boy" network. Moreover, though women were rarely mentioned in dominant news media stories where affirmative action was assumed to be about race, a number of political groups sought to include women in their campaign either for or against affirmative action. Neoconservative groups such as the Independent Women's Forum (IWF) joined forces with affirmative action opponents, arguing that this policy was "injurious" to their husbands and sons. In their view, the doors of economic opportunity were wide open to women and the "glass ceiling" was a myth. Women who didn't work hard enough or long enough had only themselves to blame if they weren't successful. The IWF called for women to "stand by their men" and oppose affirmative action. At the same time, feminist groups such as the National Organization for Women worked to support affirmative action policy.

As I found within this broader context, women lawyers had varied perspectives about affirmative action. Most supported it, though not without ambivalence. They recognized affirmative action as an important remedial policy in addressing the problem of discrimination, but also sometimes worried about its fairness to individuals. In addition, the supporters often felt that they worked under a cloud of suspicion in the workplace, that is, their male colleagues perceived that women were "less committed" to professional obligations than men were, and many women complained about the problems they encountered when requesting or taking family leaves from work. The few who opposed affirmative action, who also happened to be senior counsel members (or the equivalent of partners) in the Legal Department, not only embraced the rhetoric of "white male innocence and injury," but also castigated their younger female colleagues for not working hard enough and complaining about discrimination when things did not go their way. Unlike her white colleagues, the one black woman attorney in the Legal Department told yet another story, which provided insight into how racism and sexism operate together to disadvantage women of color. She felt she had to work against the assumption of "black intellectual inferiority" to prove that she was a competent professional. As I have shown, the resistance women attorneys faced (many of whom eventually left the Legal Department) served to reproduce whiteness as a structure of inequality in this workplace, and masculinity as well. Put another way, these practices sustained a professional workplace that was predominantly white and male.

My short story "Small Talk" continues to examine the intersections of race and gender by focusing on Robin Healy, an African American trial attorney, who is having dinner with two white men following an interview at their law firm. While this fictional account explores interracial and cross-gender dynamics, it also works to illuminate the thoughts and feelings behind the discomfort provoked by such interactions. In my commentary following the short story, I develop the concept of "ambivalent racism" to make sense of what *might* lie behind silence and discomfort that I found in the white male attorneys' personal narratives. This term is intended to conceptualize the feelings, thoughts, and practices of Bill Mankowitz, one of the central characters in the story, as a white man who is simultaneously racist and not racist. Put another way, his racist talk, feelings, and actions may exist simultaneously with other talk, thoughts, and behavior that may be construed as not racist. This not only provides some insight into why many of the white male lawyers I interviewed might deny racism as they practiced exclusionary behavior—their ambivalent racism made it difficult for them to fully elaborate their position—but also points to problems with sociological theories that do not fully embrace contradiction and ambivalence within their theoretical frameworks.

As I have argued, each method used in this study provides a different angle of vision on the affirmative action debate. Alone, each methodological source has both strengths and limitations. While print news media and Hollywood film work to supply stories about racial inequality for American cultural memory, they do not provide an accurate account of the material fact of continuing discrimination against people of color and white women in the United States. Nor do they tell us how elites interpret these accounts. Personal narratives, on the other hand, enable us to understand the varied meanings that the male and female attorneys I interviewed attributed to the affirmative action debate across time. In the case of many white male attorneys, however, their silences and hesitations made it more difficult to apprehend how they felt about this policy. My short story offers a possible interpretation of the meanings behind these silences. Together they provide a multifaceted account that not only details the historically specific discursive context for the debate and elite raced and gendered understandings of affirmative action and discrimination, but also a window into what might lie behind silences about race and gender discrimination.

Directions for Future Research

My research on the intersections between cultural memory and personal memory in the backlash against affirmative action and role of white elites in perpetuating raced and gendered forms inequality suggests a number of productive lines of inquiry for future research. First, my theoretical argument about "racing for innocence" suggests that more research needs to be done about the role that elites play in the reproduction of inequality in other workplace organizations, and also in studies of whiteness. For example, how do whiteness and masculinity as structures of inequality operate in the Gramscian notion of "common sense" in other occupations and professions?[1] Are there cases where white women and people of color do not experience tokenized forms of inclusion? If so, what strategies and practices might work to counter racial and gendered form of exclusion?

Historical studies, too, need to focus more on the role of white elites in the 1970s, '80s, and '90s in changing the terrain of America's political and economic landscape. Indeed, as my research shows, whiteness as a structure of inequality often works hand in hand with neoliberal reform. As noted in the Introduction, many historians who study this time period blame white working-class people for the resurgence of the New Right and backlash politics. One excellent, recent exception that examines deregulation in the airline industry and its effects on labor organizing among flight attendants from the 1970s to the present provides unique insight into this era. As American Studies scholar Ryan P. Murphy finds, academic economists and financial tycoons such as Carl Icahn (whom Hollywood portrayed as Gordon Gekko in the 1980s film *Wall Street*) played central roles in supplying the economic logic, cultural framework, and capital necessary to dismantle the airline industry, cripple organized labor, and, in the case of Icahn, to significantly bolster his already considerable financial holdings.[2] Murphy's study demonstrates not only the importance of attending to workers who struggled against these changes, but also to the white elites who worked to change the financial and banking requirements for buyouts as well as the federal terrain for union organizing. Murphy's study, as well as my own, point to the importance of conducting research on the role of white male elites in promulgating neoliberal reforms that contributed to their own financial gains while dispossessing others.

This kind of research is all the more crucial in our current political and economic climate where processes of deregulation, financialization, deunionization, and other neoliberal reforms have granted immense power to corporations.[3] Certainly, big business has long played a central role in our economy, but two recent court decisions—*Citizens United v. Federal Election Commission* and *Wal-Mart Inc. v. Dukes*—have given it more clout in American politics and the economy.[4] In the *Citizens United* decision, for example, the United States Supreme Court ruled that corporate funding of political broadcasts of candidate elections *cannot* be limited, thereby rendering special interest groups and lobbyists even more power in Washington D.C., while undermining the smaller political contributions of average Americans. In the other Supreme Court case, a group of women (that included 1.5 million employees) brought a class action lawsuit against Wal-Mart for sex discrimination. The Court ruled that the women failed to meet the "commonality" requirement necessary for filing a class action lawsuit. Put another way, the court denied these plaintiffs legal status as a "class," rendering it more difficult for other groups of workers to file similar kinds of discrimination lawsuits in the future.[5] These two cases as well as my own research underscore the need for more studies on corporations, elites, and their practices. This is not to undermine the incredibly important and influential scholarship being done on new social movements and activism by gays, lesbians, people of color, feminists, recent immigrants, and people on welfare; but rather to emphasize that now more than ever, we need to look at elite practices that have made it so difficult for these groups to organize, provide sustainable livelihoods for themselves and their families, and take legal action when necessary.

In addition to studies of elites, my findings about the role of cultural memory via the news media and Hollywood films in reproducing normative understandings of whiteness also raise questions for future research. For instance, Do more recent Hollywood films continue to deploy the genre of "white racial progress"? Do the tropes of "white male innocence" appear in other policy debates, such as welfare and immigration reform? If so, to what effect? In a recent study, sociologists Adia Harvey Wingfield and Joe Feagin found that the mainstream news media played a significant role in framing the Presidential election of Barack Obama. As they argue, "the white racial frame of the media" (by which they mean the way the media consistently depicts most whites as more moral, intelligent, and hardworking than most people of color, as a means of rationalizing white superiority) simultaneously produced "colorblind" narratives of race relations while maintaining white privilege. To give one example, in reporting on Obama's campaign and election, a number of articles from mainstream publications described these events as evidence of a "post-racial" America. What is not mentioned in these accounts is the fact of continuing racial inequality in the United States. By neglecting to report on such facts, mainstream news stories perpetuate the illusion that we live in a colorblind society.

While Wingfield and Feagin's research points significantly to the ways that the mainstream media continues to frame racial issues with a white audience in mind, what also requires attention is how different groups of Americans interpret these accounts. As I found in my research, white male attorneys often drew upon anti-affirmative-action rhetoric to buttress their own arguments about why such policies were no longer necessary. Conversely, though white women and people of color were aware of these arguments and often referenced them in their interviews, most provided interpretations that countered the media's simplistic binary of two and only two sides to this issue. As media scholars have long recognized, news stories do not determine how individuals will make sense of social issues, but rather facilitate our understanding by providing key terms and rhetoric. With the increasing influence of blogs and other forms of social media in the last ten to fifteen years, more attention is needed to the sources that Americans are most likely to rely upon for important social issues and how they interpret them.

Finally, living in an era of "colorblindness," where many white Americans, particularly elites, may consider it inappropriate or impolite to discuss racial issues openly and honestly, my research compels scholars to consider various methodological strategies that might enable them to unpack silences when it comes to matters of race. Ethnographic studies where researchers have access to fieldwork observations as well as interviews suggest one possible way to work through this impasse. For instance, in her important study, *Colormute: Race Talk Dilemmas in American Schools*, education scholar Mica Pollack found that teachers and administrators in the California high school she studied often avoided mentioning race directly when referring to students of color.[6] To give one example, teachers often referred to African American students whom they considered problematic as "the students who hang out in the halls" after the bell rang for class. Here, Pollack argues that these teachers were not colorblind—they did indeed notice race—but rather were "colormute." Because race had become such a contentious issue in this particular high school, and parents were quick to blame teachers for what they perceived as failures in the school system, teachers learned to be careful about what they said about race. (Significantly, too, her study took place in the wake of the passage of Proposition 209.) As Pollack argues, "blame" has become an explosive word in discussions about school failure. Parents, teachers, and administrators are all blamed by one another for student failure. As Pollack suggests, discussions revolving around blame do not solve the problems of school districts beleaguered with financial problems. Nor do "colormute" discussions work to improve problems in schools with considerable racial and ethnic diversity. Her research points importantly not only to methodological strategies scholars might use to look behind the evasions of "colormute" discourse, but also to the potential of more fruitful and productive discussions when blame can be left aside as we talk more openly about racial matters.

Of course, ethnographers aren't always able to compare fieldwork observations with interview material, particularly in the case of elites. As numerous scholars have pointed out, elites, especially in the private sector, are an enormously difficult group to study. They may deny requests to corporate archives or in some cases destroy such records altogether, decline requests for fieldwork and interviews, or, if they do grant interviews, choose not to fully participate.[7] Moreover, they have the power and influence to craft their own public personas—either through glossy corporate advertising brochures or carefully edited memoirs and autobiographies. All these practices create limits to the production of knowledge about elites.

This is one of the reasons I turned to fiction as an alternative methodological strategy in my own research. When I returned to the field in the late 1990s, I had more limited access to informal discussions about race and thus was compelled to rely more heavily on my interview material. As I have shown, my questions about race and affirmative action often provoked discomfort and silence among white male attorneys. My short story, "Small Talk," not only provides a methodological strategy for imagining a social situation that I did not have access to (i.e., a dinner following a professional job interview), but also a means of reading behind the silences. Following the lead of queer-of-color theorist Roderick Ferguson, who argues that fiction by African American writers such as Ralph Ellison provided a critique of canonical sociology's theories of race relations, I used fiction as means of countering and complementing sociological theories about white racism.[8] In analyzing my short story, I developed the concept of "ambivalent racism" as a means of apprehending what might lie behind white elites' hesitation and silences about race. Certainly, fictionalizing goes beyond what many social scientists and historians regard as acceptable rhetorical modes. Still, my approach recalls one of the challenges associated with studying elites: the particular nature of the truths revealed through life story analysis and the acts of empathy or imagination they entail. Importantly, the "truths" that emerge from the analysis of the white male lawyers' personal narratives may be unknowable; but, as I have argued, fiction provides one way of moving behind their silence. It creates an epistemological vantage point that is complex, contingent, and subject to interpretation.

Still "Racing for Innocence"

When I present my research to various audiences, one question that inevitably arises is whether my findings from the 1990s about "racing for innocence" and elite white men's participation in the backlash against affirmative action are relevant today. As many have asked: Isn't the backlash against affirmative action over? Haven't we resolved the question of whether this policy is necessary? Do lawyers of color and white women professionals still encounter exclusionary practices at work?

A number of prominent events, such as lawsuits and Supreme Court decisions, suggest that the backlash against affirmative action has continued, while more recent sociological research shows that discrimination continues to be a problem for people of color and white women in a number of occupations and professions. As the millennium began, for example, two important suits were filed against the University of Michigan that ultimately went to the United States Supreme Court. In the first case, white plaintiffs Jennifer Gratz and Patrick Hamacher complained that the University's undergraduate admissions process unfairly discriminated against them. Around the same time, another white applicant, Barbara Grutter, brought suit against the University's law school, which had a different admissions process, requirements, and pool of applicants. She too argued that the use of race in admissions unfairly discriminated against her.[9] In 2003, the U.S. Supreme Court ruled in *Gratz v. Bollinger* that the University of Michigan's point system for undergraduate admissions was too mechanistic in its use of race (points were awarded to underrepresented groups based on ethnicity) in its admission process and was, therefore, unconstitutional.[10] In the second case, *Grutter v. Bollinger*, the Court upheld the University's law school admissions policy because it drew upon a more limited consideration of race. Justice Sandra Day O'Connor, who cast the deciding vote in the *Grutter* decision, wrote in her majority opinion that the United States had *not* yet reached a point where affirmative action was no longer needed.[11]

Despite Justice O'Connor's ruling, the backlash continued in Michigan. Not long after these Court decisions were announced, Ward Connerly, former University of California Regent, and his allies in Michigan launched a campaign in the state against affirmative action. Borrowing language directly from the Civil Rights Initiative in California, they succeeded in getting Proposition 2, the Michigan Civil Rights Initiative, on the November 2006 ballot. Like Californians, the majority of Michigan voters endorsed the Proposition and it went into effect in December 2006.[12]

Two years later, two other events came to national attention, again raising the question of whether affirmative action was necessary. In 2008, Barack Obama was elected as the first African American to the office of President of the United States.[13] Immediately after the election, media pundits around the country proclaimed that the color line in the United States had collapsed. As mentioned earlier, op-ed pieces with headlines such as "Obama Elected President as Racial Barrier Falls," "Race, Post Race," and "Is Race Out of the Race?" all argued that the election of a black President meant that we now live in a "post-racial society."[14] As these editorials suggested, if the United States elected a black President, remedial policies such as affirmative action were no longer needed. Then, in November 2010, the majority of voters in the state of Arizona passed Proposition 107, which banned the consideration of race, ethnicity, or gender in state government, including public colleges and universities.[15] Here again, critics of affirmative action argued that the policy was unnecessary. As an editorial writer in the *Arizona Republic* argued:

> Affirmative action wasn't meant to be a perpetual-motion machine. The policy served an important purpose, making up for missing opportunities in education and the workplace. But over time, the drawbacks have come to outweigh the advantages. Voters should pull the plug.[16]

For Ward Connerly, who now heads a California-based anti-affirmative-action organization (the American Civil Rights Institute), passing Proposition 107 in Arizona was part of his organization's broader strategy to dismantle affirmative action in all fifty states. In addition to Arizona, California, Florida, Michigan, Nebraska, and Washington have all passed initiatives banning the policy. (Only one state, Colorado, rejected a state ban in 2008.[17]) Though Texas has not passed a statewide ban, the *Hopwood* Federal Court of Appeals decision barred the consideration of race in admissions to public universities in the Lone Star State.[18]

Though the backlash against affirmative action continues, it is not without opposition. In Texas, an educational coalition fought back after the 1996 *Hopwood* ruling. This coalition sought to increase minority enrollments through what became known as the "Texas 10 percent plan." This plan, which went into effect in 1997, offered admission in flagship universities to all high school students who graduated in the top ten percent of their class, regardless of standardized test scores.[19] Legislators reasoned that because Texas, like many states, has high schools that are predominantly black or Latino, the plan would reintegrate higher education by increasing enrollments of racial and ethnic minority students as well as boost enrollments for rural whites.[20]

Following the ban on affirmative action in two other states, both the University of California and Washington state created university admissions plans that considered academic performance in the context of a student applicant's socioeconomic status, such as "low family income," "first generation to attend college," and "disadvantaged social or economic environment."[21] Because so many blacks and Latinos come from low-income backgrounds, the reasoning was that using socioeconomic background as a criterion would assist students of color as well as disadvantaged white students. The results in California have been mixed. After a precipitous decline in racial and ethnic minority enrollments in the wake of Proposition 209—freshman minority enrollment at UC Berkeley, for example, declined by 50 percent—the University of California ushered in its new socioeconomic program.[22] Though black and Latino enrollments rose again, the majority of these students were not enrolled at UC's flagship campuses in Berkeley or Los Angeles, but at the less selective campuses such as UC Riverside.[23] This means that fewer students of color were attending the very schools that routinely send students to professional and graduate programs.

Back in Michigan, affirmative action advocates filed a brief with the Sixth Court of Appeals challenging the constitutionality of Michigan's Civil Rights Initiative. In July 2011, a panel of three judges from the Court overturned the referendum. As of this writing, Michigan Attorney General Bill Schuette has challenged the ruling, asking for a full review from all six Court judges.[24] Meanwhile, in Texas two white women challenged the application of the *Grutter* decision to the admissions process at the University of Texas, arguing that it disproportionately benefited Hispanics. This case, *Fisher v. the University of Texas*, will go to the U.S. Supreme Court in the fall of 2012.[25] Given the recent *Wal-Mart* Supreme Court decision, which makes it more difficult for people of color and white women to file class action lawsuits, the future of cases such as the one in Texas are immensely important. The muting of anti-discrimination law through the *Wal-Mart* decision means that affirmative action remains one of the few protections against discrimination.

While debate about the future of affirmative action continues, the reality remains: Race is a fundamental organizing principle of structural inequality in the United States. As sociologists Jennifer Lee and Frank Bean point out in their book, *The Diversity Paradox*, race still "affects where one lives, what schools one attends, how much education one attains, how much one earns, and how much wealth one accumulates, and whom one marries."[26] Other findings from recent sociological research demonstrate that people of color and white women continue to face discrimination in hiring and promotion. A recent field experiment study in New York City by Devah Pager and her colleagues found that employers still prefer to hire whites over blacks or Latinos in low-wage jobs—even when whites have criminal records.[27] More pertinent to my findings on lawyers, recent reports conducted by the American Bar Association, as well as other research, show that progress is still painfully slow for racial and ethnic minorities as well as white women in the legal profession.[28]

In addition to these important studies, a number of sociologists have argued that diversity rather than affirmative action became an increasing public focus in workplace in the 1990s and beyond.[29] Despite this seemingly progressive focus, the racial and ethnic composition of many professional workplaces has not changed dramatically. Part of this is because diversity has come to have many meanings beyond race or gender, such as geographic region, religious affiliation, or political affiliation.[30] Moreover, there is now a tendency for many corporations to claim in promotional materials and publications that they value diversity as a means of "selling" their products and services to consumers.[31] For example, in her excellent study, *Inside Out: Lesbian and Gay Workplace Rights*, Nicole Raeburn argues that movements within Fortune 500 corporations to include gays and lesbians often do so in an attempt to increase their customer base. In other words, corporations "sell" diversity as a commodity as a means of increasing profits. For business leaders, then, diversity is not about leveling the playing field as pro-affirmative-action advocates might argue, but rather it's a means of celebrating a few token hires as a way to improve their corporate image to ratchet up profits.

Finally, racial and class inequality increased yet again after the 2008 stock market crash, the marked decline in the value of homes, foreclosures across the nation, and rising unemployment resulting from the recession. A 2011 PEW study found that in the wake of the foreclosures following the stock market crash, white wealth increased to *twenty* times that of African Americans and thirteen times that of Hispanics.[32] As sociologists Melvin Oliver and Thomas Shapiro argue in their classic study, *White Wealth/Black Wealth*, gaps in the accumulation of wealth between whites and African Americans have long existed which, in turn, have contributed to black/white inequality over generations. What the recent PEW study findings demonstrate is that the recession has exacerbated the differences that Oliver and Shapiro first documented the 1990s.[33] Put another way, recent economic conditions sharply curtailed social mobility for many Americans, while those who lost jobs are scrambling to find employment and stay afloat financially in an increasingly tight job market. As the research I have reviewed demonstrates, not only has racial and gender discrimination continued in the United States, but also, with the recent economic downturn, things have gotten much worse for many American families, especially for families of color.

The gap between the fact of continuing racial discrimination in the United States and corporate portrayals of diverse workplaces where people of color, white women, and gays and lesbians are giddily embraced recalls the wily machinations of the Wizard of Oz. In my rendition, the wizard who hides behind the curtain creates the illusion of a happy "diversity" in American workplaces where race, gender, and sexual preference no longer matter and everyone gets along. He makes movies celebrating the accomplishment of "white racial progress" and writes news stories proclaiming the achievement of a "post-racial society." Certainly, my research paints a far more complicated historical portrait of the operation of cultural memory through an examination of journalistic practices, cinematic representations, and neoliberal and neoconservative political discourse, as well as the practices of white male elites and representations of racism through fiction. Still, academic research about racial and gender inequality continues to receive little attention in the news media. It's time to pull back the curtain.

Reference Matter

Appendix A

Reflections on Methodology

Personal narratives, such as the career life histories I draw from in this book, do not exist apart from the social context and processes through which they are created. Rather, they were shaped by an interaction in a particular historical moment between two people: "one with a unique personality traits and particular interests at a particular time of life, who answers a specific set of questions asked by another person with unique personality traits and interests at a particular time of life"[1] The first section of this Appendix examines my interactions with the lawyers I interviewed and considers how my positionality as a lesbian, white woman, and professional may have influenced what people told me in their interviews. Further, it addresses the methodological strategy I employed for negotiating the issue of "truthfulness" in my ethnographic research.

In the second section, I discuss the process of writing "Small Talk," the short story in Chapter 5. I wrote this section in part because it is unusual for an ethnographer to write fiction, and some readers may be curious about how I came to do so. At the same time, it serves as a means of rendering visible the process of revision that led to the final version of the story.[2] As I argue, fiction writing entails a different kind of process than ethnographic writing and thinking. Further, as I show, even here, the kinds of dynamics I uncovered in my research surrounding racial issues—discomfort, silence, and denial—also emerged in some of the workshops where I discussed my work-in-progress.

Researching Race in an Era of Colorblindness

One of the main sources for this book were work life histories from attorneys I interviewed first in 1989 and again ten years later in 1998 and 1999. Like other forms of personal narratives, life histories are not only products of particular forms of storytelling, such as the genre of autobiography, but their specific social, historical, and institutional contexts. In addition, their analysis is also constructed through the relationship between the narrator (the person who tells the story) and the analyst (the person who interprets it). As Mary Jo Maynes, Barbara Laslett, and I argue, attention to this relationship is important because this collaborative—though seldom equal—relationship inevitably shapes the form and content that a personal narrative takes.[3] To paraphrase historian Susan Geiger, what this means for feminist scholars is that we have a responsibility to publish *what* we know as well as *how* we think we know it and *where* we are situated in the act of trying to understand.[4] My intent is to describe my relationship to the people I interviewed in order to give readers a sense of how their life stories came to be shaped. As I suggest, a person whose positionality differs from my own might evoke stories with different emphases or different kinds of narrative themes. My point then is not to discount personal narratives as evidence, but rather to make the method of their production visible.[5]

In my first book, *Gender Trials: Emotional Lives in Contemporary Law Firms,* I detailed how my positionality as a white woman, a UC Berkeley graduate student, and a former paralegal not only influenced my relationships with paralegals and litigation attorneys, but also evoked particular kinds of stories about their workplace lives.[6] When I returned to the Legal Department ten years later in 1999, many things about my professional life had changed. I returned *not* as a graduate student but as a professional—a tenured professor from a public research university. My work life as a paralegal was long behind me, and my position as a university professor rendered my professional status more or less equivalent to the lawyers whom I interviewed.

In addition to these changes in my professional life, there were also shifts in the broader historical and national context and within the state of California itself that I detail in the first two chapters of this book. When I initially began this study in 1989, a backlash against affirmative was already well under way across the United States. At the time, the media focused its attention on the few incidents of "reverse discrimination," thereby creating the trope of "white male innocence and injury." At the same time, there was a resurgence of a conservative and neoliberal agenda with Presidents Ronald Reagan and George H.

Bush in the 1980s, which led the assault against the welfare state, affirmative action, and other forms of federal assistance.[7]

Importantly, then, when I reentered the field in 1999, Proposition 209 had already passed and debate about affirmative action continued to dominate the state and national newspaper stories and editorials. Asking people whom I did not know well (though not in all cases) about a controversial topic in an era of "colorblindness" seemed a difficult, if not impossible, task. Further, with the advent of the Civil Rights Act of 1964, as well as subsequent policies and legislation, it was no longer legally permissible for employers refuse to hire racial or ethnic minorities or women simply because they were African American or female. Consequently, I worried that people would not talk to me candidly about these issues, or would dissemble politely, or would simply dismiss my questions. My early sense that interviewing people about affirmative action would be difficult came out in one of my first interviews with Jason, a thirty-seven-year-old white lawyer (Chapter 3). In response to my first question about affirmative action, he exclaimed, "Wow, that's a loaded question! I mean, you know, affirmative action is such a controversial issue. I bet you have a hard time getting people to talk about this in a [pauses], a kind of straightforward way— especially here."

While Jason was forthcoming in his views about affirmative action, as I was to discover, his responses to my questions proved to be the exception— few white men were as candid as he was. Most of the white male attorneys interviewed described their work environment and their work in quite positive terms; however, their narratives stopped short with long, uncomfortable silences when I began asking questions about affirmative action policy. As discussed in Chapter 3, these lengthy silences were often followed by complaints in hushed tones about "having to be careful" about what was said at work. In probing for details, I often came up against their reluctance to provide specific examples.

I often wondered whether they would have been more candid with a person who stated from the outset that they were opposed to affirmative action. I refrained from voicing my own position in the interviews unless directly asked, though my questions may have signaled my own supportive stance. It is also possible that being a white and female academic signaled to them a more liberal perspective. Further, my short spiky haircut and tailored pantsuit may have hinted at my sexual persuasion. Certainly, academics, especially gay and lesbian academics, are assumed to be liberal, and white women are among the social groups who benefit from affirmative action policy. So it is possible that the white male attorneys would have been more candid with a white male interviewer or someone who held an anti-affirmative-action position, though I have no way of knowing for sure.

Conversely, with the African American men and woman I interviewed, I had the sense, for the most part, that the interviews went much better. These people were more forthcoming about their views and generous with their time. As many scholars have suggested, in interracial interviews where researchers are white and their subjects are people of color, narrators may be less forthcoming, particularly when the issue under discussion is race.[8] However, because I had worked with Randall Kingsley, one of the African American lawyers, when I was a paralegal in the 1980s, he was—perhaps for that reason—more candid during his interview. As I discovered in later interviews, he had "vetted" me for the other two black attorneys whom I knew less well. They both told me that Randall had indicated that I was "trustworthy" and encouraged them to talk to me.

White women were also more likely than white men to be forthcoming in their interviews. Here I suspect that my status as a white woman and as another professional made rapport easier to accomplish than with white men. For example, when discussing sex-based discrimination, white women often followed descriptions of problems they encountered at work, especially as mothers with children, with comments such as, "But you probably know what I am talking about" or "I suspect this happens to college professors, too." In these cases, I was quick to acknowledge that I didn't have children, but I validated their experiences either by pointing to research that confirmed their concerns more generally among women professionals or mentioning friends who faced similar problems.

In interviews with Kathryn and Isabella, whose positions on affirmative action were quite different from my own, I worked hard to listen to what they had to say and understand their point of view (Chapter 4). At times, I suspect I was less than successful. For example, when Isabella told me that she couldn't take women seriously who complain about discrimination, I countered by asking, "But, isn't it true that BC was sued for sex and race discrimination in the 1970s and that's why the consent decree was ordered by the court in the first place?" She was quick to point out that had all happened "*a very* long time ago" (emphasis in original). I countered her position again by asking about the difficulties of "balancing work and family," adding that research showed "contemporary workplaces have been resistant to accommodating family and medical leaves to women who have childcare . . . responsibilities," Her response was definitive and vehement: "That has nothing to do with discrimination. You're talking about *personal* choices that individuals make. . . . We're *not* responsible for accommodating personal decisions" (emphasis in original).

My sense at the time was that she was irritated with me for raising these questions and realized that I didn't share her position. Nonetheless, she didn't cut the interview short as one white male attorney had done. However, it's important to note that while other women, including Kathryn, whom I also challenged in a number of questions, thanked me when the interview ended, Isabella did not. Unlike the other women who I felt enjoyed talking about their experiences to an attentive audience, Isabella seemed far more defensive—even prickly—by the end of the interview. And, it is possible this influenced what she told me in her interview.

Despite the fact that most white women and people of color seemed more open in my interviews with them, there remains the issue of whether their accounts were "true" ones. In fact, many historians and social scientists consider life histories to be problematic as a form of evidence, because they are unreliable. Narrators may not recall events accurately, they may omit material they find personally embarrassing, or they might even fabricate a story. Further, elites, more than other social groups, may wish to preserve a particular public image and edit their life stories accordingly.[9] How, then, do we assess the truthfulness of their personal narratives?

In addressing this question, sociologist R. W. Connell argues that researchers need to compare life stories with other kinds of evidence to assess their veracity, while at the same time taking seriously the efforts of narrators "to speak the truth."[10] This does not mean taking personal narrative evidence at face value, but rather being prepared to read it in a context and to interpret it. As historian Mary Jo Maynes argues, "[e]ffective analyses of personal narratives must take into consideration that any rendition of the past has to be seen in the context of its motives in the present (that is, at the time of the telling), its symbolic power, and its contextual framing."[11]

In comparing narrators' accounts against other sources of evidence, researchers may uncover significant discrepancies. While such discoveries are crucial to analysis, I am not proposing that analysts determine the truth of a narrator's words solely in terms of their factual accuracy or the reliability of memory. Important insights can also be gleaned from discrepancies and mistakes.[12] Whether or not a story is true in the factual sense, narrators *act* on the basis of *the sense they make* of a particular experience within a particular context. The researcher's responsibility is to provide enough information to bring to light the reasons why narrators tell the stories they do.

Chapter 3 provides an example of getting at the truthfulness of two divergent accounts of African American lawyer Randall Kingsley's reasons for leaving the BC Legal Department for another job. While the majority of the white attorneys interviewed told me stories of his leave-taking that emphasized Randall's lack of "fit" and "qualifications" for the job, Randall's own narrative focused on dissatisfaction with his colleagues and a myriad of small discriminatory acts. There, I explored a number of other possible sources of evidence to support each side of the story; and, importantly, though I uncovered further evidence to support Randall's narrative, I did not summarily dismiss the stories the white lawyers told about his departure as false. In fact, my central concern lay in trying to figure out how two such different interpretations of the same episode existed. While this is explained more fully in the chapter, I want to emphasize here that rather than simply labeling personal narratives as true or untrue, my methodological strategy throughout this book is to contextualize such accounts, search for other sources of evidence—when possible—and consider the reasons that narrators tell the stories they do.

An Ethnographer Writing Fiction

Several years ago, I started taking fiction classes at the Loft Literary Center in Minneapolis, a nonprofit organization that supports the artistic development of writers in the local community through classes, workshops, literary readings, and other events.[13] It's located in a wonderful old building in downtown Minneapolis with unfinished blond, brick walls and high wood-beamed ceilings. In the many classes I have taken, students have come from a wide range of ages and backgrounds, but share a passion for reading fiction, poetry, and creative nonfiction. It is the kind of place that encourages aspiring writers to find, as Brenda Ueland suggests, the important things they want to write about.[14]

After years of academic writing, the process of learning to write fiction, though at times fascinating and energizing, was not an easy one for me. Although my ethnographic training helped me to pay attention to details about dialogue and settings, at other times it bled through in drafts that were not at all literary. For instance, in a workshop on my first version of "Small Talk," a white eighteen-year-old noted that I had failed to describe any of my characters' facial features in my short story.[15] Until she pointed this out, I was completely unaware that I had done so. Apparently, I had unwittingly imported ethnography's ethical practice of protecting the anonymity of subjects into a short story, thereby leaving out visual details that can be crucial to establishing fictional characters.

In addition to learning that I had failed to pay attention to details in painting a portrait of my characters, I also came up against the fraught issue of representation. Another student, a middle-aged woman of color, criticized some of the ways I represented Robin's experience as a black woman. This was certainly not surprising, as I had already given this question a lot of thought. After all, how would I as a white woman be able to accurately represent an African American woman's subjectivity? At the same time, I believed that to ignore black experiences was to reproduce a gap in much of fiction—white writers are often reluctant to portray characters of color. Further, as feminist studies scholar Jessica Petocz astutely observes, the retreat from interpretation of the lives of women of color in research by white women seems to "feign respect."[16] As she asks, how can white feminists ever advance any kind of dialogue across difference if we continue to retreat from it? Certainly, going forward may entail making mistakes, but presumably something important can be gleaned from them. Finally, by reading sociological studies of African American women professionals and relying on the personal narratives from my research, I hoped to make, at the very least, a good *first* attempt.

Though the student was interested in what I was trying to accomplish in my broader book project, as she explained, for a black woman like Robin to survive in a predominantly white workplace, she would have to work hard to make whites feel at ease around them by demonstrating that she was pleasant and accommodating in order to counter the racist stereotype of the "angry black woman."[17] Consequently, she didn't think a *smart* black attorney like Robin would let Bill have it at the end of the dinner. Further, though she appreciated my attempts to depict Robin as reticent, in her view, someone like Robin would never become a highly successful attorney because she didn't have the requisite social skills, such as engaging in small talk, that are necessary for playing the game.

Conversely, the eighteen-year-old student liked the fact that Robin told Bill off at the end of the story; she thought Bill deserved it. (I should add that in this first version of the short story, Bill had no redeeming qualities whatsoever.) Another student, an older white man, thought that I had captured Robin "perfectly as a real ball-buster" but found Bill's character "too stereotypical." The instructor, who was silent throughout the discussion, later at my prompting provided useful written comments. She thought Bill was the most interesting character in the story but needed more work to become "a sympathetic character." (She especially liked the story Bill told about "fucking a piano.") She also pointed out that Bill and Robin, despite their differences, had some things in common, such as daughters they worried about and the inability to do small talk. "Couldn't you write a story where they find some things in common, despite their differences, and possibly become friends?" the instructor asked.

The critical comments on my early draft were discouraging and, for a time, I considered ditching the story altogether and starting another one. But, part of its inspiration came from an anecdote shared with me by a black academic who, during a job interview, encountered a Bill-like character who blathered on at great length about understanding discrimination because of his white ethnicity. Her story reminded me of other Bill-like individuals I knew in real life, and I wondered what someone like Bill might learn from Robin's interpretation of the meeting. Further, most African American lawyers I interviewed had, at some point in their careers, encountered whites who seemed to think that by highlighting their status as a white ethnic minority, they shared common experiences, understood the realities of discrimination, and were thereby immune from prejudice.

Certainly, the tendency toward white solipsism in conversations about race is not a new issue. Women-of-color feminists have long written eloquently and critically about what happens in interracial discussions when the topic turns to race. Rather than listen to the distinctiveness of racist experiences, white feminists in these groups are described as quick to change the subject by referencing their own working-class or white ethnic status.[18] In light of this research, I imagined my short story as a way of *listening* to these kinds of fraught conversations. Further, to make the story understandable to white Americans who might not grasp the racial subtext, I wanted to tell the story from Robin's perspective.

Using these critical comments, I revised the short story and submitted it to another fiction class I took in the summer, as well as to my academic writing group, which is composed of ethnographers. In the second fiction class, a white middle-aged woman who worked as a marketing director at a law firm told me that my story was "unbelievable" because "minorities call all the shots these days." Though I was irritated by her comment—it sounded much like the anti-affirmative-action rhetoric I describe in this book—I tried to respond evenly with questions, such as, "What makes you think minorities call the shots today?" and "How many lawyers are people of color in the firm where you work?"

She, in turn, became red-faced and defensive and told me my story was "dated" because "everyone knows today things are better." When I explained that my story took place in 1995, she replied that that fact was "not obvious." The instructor and another white student, however, were quick to point out that I did refer to the University of California Regents' decision to get rid of affirmative action on the first page of the story, the basketball player Michael Jordan on the second, and 1995 American Bar Association report on the status of women in the profession several pages later. The rest of the class shifted around in their seats, refusing to make eye contact with me and offering little in the way of comments. One middle-aged white man did say he was surprised to learn that Robin interpreted Bill's discussion of his ethnicity as offensive; he thought Bill was struggling to find "common ground and be friendly." My sense was that most of them either didn't like the story but didn't want to say so, or didn't feel comfortable talking about its racial dynamics. "A very difficult issue to write about," one young white woman wrote at the end of my story. "I could never write about this." "Am I supposed to feel judged?" a white middle-aged man scrawled in his one-sentence commentary at the end of my story. "This would never happen today!" the marketing director declared in her round, child-like cursive comments in the margins of the last page.

The instructor and my academic writing group, however, made some important critical and constructive suggestions. One was that I should follow Robin and Bill after the end of the dinner outside or to the hospital into an entirely different situation. They pointed out that the interview situation was too constrained for the characters to fully emerge and that it was important to give them another context where they could interact and reveal other aspects of their personalities. Second, they wanted me to do more to complicate Bill as a character. As the instructor queried in her comments, "Is he supposed to be a racist and sexist jerk, a clumsy oaf incapable of behaving well in social situations, or a bit of both?"

With these questions in mind, I worked to develop Bill as a more complex character and introduced a new scene at the end of the short story—their meeting outside the San Francisco Hilton Hotel when Robin is trying to hail a cab to the hospital. That version of the story has, in turn, has gone through further revisions in a third fiction writing class and still more revisions in other classes. Part of the reason for this constant revision is that fiction writing requires attention to detail in every sentence. Descriptions of characters, their dialogue, and settings must work together to give the reader a sense who these people are and why they make the decisions they do. To give an example, one way to develop character is to show what they are wearing. Bill is the kind of person who would wear an expensive suit, but with a rumpled button-down shirt and a tie with a small spot on it, while McElroy is someone who is always impeccably dressed. If McElroy got a spot on his tie, he would probably replace it with another kept in his office for precisely that reason. This small detail not only hints that Bill is somewhat of a slob, but also suggests class differences between the two characters. As Bill tells us, he worked his way up from a working-class background; McElroy did not.

In addition to these kinds of nuances, I needed to find the right language to create dialogue for each character and a setting that worked to highlight the emotional dynamics of the story and move it forward. In the interim, I wrote another short story about Bill and his daughter, the aspiring poet, who had just "come out" to her parents as a lesbian. This gave me the opportunity to imagine Bill in a familial, rather than professional, relationship. When I came back to "Small Talk," I used some of the things I had learned about Bill in writing the other story to create a more complicated character.

Before moving on to conclude my discussion about the process surrounding my revisions of "Small Talk," I want to pause to shine a light on some of the racial dynamics that emerged in my writing classes. Much like the white male attorneys I interviewed, who seemed uncomfortable discussing race openly, many (though certainly not all) of the white workshop participants in the two classes I have described either seemed uncomfortable discussing racial discrimination or, in the case of the law firm marketing director, oblivious to the fact it still exists in contemporary workplaces. In contrast, when one student of color, much like Randall the African American attorney in Chapter 3, discussed representations of race as a problem in my short story, most of the students as well as the class instructor became silent. The majority were unwilling to either support her interpretation or offer one of their own.

Afterwards, much like Randall's boss, who complained to others that Randall had called him a racist, two white students spoke to me individually saying how much they liked my story and how sorry they were that I had been "blasted" for writing about race. I said that I hadn't felt "blasted," but rather found the comments useful in helping me to draw a more complex portrait of Robin that avoided racist stereotypes. Further, I told them I was disappointed that more people hadn't engaged during the workshop. I wanted to learn more about how to improve my short story and felt that only two or three people had taken me seriously enough to provide comments. (Neither of these students had spoken during the discussion of my short story.) They both seemed taken aback by my comments and somewhat embarrassed, but promised to provide written comments. (Neither one did so.) By the time I got home, I felt annoyed with them and with the instructor for practicing what I regarded as conflict avoidance.

Later that day, I e-mailed the instructor to say that I was disappointed by the class discussion. I pointed out that in other workshops, students had received feedback from many other students and I had heard only from three. Since she herself hadn't provided comments in class, I asked that she do so. In a detailed response, the teacher noted that I had written about an issue that addressed the student of color's "vulnerabilities," and suggested that I not take the student's comments "personally" because my story was a "good one." She then provided the comments I mentioned above. Again, I was irritated, but this time because I felt she was *personalizing* the comments I had received and ignoring the broader issue I raised about *structural dynamics* in the classroom and her responsibility as a teacher to facilitate discussion.

To be clear, I raise these issues now not to vilify the instructor or the white students in the workshop, but rather to underscore how even in this one class-room situation in the Upper Midwest many years after I had conducted my research on the backlash against affirmative action in California, it was difficult for most white students and one teacher to engage openly in discussions about race. Living in a state where the stereotypical phrase "Minnesota nice" is often used to describe long-term residents who display a pleasant, friendly exterior when they may feel otherwise, I am frequently reminded that I am much less tolerant than others of suppressing disagreement.[19] I know that my direct ap-proach is often perceived as at odds with what others may understand as "civil-ity" or their own desire for the avoidance of conflict. Certainly, this could have played a part in class discussions.

At the same time, it's possible that this is not a uniquely Minnesota phe-nomenon. Contemporary fiction, especially by Anglo European authors, that focuses on racial inequality or other political issues is not typical in the United States. American novels, for instance, are much more likely than French or Brit-ish fiction to focus on relationships—familial, personal, or romantic—rather than on politically loaded issues such as race, social class, immigrant status, or other forms of structural inequality.[20] "Small Talk" may have struck those who are accustomed to a different genre as unusual and therefore difficult to discuss.

That said, it strikes me that we are ever to move beyond the gap between white Americans' professed ideal of colorblindness and their racially exclusion-ary practices, we all have to learn to talk frankly and openly about racial issues. I am not suggesting this might be easy, and from past experiences, I know that these conversations can be especially fraught. People of color are likely to have their experiences and perspectives dismissed or misunderstood by Anglo Americans, while whites often respond with guilt or denial. But, as feminist philosopher Jane Flax argues, post-structuralist critique suggests that none of us is "innocent" of power.[21] Put another way, we are all implicated in some way within structures of privilege and disadvantage. Consequently, we have to recognize the ways we are all involved in the "dirty process of racializing and gendering others."[22]

At the same time, I realize that my call for open dialogue and debate may be difficult for another reason. Unlike in the United Kingdom, where there is a long history of and an elaborate language for discussing social class and privilege, in the United States we understand our history as a rejection of the status hierarchies inherent in aristocracy and a celebration of the ideals of equality and individual rights under democracy.[23] What this means is that our dominant discourse does not provide a language for talking social class, race, and gender in structural terms. As my work life history interviews reveal, there is a tendency to reduce racial and gendered structural inequalities to the individual level with phrases such as "He's not qualified" or "She's "not committed." At the same time, however, tensions emerged between this individualist and meritocratic discourse and another that derives from the civil rights movement and later from the women's movement, one emphasizing the history of discrimination against people of color and white women. The traces of this second discourse emerge in the white women lawyer's ambivalent stance about affirmative action, and more obliquely in the white male attorneys' hesitations, silences, and vehement denials. Perhaps one fruitful place to begin is by addressing the heart of this tension.

Returning to my discussion about the revisions I made for "Small Talk," I should add that in summarizing my revisions, I may have given the impression that this was an orderly process where one insight logically led to the next, thereby improving the short story. Perhaps what I have not emphasized enough is the role of imagination in this process. As acclaimed Japanese author Haruki Murakmi emphasizes, in writing fiction, you have to sit your desk, "focusing your mind like a laser beam, imagining something out of a blank horizon, creating a story, selecting the right words, one by one . . ."[24] Put another way, you have to let your imagination go and allow your characters guide the story. To give an example of what that means, I didn't know when I was rewriting "Small Talk" for the tenth or eleventh time what Bill would do when he encountered Robin on the street after their dinner. Further, when he offered Robin a ride to the hospital, I didn't know in advance how Robin might respond. I had to get inside each character's head to *imagine* what she or he might do.

After spending the summer of 2010 writing fiction for two different courses—one focused on flash fiction, that is, stories of fewer than 1,500 words, and another on intermediate fiction—I had to revise an academic paper for a presentation at the annual American Sociological Association meeting. Initially, it felt like pulling teeth. I had to keep reminding myself to make an argument and ground it in the relevant theoretical work. This required not imagination, but a prosaic recitation of extant literature. Then, piece by piece, I worked to lay out evidence to support my argument. This felt completely counterintuitive to the creative work I had been doing, which reminded me that writing for a scholarly audience is not only an entirely different process and generic form, but also a distinct way of knowing.

The disjuncture I felt in trying to move from writing fiction back to writing an academic paper ties in with this book's argument about the distinctiveness of these two epistemologies. In fiction, we try to create characters and situations that are complex but believable, while as ethnographers we search for patterns of talk and behavior to make arguments that reconstruct or modify existing theory. Moreover, unlike short story writers, as ethnographers we seldom provide enough detail to construct individual personalities, in part because we are bound by the ethical strictures of anonymity and confidentiality.[25] Further, each form makes different claims about truth. In creative writing, we aspire to verisimilitude in developing characters. We write "true" stories in the sense that we try to create *believable* fictional characters.[26] In anthropology and sociology, we rely on what actual people tell us in order to document patterns as well as variations to describe dominant cultural beliefs and practices and make credible theoretical arguments. Thus, "truth" has different indexical claims in fiction and in ethnography.

At the same time, as I have shown with respect to white male attorneys, ethnographic research provides a source for the "truthful" but perhaps not the "real."[27] Put another way, while this group of lawyers told me what they considered important, their silences and hesitations hinted that their work life history interviews did not provide a source for their actual understandings of race and racism. Rather, they may have felt reluctant, afraid, or ambivalent about revealing what they actually thought and felt. It is precisely this limitation in my ethnographic research that led me to pursue fiction as another way of knowing.[28]

As I have argued, ethnography and fiction are both important generic forms; one is no better than the other. By bringing them together, my intent has been to show how each complements the other by providing, on one hand, details about historically and culturally distinctive patterns of behavior; and, on the other hand, individual subjectivity and meaning. My ethnographic research highlights the dominant discursive practice of "racing for innocence" among a group of white men in a particular historical time and place, while "Small Talk" suggests what *might* lie behind their silences. I leave it for readers to assess whether I have done each one successfully.

Appendix B

Hollywood Films

Detailed below is the full list of Hollywood movies in my sample that exceeded $3 million in box office receipts between 1987 and 1999 and focused on racial themes. Box office receipts are in millions of dollars, and figures have been rounded up to the next million when they exceed $500,000. (This information comes from Internet Movie Database.) The next column lists the general category of the film, such as historical drama, comedy, or white racial progress, followed by the particular perspective taken in the film. For instance, *American Me* is a historical drama and takes the perspective of a Chicano man, while *B*A*P*S** is a comedy about black female friendship and takes the perspective of one of the African American women in the film.

Title/Year released	Receipts (in millions of $)	Topics/Central perspective
American History X (1998)	7	white racial progress; white male
American Me (1992)	13	historical drama; Chicano
Amistad (1997)	60	historical; racial progress; white male
Amos and Andrew (1993)	10	black-white buddy comedy; black male
B*A*P*S* (1997)	7	black female friendship; black female
The Bonfire of the Vanities (1990)	16	car accident; white male
Bulworth (1998)	26	white racial progress; white male
City Hall (1996)	20	shooting in NYC; white male
The Color Purple (1985)	94	historical drama; black female
Cop and a ½ (1993)	32	black-white buddy; white male
Cry Freedom (1987)	6	white racial progress; white male
Dances with Wolves (1990)	184	historical; racial progress; white male

168

Appendix B

Title/Year released	Receipts (in millions of $)	Topics/Central perspective
Dangerous Minds (1995)	5	white racial progress; white female
Dead Presidents (1995)	24	Vietnam vets; black male
Deep Cover (1992)	17	police drama; black male
Devil in a Blue Dress (1995)	16	historical drama; black male
Do the Right Thing (1989)	27	historical drama; black male
Driving Miss Daisy (1989)	106	historical drama; white female
A Dry White Season (1989)	4	white racial progress; white male
A Family Thing (1996)	10	family drama; white male
The Five Heartbeats (1991)	9	historical drama; black male
Gattaca (1997)	12	science fiction; white genetic underclass
Get on the Bus (1996)	6	historical drama; black male
Ghosts of Mississippi (1996)	13	white racial progress; white male
The Glass Shield (1994)	3	police drama; black male
Glory (1989)	26	historical; racial progress; white male
Heart Condition (1990)	4	black-white buddy; white male
Higher Learning (1995)	38	racial dynamics in college; ensemble
Hoodlum (1997)	23	historical drama; ensemble
The Hurricane (1999)	51	historical drama; black male
Jerry Maguire (1996)	154	black-white buddy; white male
The Joy Luck Club (1993)	33	family; Asian American female
Jungle Fever (1991)	32	interracial romance; black male
The Last of the Mohicans (1992)	35	historical drama; mixed race male
Liberty Heights (1999)	4	historical drama; white male
The Long Walk Home (1990)	5	historical; racial progress; white female
Losing Isaiah (1995)	8	racial progress; white female
Malcolm X (1992)	48	historical drama; black male
Men of Honor (1999)	49	military; black male
Mi Vida Loca (1993)	3	female friendship; Latina
Mississippi Burning (1988)	34	racial progress; white male
Mississippi Massala (1991)	7	interracial romance; black male
Panther (1995)	7	historical drama; black male
Posse (1993)	18	historical drama; black male
Rising Sun (1993)	63	police drama; black male
Rosewood (1997)	13	historical drama; black male
Set It Off (1996)	36	bank heist; black female
The Shawshank Redemption (1994)	28	prison; black male
She's Gotta Have It (1986)	7	romance; black ensemble
Stand and Deliver (1988)	14	racial progress; Latino
Surf Ninjas (1993)	4	comedy; Asian American male
Surviving the Game (1994)	7	thriller; black male
Tales from the Hood (1995)	12	drug dealing; black male
Thunderheart (1992)	22	murder investigation; mixed race male
A Time to Kill (1996)	145	white racial progress; white male
True Identity (1991)	5	comedy; black male
A Walk in the Clouds (1995)	50	historical; racial progress; white male
White Man's Burden (1995)	4	future dystopia; white male
The Wood (1999)	25	buddy film; black male

Notes

Introduction

1. The name of this workplace organization and all the individuals interviewed are pseudonyms.

2. The corporation also held a two-day mandatory workshop on affirmative action and sexual harassment policies that I attended in 1989.

3. Jennifer L. Pierce, *Gender Trials: Emotional Lives in Contemporary Law Firms*, Berkeley and Los Angeles: University of California Press, 1995, p. 201.

4. Renee Blank and Sandra Slipp, "White Male: An Endangered Species?" *Management Review* (September 1994): 28–32; and Frederick Lynch, *Invisible Victims: White Males and Affirmative Action*, New York: Praeger, 1991. Also, see Chapter 1 in this volume.

5. Faye Crosby and Diana Cordova, "Words Worth of Wisdom: Toward an Understanding of Affirmative Action," in Faye Crosby and Cheryl VanDeVeer, eds., *Sex, Race, and Merit: Debating Affirmative Action in Education and Employment,* Ann Arbor: University of Michigan Press, 2000.

6. Barbara Reskin, *The Realities of Affirmative Action in Employment*, Washington, D.C.: American Sociological Association, 1998.

7. Crosby and Cordova, "Words Worth of Wisdom: Toward an Understanding of Affirmative Action."

8. *The Regents of the University of California v. Bakke.* See Chapter 1 for a discussion of the *Bakke* decision.

9. William Honan, "Admission Change Will Alter Elite Campuses, Experts Say," *New York Times*, July 22, 1995, p. 7. For a discussion of faculty and students, see Editorial, "Harmful Split Between UC Regents and Faculty," *San Francisco Chronicle*, December 9, 1995, p. A20; Edward Epstein and Henry Lee, "UC Students Rally for Affirmative Action, Thousands Skip Classes, Some Clash with Police," *San Francisco Chronicle*, October 13, 1995, p. A1.

10. The Regents also charged the academic senate with developing a set of "supplemental criteria" that would give consideration to "individuals who suffered economic

disadvantage." See Roopali Mukherjee's *The Racial Order of Things: Cultural Imaginaries in the Post-Soul Era*, Minneapolis, MN: University of Minnesota Press, 2006, p. 1.

11. Mukherjee, *The Racial Order of Things*, pp. 24–25. For other discussions of affirmative action and Proposition 209 in California, see Dana Takagi's *The Retreat from Race: Asian American Admissions and Racial Politics*, New Brunswick, NJ: Rutgers University Press, 1992; and Lydia Chávez, *The Color Bind: California's Battle to End Affirmative Action*, Berkeley and Los Angeles: University of California Press, 1998. For a discussion of the politics of affirmative action in Texas, see Lani Guinier and Gerald Torres, *The Miner's Canary: Enlisting Race, Resisting Power, Transforming Democracy*, Cambridge, MA: Harvard University Press, 2002. For a discussion of affirmative action in Michigan, see Patricia Gurin, Jeffrey Lehman, and Earl Lewis, *Defending Diversity: Affirmative Action at the University of Michigan*, Ann Arbor: University of Michigan Press, 2004.

12. Andrew Sullivan, "Let Affirmative Action Die," *New York Times*, July 23, 1995, p. 15; Edward Esptein and Susan Yoachum, "Affirmative Action Showdown: UC Regents Seem Poised to End Preferences," *San Francisco Chronicle*, July 20, 1995, p. A1.

13. Here, I am referring to survey research from sociologists and political scientists. For a summary of academic surveys and newspaper opinion polls, see Fred Pincus, *Reverse Discrimination: Dismantling the Myth*, Boulder, CO: Lynne Rienner, 2003, p. 6. Also, see Howard Schuman, Charlotte Steeh, Lawrence Bobo, and Maria Krysan, *Racial Attitudes in America: Trends and Interpretations*, Cambridge, MA: Harvard University Press, 1997; Jim Sidanius, Pam Singh, John Hetts, and Chris Feerico, "'It's Not Affirmative Action: It's the Blacks': The Continuing Relevance of Race in American Politics," in David Sears, Jim Sidanius, and Lawrence Bobo, eds., *Racialized Politics: The Debate About Racism in America*, Chicago: University of Chicago Press, 2000, pp. 191–235. Also, see Lawrence Bobo, who argues that white attitudes are not completely monolithic in his "Race, Interests, and Beliefs about Affirmative Action," *American Behavioral Scientist*, 41 (April 1998): 985–1003; and "Race and Beliefs About Affirmative Action: Assessing the Effects of Interests, Group Threat, Ideology, and Racism," in *Racialized Politics*, pp. 137–164.

14. John Dovidio, John Mann, and Sam Gaertner. "Resistance to Affirmative Action: The Implications of Aversive Racism," in Fletcher Blanchard and Faye Crosby, eds., *Affirmative Action in Perspective*, New York: Springer-Verlag, 1989, pp. 83–97; Joleen Kirschenman and Kathryn Neckerman, "We'd Love to Hire Them, But . . . : The Meaning of Race for Employers," in Christopher Jencks and Paul Peterson, eds., *The Urban Underclass*, Washington, DC: Brookings Institution, 1991; Doug Massey and Nancy Denton, *American Apartheid: Segregation and the Making of the Underclass*, Cambridge, MA: Harvard University Press, 1993; Willie Avon Drake and Robert Holsworth, *Affirmative Action and the Stalled Quest for Black Progress*, Urbana: University of Illinois, 1996; Howard Schuman, Charlotte Steeh, Lawrence Bobo, and Maria Krysan, *Racial Attitudes in America: Trends and Interpretations*, Cambridge, MA: Harvard University Press, 1997, revised edition; William Julius Wilson, *When Work Disappears*, Chicago: University of

Chicago Press, 1997; Deirdre Royster, *Race and the Invisible Hand: How Social Networks Exclude Black Men from Blue-Collar Jobs*, Berkeley and Los Angeles: University of California Press, 2003; Devah Pager, Bruce Western, and Bart Bonikowski, "Discrimination in a Low-Wage Labor Market: A Field Experiment," *American Sociological Review*, 74, 5 (October 2009): 777–799; and Jennifer Lee and Frank Bean, *The Diversity Paradox: Immigration and the Color Line in 21st Century America*, New York, NY: Russell Sage Foundation, 2010.

15. Marita Sturken, *Tangled Memories: The Vietnam War, The AIDS Epidemic and The Politics of Remembering*, Berkeley and Los Angeles: University of California Press, 1997, p. 1.

16. Sturken, *Tangled Memories*, p. 1.

17. A personal narrative is a retrospective first-person account of an individual's life, including sources such as oral histories, autobiographies, and in-depth interviews that cover a substantial portion of a life. See Mary Jo Maynes, Jennifer Pierce, and Barbara Laslett, *Telling Stories: The Use of Personal Narratives in the Social Sciences and in History*, Ithaca, NY: Cornell University Press, 2008.

18. See Howard Winant, *The New Politics of Race: Globalism, Difference, Justice*, Minneapolis: University of Minnesota Press, 2004, p. xiii. For historians, see Dave Roediger, *Colored White: Transcending the Racial Past*, Berkeley and Los Angeles: University of California Press, 2002; and Peggy Pascoe, *What Comes Naturally: Miscegenation Law and the Making of Race in America*, New York, Oxford University Press, 2009. For social scientists, see Eduardo Bonilla-Silva, *Racism Without Racists: Color-Blind Racism and the Persistence of Racial Inequality in America*, New York: Rowman & Littlefield, 2003; Charles Gallagher, "Transforming Racial Identity Through Affirmative Action," in Rodney Coates, ed., *Race and Ethnicity: Across Time, Space and Discipline*, Boston: Brill Publishers, 2004, pp. 153–170; and Jennifer L. Pierce, "'Racing for Innocence': Whiteness, Corporate Culture, and the Backlash Against Affirmative Action," *Qualitative Sociology*, 26, 1 (2003): 53–71. For cultural studies scholars, see Mukherjee, *The Racial Order of Things*.

19. Howard Winant, "Behind Blue Eyes: Contemporary White Racial Projects," in his *The New Politics of Race*, p. 57.

20. Lisa Duggan, *The Twilight of Equality: Neoliberalism, Cultural Politics, and the Attack on Democracy*, Boston: Beacon Press, 2004.

21. For the classic sociological study which argues that working-class Americans are more authoritarian than the middle-class, see Theodore Adorno, *The Authoritarian Personality*, New York: Harper, 1950. For more recent studies of white working-class men, see, Michelle Fine, Lois Weiss, Judi Addleston, and Julia Marusza, "(In)secure Times: Constructing White Working-Class Masculinities in the Late Twentieth Century," *Gender & Society*, 11, 1 (February 1997): 52–68; Michelle Lamont, *The Dignity of Working Men: Morality and the Boundaries of Race, Class and Immigration*, Cambridge, MA: Harvard University Press, 2000; Monica McDermott, *Working-Class White: The Making and Unmaking of Race Relations*, Berkeley and Los Angeles: University of California

Press, 2006; and Kris Paap, *Working Construction: How White Men Put Themselves and the Labor Movement in Danger*, Ithaca, NY: Cornell University Press, 2005. For exceptions that focus on elite whites, see Joe Feagin and Eileen O'Brien, *White Men on Race: Power, Privilege, and the Shaping of Cultural Consciousness*, Boston: Beacon, 2004.

22. I draw here from the important scholarship in critical whiteness studies. See Karen Brodkin, *How the Jews Became White Folks and What This Says about Race in America*, New York: Routledge, 1999; Vincent Crapanzano, *Waiting: The Whites of South Africa*, New York: Random House, 1985; Cheryl Harris, "Whiteness as Property," *Harvard Law Review*, 106, 8: 1709–1791; Abby Ferber, *White Man Falling*, New York; Rowman & Littlefield, 1998; Fine, Weiss, Addleston, and Marusza, "(In)secure times," pp. 52–68; Ruth Frankenberg, *White Women, Race Matters*, Minneapolis: University of Minnesota Press, 1990; Charles Gallagher, "White Reconstruction in the University," *Socialist Review*, 24 (1-2) (1995): 165–185; John Hartigan, *Racial Situations: Class Predicaments of Whiteness in Detroit*, Princeton, NJ: Princeton University Press, 1999; Matthew Frye Jacobson, *Whiteness of a Different Color: European Immigrants and the Alchemy of Race*, Cambridge, MA: Harvard University Press, 1999; Ira Katznelson, *When Affirmative Action Was White: An Untold History of Racial Inequality in Twentieth-Century America*, New York: Norton, 2005; George Lipsitz, *The Possessive Investment in Whiteness: How White People Benefit from Identity Politics*, Philadelphia: Temple University Press, 1998; Birgit Brander Rasmussen, Eric Klineberg, Irene Nexica, and Matt Wray, eds., *The Making and Unmaking of Whiteness*, Durham, NC: Duke University Press, 2001; Pamela Perry, *Shades of White: White Kids and Racial Identities in High School*, Durham, NC: Duke University Press, 2002; Michael Brown, Martin Carnoy, Elliot Curie, Troy Duster, David Oppenheimer, Marjorie Schultz, and David Wellman, eds., *White-Washing Race: The Myth of a Color-Blind Society*, Berkeley and Los Angeles: University of California Press, 2003; David Roediger, *The Wages of Whiteness: Race and the Making of the American Working Class*, New York: Verso, 1991; Roediger, *Colored White*; France Winddance Twine, *A White Side of Black Britain: Interracial Intimacy and Racial Literacy*, Durham, NC: Duke University Press, 2010; France Winddance Twine and Charles Gallagher, "The Future of Whiteness: A Map of the Third Wave," *Ethnic and Racial Studies*, 31, 1 (January 2008): 4–24; McDermott, *Working-Class White*; and Paap, *Working Construction*.

23. Lipsitz, *The Possessive Investment in Whiteness*, p. 233.

24. Lipsitz, *The Possessive Investment in Whiteness*, pp. 20–21.

25. See Note 22 on whiteness studies. For exceptions, see Feagin and O'Brien, *White Men on Race*.

26. Thomas Frank, *What's the Matter with Kansas? How Conservatives Won the Heart of America*, New York: Metropolitan Books, 2004; Thomas Sugrue, *The Origins of the Urban Crisis: Race and Inequality in Detroit*, Revised Edition, Princeton, NJ: Princeton University Press, 2005; Lisa McGirr, *Suburban Warriors: The Origins of the New American Right*, Princeton, NJ: Princeton University Press, 2002; and Bethany Moreton, *To Serve God and Wal-Mart: The Making of Christian Free Enterprise*, Cambridge, MA: Harvard

University Press, 2009. For an exception to this historiography that provides a more complex account of racism among working-class whites, see Jefferson Cowie, *Stayin' Alive: The 1970s and the Last Days of the Working Class*, New York: The New Press, 2010.

27. For a discussion of "accumulation by dispossession" under neoliberal economic reforms, see David Harvey, *The New Imperialism*, New York: Oxford University Press, 2003. For use of this term in other work, see Gillian Hart, *Disabling Globalization: Places of Power in Post-Apartheid South Africa*, Berkeley and Los Angeles: University of California Press, 2001; and Ryan P. Murphy, "The Gay Land Rush: Race, Gender, and Sexuality in Post-Welfare Minneapolis," in The Twin Cities GLBT Oral History Project, eds., *Queer Twin Cities*, Minneapolis: University of Minnesota Press, 2010.

28. Wendy Leo Moore, *Reproducing Racism: White Space, Elite Law Schools, and Racial Inequality*, Lanham, MD: Rowman & Littlefield, 2006, p. 2.

29. Pascoe, *What Comes Naturally*; Derrick Bell, *Race, Racism, and the Law*, 4th edition, New York: Aspen Press, 2000; Haney Lopez, *White by Law: The Legal Construction of Race*, New York: New York University Press, 2000; and Jacobson, *Whiteness of a Different Color*.

30. Here I draw from feminist sociologist Joan Acker's theoretical work on gendered and racialized class practices. As she argues, "inequality regimes" within workplace organizations are reproduced through hiring, salary decisions, promotions, informal rules about attire, and other practices. For example, a restaurant employer may hire only attractive, white women for waitressing jobs. See Joan Acker, *Class Questions, Feminist Answers*, Lanham, MD: Rowman & Littlefield, 2006, p. 50.

31. See Pierce, *Gender Trials*, for a complete discussion of methods used in the first phase of this research and more specifically the issue of ethics in doing covert research.

32. Ruth Behar, *Translated Woman: Crossing the Border with Esperanza's Story*, Boston: Beacon Press, 1993, pp. 12–13.

33. See Donna Haraway, "Situated Knowledges: The Science Question in Feminism as a Site of Discourse on the Privilege of Partial Perspective," *Feminist Studies*, 14, 3 (1988); Patricia Hill Collins, *Black Feminist Thought, Knowledge, Consciousness, and the Politics of Empowerment*, Boston: Unwin Hyman, 1990; Susan Krieger, *Social Science and the Self: Personal Essays on an Art Form*, New Brunswick, NJ: Rutgers University Press, 1990; Barbara Laslett, "Unfeeling Knowledge: Emotion and Objectivity in the Sociology of Knowledge," *Sociological Forces*, 5 (1990): 413–433; Sandra Harding, *Whose Science? Whose Knowledge?* Ithaca, NY: Cornell University Press, 1991; and Maynes, Pierce, and Laslett, "Personal Narrative Research as Intersubjective Encounter," in *Telling Stories*.

34. Pierce, *Gender Trials*.

35. Elizabeth Chambliss, "Miles to Go: The Progress of Minorities in the Legal Profession," American Bar Association Report, accessed on October 10, 2010, from http://www.law.harvard.edu/programs/plp/pdf/Projects_MilesToGo.pdf; John Heinz, Robert Nelson, Rebecca Sandefur, and Ed Laumann, *Urban Lawyers: The New Social Structure of the Bar*, Chicago: University of Chicago Press, 2005; Mary C. Noonan, Mary E.

Corcoran, and Paul N. Courant, "Is the Partnership Gap Closing for Women? Cohort Differences in the Sex Gap in Partnership Chances," *Social Science Research*, 37 (2008); N. Reichman and J. Sterling, "Sticky Floors, Broken Steps, and Concrete Ceilings in Legal Careers," *Texas Journal of Women and the Law*, 27 (2004); Rebecca Sandefur, "Staying Power: The Persistence of Social Inequality in Shaping Lawyer Stratification and Lawyers' Persistence in the Profession," *Southwestern University Law Review*, 36, 3 (2007).

36. Heinz, Sandefur, and Laumann, *Urban Lawyers*, pp. 22–23.

37. Heinz, Sandefur, and Laumann, *Urban Lawyers*, pp. 22–23.

38. Michael Burawoy, "Introduction," in Michael Burawoy, Alice Burton, Ann Arnett Ferguson, and Kathryn J. Fox, *Ethnography Unbound: Power and Resistance in the Modern Metropolis*, Berkeley and Los Angeles: University of California Press, 1991.

39. W. Lance Bennet, *News: The Politics of Illusion*, New York: Longman Press, 1983; W. Lance Bennet and Robert Entman, eds., *Mediated Politics: Communication and the Future of Democracy*, New York and Cambridge, UK: Cambridge University Press, 2001; and Robert Entman and Andrew Rojeki, *The Black Image in the White Mind: Media and Race in America*, Chicago: University of Chicago Press, 2000.

40. Sturken, *Tangled Memories*, p. 99.

41. Of course, some ethnographers are able to apprehend innermost thoughts and feelings, especially when fieldwork is done covertly. One example is Monica McDermott, who in *Working-Class White* recounts her covert fieldwork as a clerk in convenience stores in order to observe interracial interactions between customers and clerks.

42. For example, see Paul Stoller on his reasons for writing fiction and ethnography in separate volumes in "The Griot's Many Burdens—Fiction's Many Truths," in Arthur Boechner and Carolyn Ellis, eds., *Ethnographically Speaking: Autoethnography, Literature, and Aesthetics*, Walnut Creek, CA: Altamira Press, 2002; as well as in Stoller's novel, *Jaguar: A Story of Africans in America*, Chicago: University of Chicago Press, 1999. Also see Carolyn Ellis's *The Ethnographic I: A Methodological Novel About Autoethnography*, Walnut Creek, CA: Altamira Press, 2006, in which she combines ethnography and fiction into a blended form. In addition, critical race theorists such as Derrick Bell, Patricia Williams, and Gary Delgado have used storytelling as a method of critically assessing legal issues. See, Derrick Bell, *And We Are Not Saved: The Elusive Quest for Racial Justice*, New York: Basic Books, 1987, and *Faces at the Bottom of the Well: The Permanence of Racism*, New York: Basic Books, 1992; Patricia Williams, *Alchemy of Race and Rights*, Cambridge, MA: Harvard University Press, 1991; and Gary Delgado, *The Rodrigo Chronicles: Conversations About America and Race*, New York: New York University Press, 1995. More recently, political scientist Ruth O'Brien used short stories written by novelists as a means of investigating broader issues about discrimination, Ruth O'Brien, ed., *Telling Stories Out of Court: Narratives about Women and Workplace Discrimination*, Ithaca, NY: Cornell University Press, 2008.

43. Margery Wolf, *A Thrice-told Tale: Feminism, Postmodernism, and Ethnographic Responsibility*, Stanford, CA: Stanford University Press, 1992.

44. Barbara Brinson Curiel, "My Border Stories: Life Narratives, Interdisciplinarity, and Post-Nationalism in Ethnic Studies," in John Carlos Rowe, ed., *Postnationalist American Studies*, Berkeley: University of California Press, 2000.

45. Robert Owen Butler, *From Where You Dream: The Process of Writing Fiction*, edited and with an introduction by Janet Burroway, New York: Grove Press, 2005.

46. For discussions of the particular value of fiction and the questions it raises about subjectivity and morality, see Ruth O'Brien, "Introduction: Women's Work, Writing Politics, Sharing Stories," in her *Telling Stories Out of Court*, p. 5. Also, see Francine Prose, *Reading Like a Writer: A Guide for People Who Love Books and For Those Who Want to Write Them*, New York: Harper Perennial, 2006; and Butler, *From Where You Dream*.

Chapter 1

1. *The Regents of the University of California v. Bakke* 438 U.S. 265 (1978). For important discussions of this case, see Fred Pincus, *Reverse Discrimination: Dismantling the Myth*, Boulder, CO: Lynne Rienner, 2003; Howard Ball, *The Bakke Case: Race, Education and Affirmative Action*, Lawrence: University of Kansas Press, 2000; Bernard Schwartz, *Behind Bakke: Affirmative Action and the Supreme Court*, New York: New York University Press, 1988; and John David Skrentny, *The Ironies of Affirmative Action: Politics, Culture, and Justice in America*, Chicago: University of Chicago Press, 1996, pp. 225–226.

2. A number of plaintiffs in the late 1980s and 1990s brought lawsuits for "reverse discrimination" and the courts ruled on the plaintiff's behalf. See, *City of Richmond v. J.A. Croson Co.* 488 U.S. 469 (1988); *Adarand Constructors, Inc. v. Pena* 515 U.S. 200 (1995); and In *Hopwood v. Texas* 78 Fed 3d 932 (5th Cir. 1996).

3. Matthew Frye Jacobson, *Roots Too: White Ethnic Revival in Post-Civil Rights America*, Cambridge, MA: Harvard University Press, 2006, p. 100. Also, see Thomas Ross, "The Rhetorical Tapestry of Race: White Innocence and Black Abstraction," *William & Mary Law Review*, 32, 1 (1990).

4. Sociologist Charles Gallagher argues that affirmative action also served to bring whiteness as a racial category to public attention. See Charles Gallagher, "Transforming Racial Identity Through Affirmative Action," in Rodney Coates, ed., *Race and Ethnicity: Across Time, Space and Discipline*, Boston: Brill Publishers, 2004.

5. *The Regents of the University of California v. Allan Bakke* 438 U.S. 265 (1978).

6. Ross, "The Rhetorical Tapestry of Race," p. 34.

7. Ross, "The Rhetorical Tapestry of Race," p. 34.

8. Leo Marx, *The Machine and the Garden*, New York: Oxford University Press, 1964; Perry Miller, *The New England Mind*, Boston: Beacon Press, 1961; Henry Nash Smith, *Virgin Land: The American West as Symbol and Myth*, Cambridge, MA: Harvard University Press, 1950. For a critique of this literature, see David Noble, *The End of American History: Democracy, Capitalism, and the Metaphor of Two Worlds in Anglo-American Historical Writing, 1890–1980*, Minneapolis: University of Minnesota Press, 1985; and *Death of a Nation*, Minneapolis: University of Minnesota Press, 2002.

9. Gay Tuchman, *Making News: A Study in the Social Construction of Reality*, New York: Free Press, 1980; W. Lance Bennet, *News: The Politics of Illusion*, New York: Longman Press, 1983; W. Lance Bennet and Robert Entman, eds., *Mediated Politics: Communication and the Future of Democracy*, New York: Cambridge University Press, 2001; Robert Entman and Andrew Rojeki, *The Black Image in the White Mind: Media and Race in America*, Chicago: University of Chicago Press, 2000.

10. Like sociologist Dana Takagi, I purposefully use the term "facilitate" as opposed to "caused" in an effort to connote how perceptions of affirmative action were nourished by the language and rhetoric of the debate. See Dana Takagi, *The Retreat From Race: Asian American Admissions and Racial Politics*, New Brunswick, NJ: Rutgers University Press, 1992, p. 8.

11. Tuchman, *Making News*; and William Gamson, *Talking Politics*, New York: Cambridge University Press, 1992.

12. Marita Sturken, *Tangled Memories: The Vietnam War, the AIDS Epidemic, and the Politics of Remembering*, Berkeley and Los Angeles: University of California Press, 1997, p. 9.

13. Thomas Frank, *What's the Matter with Kansas? How Conservatives Won the Heart of America*, New York: Metropolitan Books, 2004; Thomas Sugrue, *The Origins of the Urban Crisis: Race and Inequality in Postwar Detroit*, Princeton, NJ: Princeton University Press, 2005, revised edition; Lisa McGirr, *Suburban Warriors: The Origins of the New American Right*, Princeton, NJ: Princeton University Press, 2002; and Bethany Moreton *To Serve God and Wal-Mart: The Making of Christian Free Enterprise*, Cambridge, MA: Harvard University Press, 2009.

14. From the Internet Movie Database, Road to the Oscars, "Awards for Rocky," accessed on January 24, 2012, from http://www.imdb.com/title/tt0075148/awards

15. Roger Ebert, "Rocky," *The Chicago Sun-Times*, January 1, 1976.

16. Jacobson, *Roots Too*, p. 101.

17. Historian Elizabeth Lasch-Quinn and journalist Susan Faludi make similar arguments about the perception of white male disadvantage. Lasch-Quinn calls this discourse, "black assertion, white submission," in *Race Experts: How Racial Etiquette, Sensitivity Training, and New Age Therapy Hijacked the Civil Rights Movement*, New York: Norton, 2001. Faludi highlights male injury and disadvantage, though she pays less attention to race, in *Stiffed: The Betrayal of American Men*, New York: Morrow, 1999.

18. A number of writers have focused on male injury and white male injury; see Frank, *What's the Matter with Kansas?*; Sugrue, *The Origins of the Urban Crisis*; Lisa Marie Comacho, "The People of California are Suffering: The Ideology of White Injury in Discourses of Immigration," *Cultural Values*, 4, 4 (October 2000): 389–413; McGirr, *Suburban Warriors*; Moreton, *To Serve God and Wal-Mart*; and Faludi, *Stiffed*. Also, for important theoretical work on how identity politics as "injury" translates into "rights" claims, see political theorist, Wendy Brown, *States of Injury: Power and Freedom in Late Modernity*, Princeton, NJ: Princeton University Press, 1995.

19. Gamson, *Talking Politics*. On the debate surrounding Asian American admissions, see Takagi, *The Retreat from Race*, pp. 9–10. Also see Robyn Stryker, Martha Scarpellion, and Mellisa Holtzman, "Political Culture Wars 1990s Style: The Drum Beat of Quotas in the Media Framing on the Civil Rights Act of 1991," *Research in Social Stratification and Mobility*, vol. 17 (1999): 33–106; and Terry Anderson, *The Pursuit of Fairness: A History of Affirmative Action*, New York: Oxford University Press, 2005, p. 166.

20. Frederick Lynch, *Invisible Victims: White Males and the Crisis of Affirmative Action*, New York: Praeger, 1991 [1989].

21. Frederick Lynch and William Beers, "'You Ain't The Right Color Pal': White Resentment of Affirmative Action," *Policy Review*, 51 (Winter 1990): 64–67; and Frederick Lynch, "Surviving Affirmative Action (More or Less)," *Commentary* (August 1990): 44–47.

22. Lynch, *Invisible Victims*, p. 124. Also cited in Anderson's *The Pursuit of Fairness*, pp. 228–229.

23. Joseph Adelson's book review of *Invisible Victims* in *Academic Questions*, 4, 1 (Winter 1990–1991): 90–93.

24. Shelby Steele, "A Negative Vote on Affirmative Action," *The New York Times Magazine*, May 13, 1990, p. 46; and *The Content of Our Character: A New Vision of Race in America*, New York: Harper, 1991.

25. Shelby Steele, "A Negative Vote on Affirmative Action," p. 46.

26. Angela Dillard, *Guess Who's Coming to Dinner Now? Multicultural Conservatism in America*, New York: New York University Press, 2001.

27. Howard Winant, *The New Politics of Race: Globalism, Difference, Justice*, Minneapolis: University of Minnesota Press, 2004, p. 57.

28. Roopali Mukherjee, *The Racial Order of Things: Cultural Imaginaries of the Post-Soul Era*, Minneapolis: University of Minnesota Press, 2006.

29. Thomas Edsall and Mary Edsall, *Chain Reaction: The Impact of Race, Rights, and Taxes on American Politics*, New York: Norton, 1992. There is extensive literature on deindustrialization, the rise of the service economy, and the decline of union mobilization in the United States. See Daniel Bell, *The Coming of Post-Industrial Society*, New York: Basic Books, 1973; Barry Bluestone and Bennett Harrison, *The Deindustrialization of America: Plant Closings, Community Abandonment, and the Dismantling of Basic Industry*, New York: Basic Books, 1982; Kim Moody, *An Injury to All: The Decline of American Unionism*, London: Verso, 1988; Robert B. Reich, *The Work of Nations: Preparing Ourselves for 21st Century Capitalism*, New York, Vintage Books, 1991; Stephen Herzenberg, John Alic, and Howard Wial, *New Rules for a New Economy: Employment and Opportunity in Postindustrial America*, Ithaca, NY: Cornell University Press, 1998; Kathleen Barker and Kathleen Christiansen, *Contingent Work: American Employment Relations in Transition*, Ithaca, NY: Cornell University Press, 1998; Jacki Rogers *Temps: The Many Faces of the Changing Workplace*, Ithaca, NY: Cornell University Press, 2000; Vicki Smith *Across the Great Divide*, Ithaca, NY: Cornell University Press, 2001; Margaret Nelson and Joan Smith; *Working Hard and Making Do*, Ithaca, NY: Cornell University Press, 1999.

30. Edsall and Edsall, *Chain Reaction*, p. 11

31. Eleanor Holmes Norton, "Affirmative Action in the Workplace," in G. E. Curry, ed., *The Affirmative Action Debate*, Reading, MA: Addison-Wesley, 1996, pp. 39–48.

32. Sharon Collins, *Black Corporate Executives: The Making and Breaking of a Black Middle Class*, Philadelphia: Temple University Press, 1996.

33. For statistics on management, see U.S. Glass Ceiling Commission, *Good for Business: Making Full Use of the Nation's Human Capital: A Fact Finding Report for the Federal Glass Ceiling Commission*, Washington D.C.: GPO, 1995; on discrimination, see, Michael Fix and Margery Turner, *A National Report Card on Discrimination in America*, Washington D.C.: Urban Institute, 1998.

34. William G. Bowen and Derek Bok, *The Shape of the River: Long Term Consequences of Considering Race in College and University Admissions*, Princeton, NJ: Princeton University Press, 1998.

35. David Karen, "'Achievement' and 'Ascription' in Admission to an Elite College: A Political-Organizational Analysis," *Sociological Forum*, 6 (1999).

36. Bowen and Bok, *The Shape of the River*, p. 10.

37. Peter Applebome, "The Debate on Diversity in California Shifts," *New York Times*, June 4, 1995, sec. 1, p. 1.

38. *Businessweek*, January 31, 1994; and *TIME*, April 9, 1990.

39. *Newsweek*, April 3, 1995, pp. 24–25.

40. *NBC Nightly News*, July 19, 1995.

41. Ramon McLeod, "White Men's Eroding Economic Clout Contributes to Backlash," *San Francisco Chronicle*, March 20, 1995, p. A7; Susan Yoachum, "Affirmative Action Facing Hard Times, Whites Take Initiative against Preferential Hiring," *San Francisco Chronicle*, March 20, 1995, p. A1; Jamie Becket, "White Firefighters Say San Jose Rigged Examination, Suit Claims Test Favored Minorities," *San Francisco Chronicle*, July 28, 1995, p. A1; Yumi Wilson, "Men: Many Whites Say They Feel Cheated," *San Francisco Chronicle*, May 10, 1995, p. A8; "Don't Forget About White Males" and "White Guy's Revenge," letter to the editor, *San Francisco Chronicle*, November 23, 1994. Interestingly, these articles all appeared in the *Chronicle*, but not *The New York Times*. For an exception to these headlines, see Jonathan Marshall, "Don't Tie Anger to Low Wages / Experts Debunk Conventional Wisdom on the 'Angry White Male' View," *San Francisco Chronicle*, May 29, 1995, p. D1.

42. Quoted in William Honan, "Regents Prepare for Storm on Affirmative Action," *New York Times*, July 19, 1995, p. A1.

43. Benjamin Lu, "Letter to the Editor," *New York Times*, September 18, 1998, p. A28.

44. James Traub, "The Class of Prop. 209," *New York Times Magazine*, May 2, 1999, sec. 6, p. 44. Also, see media scholars Entman and Rojeki who also use this term "zero-sum calculus" in *The Black Image in the White Mind*, p. 118.

45. Entman and Rojeki, *The Black Image in the White Mind*, p. 118.

46. Herman Beitch, "Letter to the Editor," *San Francisco Chronicle*, May 13, 1995.

47. Anderson, *The Pursuit of Fairness*, p. 232.

48. Associated Press, "Affirmative Action Should Focus on Poor People, Gingrich Says," *New York Times*, June 17, 1995, sec. 1, p. 9.

49. Seth Mydans, "A Challenge to the Concept of Disadvantaged," *New York Times*, June 18, 1995, p. A16.

50. Wilson, "Men: Many Whites Say They Feel Cheated," p. A8.

51. Yoachum, "Affirmative Action Facing Hard Times," p. A1.

52. George Lipsitz, *The Possessive Investment in Whiteness: How White People Benefit from Identity Politics*, Philadelphia: Temple University Press, p. 223.

53. Lipsitz, *The Possessive Investment in Whiteness*, pp. 223–234.

54. See for example, John Boudreau, "Effort to Outlaw Affirmative Action Promoted in California," *Washington Post*, December 27, 1994, p. A3; and Nicholas Lehmann, "California, Here We Come . . . ?" *TIME*, October 7, 1996. For a set of interviews conducted with Woods, see Lydia Chávez, *The Color Bind: California's Battle to End Affirmative Action*, Berkeley and Los Angeles: University of California Press, 1998.

55. Entman and Rojeki, *The Black Image in the White Mind*, p. 122.

56. Entman and Rojeki, *The Black Image in the White Mind*; Bowen and Bok, *The Shape of the River*; Christopher Edley, *Not All Black and White: Affirmative Action and American Values*, Hill and Wang, 1998; Lani Guinier, *Lift Every Voice: Turning Civil Rights Setbacks into a New Vision*, New York: Simon & Schuster, 2003.

57. Reynolds Holding, "Gains for Minority Attorneys in SF: But They Cite Frustration of Institutional Racism . . ." *San Francisco Chronicle*, Dec 21, 1993, p. A18.

58. Holding, "Gains for Minority Attorneys in SF," p. A18.

59. "Affirmative Action Levels the Playing Field," editorial, *New York Times*, November 25, 1995.

60. *New York Times*, letter to the editor, July 19, 1998, sec. 6, p. 8.

61. James Bennet, "Clinton Debates 9 Conservatives on Racial Issues," *New York Times*, December 20, 1997, p. A1.

62. Other scholars have noted a shift to diversity approaches in corporations in the late 1990s. For example, sociologist Laurel Edelman argues that such policies don't do enough to ensure diversity in the workplace. See Lauren Edelman, "Legal Ambiguity and Symbolic Structures: Organizational Mediation of Civil Rights Law," *American Journal of Sociology*, 97, 6 (1992): 1531–1576; Edelman with Christopher Uggen and Howard S. Erlanger, "The Endogeneity of Legal Regulation: Grievance Procedures as Rational Myth," *American Journal of Sociology*, 105, 2 (1999): 406–454; and Edelman with Sally Riggs Fuller and Sharon F. Matusik, "Legal Readings: Employee Interpretation and Enactment of Civil Rights Law," *Academy of Management Review*, 25, 1 (2000): 200–216.

63. Justice Lewis Powell made this argument in the 1978 *Bakke* decision. In a separate opinion, he offered his own rationale for affirmative action, arguing that to

promote the "robust exchange of ideas" that might flow from the diversity of a student body, institutions of higher learning could give some consideration to an applicant's race.

64. Ethan Bronner, "Study Strongly Supports AA in Admission to Elite Colleges," *New York Times*, September 9, 1998, p. B10.

65. *New York Times*, letter to the editor, September 13, 1998, sec. 4, p. 20.

66. David Rosenbaum, "White House Revises Policy on Contracts for Minorities," *New York Times*, June 25, 1998, p. A1; and James Bennet, "Clinton, at Race Forum, Is Confronted on Affirmative Action," *New York Times*, July 9, 1998, p. A23.

67. Gerald R. Ford, "Inclusive America, Under Attack," editorial, *New York Times*, August 8, 1999, sec. 4, p. 15; also see Lena Williams, "Companies Capitalizing on Worker Diversity," *New York Times*, December 15, 1992, p. A1.

68. David Tuller, "True Colors: Racial Diversity May get Lip Service in Workplace, But . . ." *San Francisco Chronicle*, March 3, 1996.

69. Peter Kilborn, "A Leg Up on Ladder, But Still Far From Top," *New York Times*, June 16, 1995, p. A1.

70. Thanks to Lisa S. Park and Ryan Murphy for reminding me of this point. Other scholars have made a similar argument about selling diversity to bolster corporate profits. See Frank Dobbin and John Sutton, "The Strength of a Weak State: The Rights Revolution and the Rise of Human Resources Management Divisions," *American Journal of Sociology*, 104, 2 (1998): 441–476, and Nicole Raeburn, *Changing Corporate America from the Inside Out: Lesbian and Gay Workplace Rights*. Minneapolis: University of Minnesota Press, 2004

71. The typical news story contained three elements: (1) affirmative action as a racial (and not a gender) preference is unfair to white men; (2) the policy contributes to racial conflict; and (3) a tone implying high drama and tension dramatizing the so-called conflict.

72. "Lucky's Sex Discrimination Lawsuit—Women Win Damages," *New York Times*, December 17, 1993; Marc Sandalow, "House Panel Cites Glass Ceiling at Federal Reserve Bank for Women, Minorities," *San Francisco Chronicle*, December 2, 1993, p. A8; Jane Gross, "Big Grocery Chain Reaches Landmark Sex-Bias Accord," *New York Times*, December 16, 1993, p. A1.

73. Entman and Rojeki, *The Black Image in the White Mind*, p. 109

74. For examples, see Teresa Moore, "Black and White Youths in '2 Different Worlds,'" *San Francisco Chronicle*, January 14, 1993, p. B8; "White Guy's Revenge," *San Francisco Chronicle*; "Affirmative Action Showdown: UC Regents Seem Poised to End Preference," *San Francisco Chronicle*, July 20, 1995, p. A1; Honan, "Regents Prepare for Storm on Affirmative Action"; "Daily Cal Backs Vote by Regents, Race-Based Criteria Unfair, Students Say," *San Francisco Chronicle*, September 23, 1995; Rick Bragg, "Affirmative Action: One City's Experience; Fighting Bias with Bias and Leaving a Rift," *New York Times*, August 21, 1995, p. A1; Linda Greenhouse, "In Step with Racial Policy," *New York Times*, June 14, 1995, p. A1; Peter Applebome, "The Debate on Diversity in

California Shifts," p. A1; and Edward Lempinen, "Protesters, Polish Skirmish as Duke Debates CCRI," *San Francisco Chronicle*, September 26, 1996, p. A1.

75. Rick Bragg, "Affirmative Action," p. A1.

76. *New York Times*, Editorial Desk, "Affirmative Action Without Fear," September 19, 1994, p. A16. Also see Iver Peterson, "Justice Officials Clarify Stand in Race-Based Dismissal Case," *New York Times*, September 22, 1994, p. B6.

77. Ben Wildavsky, "UC Campus Debates Affirmative Action, Some Say Success in Diversifying Berkeley Student Body Back," *San Francisco Chronicle*, May 16, 1995, p. A1.

78. *Newsweek*, March 29, 1993; also cited in Terry Anderson, *The Pursuit of Fairness*, p. 229.

79. Susan Yoachum, "Surprises in Affirmative Action Poll, Wide Support for Cutting Programs," *San Francisco Chronicle*, March 7, 1995, p. A1.

80. Ramon McLeod, "Family Ties Help Explain Why Women Are Split, Many Worried About Husbands' Jobs," *San Francisco Chronicle*, March 31, 1995, p. A4.

81. Susan Yoachum, "Wording Affects Polls on Affirmative Action," *San Francisco Chronicle*, September 14, 1995, p. A17. Also see Lydia Chávez, *The Color Bind*.

82. Charlotte Steeh and Maria Krysan, "The Polls: Trends: Affirmative Action and the Public, 1970–1995," *Public Opinion Quarterly*, 60, 1 (1996): 128–158. Also cited in Entman and Rojeki, *The Black Image in the White Mind*, p. 112.

83. Associated Press, "Reverse Discrimination Complaints Rare, Labor Study Reports," *New York Times*, March 31, 1995, p. A23.

84. Phil McCombs, "White Guys: Their Issues Are Guns and Butter. They've Had It with Democrats. Here's an Earful," *Washington Post*, November 22, 1994, p. D1. Also cited in Anderson, *The Pursuit of Fairness*, p. 232. For a discussion of California in the context of these national politics, see Lydia Chávez, "Hitting a Nerve, the Angry White Males of 1994," chapter 2 in *The Color Bind*.

85. Anderson, *The Pursuit of Fairness*, p. 232.

86. See Frank, *What's the Matter with Kansas?*; Sugrue, *The Origins of the Urban Crisis*; Lisa McGirr, *Suburban Warriors*; and Moreton *To Serve God and Wal-Mart*.

87. Gay Tuchman, *Making News*.

88. See Susan Sward, "Generation Gap, Color Gap, Women Split on Affirmative Action," *San Francisco Chronicle*, March 31, 1995, p. A1. In this article, Sward also provides one example of ambivalence. She quotes Becky Morgan, a former Republican state senator now in the private section, who says: "The dilemma for me is in some cases we have lowered standards to accomplish diversity in our university systems . . . The flip side is that kindergarten to 12th grade is not doing enough to support kids that don't have that support in the homes. . . . But, I don't think we can totally take away the requirements and expect equity to happen. I doubt there are enough white employers who would hire people from minority communities without the encouragement of affirmative action policies."

89. Entman and Rojeki, *The Black Image in the White Mind*, pp. 108–109.

90. See John Searle, "The Storm over the University," in Paul Berman, ed., *Debating P.C.: The Controversy over Political Correctness on College Campuses*, New York: Dell, 1992. For an examination of Searle's position on affirmative action, see Carol Nicholson, "Three Views of Philosophy and Multiculturalism: Searle, Rorty, and Taylor," *Philosophy and Education* (1998), accessed on November 30, 2010, from http://www.bu.edu/wcp/Papers/Educ/EducNich.htm. For information about Professor David Kirp and his writings on education, see http://gspp.berkeley.edu/academics/faculty/kirp.html, accessed on November 30, 2010.

91. Entman and Rojeki, *The Black Image in the White Mind*.

92. Peter Kilborn, "For Many in Work Force, 'Glass Ceiling' Still Exists," *New York Times*, March 15, 1995, p. A22; and letter to the editor, *New York Times*, September 13, 1998, sec. 4, p. 20.

93. Sturken, *Tangled Memories*, p. 1.

Chapter 2

1. Janet Maslin, "A Father's Revenge for His Daughter's Rape," film review in *The New York Times*, July 24, 1996, accessed on April 28, 2011, from http://movies.nytimes.com/movie/review?res=9C03EED81639F937A15754C0A960958260

2. Roger Ebert, film review of *A Time to Kill*, in *Chicago Sun-Times*, July 26, 1996, accessed on November 29, 2011, from http://rogerebert.suntimes.com/apps/pbcs.dll/article?AID=/19960726/REVIEWS/607260302/1023. For Gene Siskel's review from *Siskel and Ebert*, see http://www.youtube.com/watch?gl=US&hl=iw&v=VfMv3DLn73s Accessed on April 29, 2011.

3. Internet Movie Database, *A Time to Kill*, accessed on May 31, 2011, from http://www.imdb.com/title/tt0117913/.

4. Theodoric Manley, "Teaching Race and Ethnic Relations: Do the Right Thing," *Ethnic and Racial Studies*, 17, 1 (January 1994): 134–163.

5. Film scholars argue that the cinematic "gaze" invites viewers to not only imagine themselves in the position of the characters, but also to take pleasure in doing so. Feminists, in particular, have been critical of how the "male gaze" hails viewers to take the position of men in objectifying women's bodies on screen and have asked how we can imagine women as "spectators." See Laura Mulvey, *Visual and Other Pleasures*, New York: Palgrave Macmillan, 2009, and Jackie Stacey, *Star Gazing: Hollywood Cinema and Female Spectatorship*, New York: Routledge, 1994. In the genre of film studied here, I suggest that the gaze is often racialized as a white one.

6. Doug Massey and Julie Denton, *American Apartheid: Segregation and the Making of the Underclass*, Cambridge, MA: Harvard University Press, 1993; Melvin Oliver and Thomas Shapiro, *Black Wealth/White Wealth: A Perspective on Racial Inequality*, New York: Routledge, 2006 [1996].

7. Marita Sturken, *Tangled Memories: The Vietnam War, the AIDS Epidemic, and the Politics of Remembering*, Berkeley and Los Angeles: University of California Press, 1997, p. 96.

8. Teshome Gabriel, "Third Cinema as Guardian of Popular Memory: Towards a Third Aesthetics," in Jim Pines and Paul Willemen, eds., *Questions of Third Cinema*, London: British Film Institute, 1989, pp. 53–64.

9. The song "Amazing Grace" is attributed to John Newton (1725–1807). See Jonathan Aitken, *John Newton: From Disgrace to Amazing Grace*, Wheaton, IL: Crossway Books, 2007.

10. Ann duCille, "The Occult of True Black Womanhood: Critical Demeanor and Black Feminist Studies," *Signs: Journal of Women in Culture and Society*, 19, 3 (1994); Gloria Anzúldua, Introduction in Gloria Anzúldua, ed., *Making Face, Making Soul/Hacienda Caras: Creative and Critical Perspectives by Feminists of Color*, San Francisco: Aunt Lute Books, 1990; and Susan Stanford Friedman, "Beyond White and Other: Relationality and Narratives of Race in Feminist Discourse," *Signs: Journal of Women in Culture and Society*, 21, 1 (1995).

11. Kelly Madson, "Legitimation Crisis and Containment: The 'Anti-Racist-White-Hero,'" *Critical Studies in Mass Communication*, 16, 4 (1999): 399–416. Madson focuses on films in the late 1980s such as *Mississippi Burning, Losing Isaiah*, and *The Long Walk Home*. As the research I conducted with Wendy Leo Moore shows, this genre continued through the end of the 1990s. See Wendy Leo Moore and Jennifer L. Pierce, "Still Killing Mockingbirds: Race and Innocence in Hollywood's Depiction of the White Messiah Lawyer," *Qualitative Sociology Review*, III, 2 (August 2007): 171–187.

12. As Hernán Vera and Andrew Gordon have argued, cinematic representations of the "white savior" in American films have long portrayed whites as noble, kind, beneficent, and powerful; "even early movies like *Gone with the Wind* (1936) and *The Littlest Rebel* (1935), though steeped in 'nostalgia for the antebellum South,' presented images of courageous, just, and kind white self." Hernán Vera and Andrew Gordon, *Screen Saviors: Hollywood Fictions of Whiteness*, Boston, MA: Rowman & Littlefield, p. 23.

13. Gregory Peck won Best Actor awards not only from the Academy of Motion Picture Arts and Sciences, but also from the Golden Globe and the Cannes Film Festival for his portrayal of Atticus Finch. The film received rave reviews from critics and won substantial movie industry nominations and awards. It has since been named one of the 100 greatest American movies, and Harper Lee's novel is still used in high school classrooms. http://www.imdb.com/title/tt0056592/awards accessed on December 9, 2010.

14. Moore and Pierce, "Still Killing Mockingbirds."

15. Only three of the films focus on white women as protagonists (*The Long Walk Home, Losing Isaiah, Dangerous Minds*), one on a Latino man (*Stand and Deliver*), and another on a man with both Anglo American and Sioux heritage (*Thunderheart*).

16. One exception is *Dances with Wolves*, where racial violence comes from the Pawnees who attack the Sioux village where the main character, Dunbar, is staying.

17. As legal scholar Robert Post argues, the figure of the lawyer is often vilified in popular culture. By contrast, in these two films, lawyers are celebrated. See Robert Post,

"On the Popular Image of Lawyers: Reflections in a Dark Glass," *California Law Review*, 75, 1 (January 1987): 379–389.

18. Janet Maslin, "For a True Story, Dipping into the Classics," film review in *The New York Times*, accessed on April 27, 2011, from http://movies.nytimes.com/movie/review?res=9F0DE7DF1431F933A15751C1A960958260.

19. Chris Hewitt, film review of *Ghosts of Mississippi*, accessed on April 27, 2011, from http://lubbockonline.com/news/010397/movie.htm

20. Figures come from the Internet Movie Database, accessed on April 27, 2011, from http://www.imdb.com/

21. One exception is in Edward J. Almos's performance of the schoolteacher Jaime Escalante in *Stand and Deliver*. Another is *Thunderheart*, which is a bit more complicated because the central character, an FBI agent played by Val Kilmer, identifies as white even though, as we learn, he has some Sioux heritage.

22. Thanks to Lisa Disch and Lisa S. Park for reminding me of this point.

23. G. W. F. Hegel, *The Phenomenology of Spirit*, trans. by A. V. Miller, Oxford, UK: Clarendon Press, 1977 [1807].

24. For studies of white working-class men, see Michelle Fine, Lois Weiss, Judi Addleston, and Julia Marusza, "(In)secure Times: Constructing White Working-Class Masculinities in the Late Twentieth Century," *Gender & Society*, 11, 1 (February 1997): 52–68; Michelle Lamont, *The Dignity of Working Men: Morality and the Boundaries of Race, Class and Immigration*, Cambridge, MA: Harvard University Press, 2000; Monica McDermott, *Working-Class White: The Making and Unmaking of Race Relations*, Berkeley and Los Angeles: University of California Press, 2006; and Kris Paap, *Working Construction: How White Men Put Themselves and the Labor Movement in Danger*, Ithaca, NY: Cornell University Press, 2005. For exceptions that focus on elite whites, see Joe Feagin and Eileen O'Brien, *White Men on Race: Power, Privilege, and the Shaping of Cultural Consciousness*, Boston: Beacon, 2004. For historical studies on white working-class men, see Thomas Frank, *What's the Matter with Kansas? How Conservatives Won the Heart of America*, New York: Metropolitan Books, 2004; Thomas Sugrue, *The Origins of the Urban Crisis: Race and Inequality in Detroit*, Revised Edition, Princeton, NJ: Princeton University Press, 2005; Lisa McGirr, *Suburban Warriors: The Origins of the New American Right*, Princeton, NJ: Princeton University Press, 2002; and Bethany Moreton, *To Serve God and Wal-Mart: The Making of Christian Free Enterprise*, Cambridge, MA: Harvard University Press, 2009. For an exception to this historiography that provides a more complex account of racism among working-class whites, see Jefferson Cowie's discussion of Dewey Burton in *Stayin' Alive: The 1970s and the Last Days of the Working Class*, New York, NY: The New Press, 2010.

25. Vera and Gordon, *Screen Saviors*.

26. Howard Schuman, Charlotte Steeh, Lawrence Bobo, and Maria Krysan, *Racial Attitudes in America: Trends and Interpretations*, Cambridge, MA: Harvard University

Press, 1997; and Paul Sniderman and Thomas Piazza, *The Scar of Race*, Cambridge, MA: Belknap Press, 1993.

27. John Dovidio, John Mann, and Sam Gaertner. "Resistance to Affirmative Action: The Implications of Aversive Racism," in Fletcher Blanchard and Faye Crosby, eds., *Affirmative Action in Perspective*, New York: Springer-Verlag, 1989, pp. 83–97; Willie Avon Drake and Robert Holsworth, *Affirmative Action and the Stalled Quest for Black Progress*, Urbana: University of Illinois, 1996; Schuman, Steeh, Bobo, and Krysan, *Racial Attitudes in America*; William Julius Wilson, *When Work Disappears*, Chicago: University of Chicago Press, 1997; Deirdre Royster, *Race and the Invisible Hand: How Social Networks Exclude Black Men from Blue-Collar Jobs*, Berkeley and Los Angeles: University of California Press, 2003; Devah Pager, Bruce Western, and Bart Bonikowski, "Discrimination in a Low-Wage Labor Market: A Field Experiment," *American Sociological Review*, 74, 5 (October 2009): 777–799; and Jennifer Lee and Frank Bean, *The Diversity Paradox: Immigration and the Color Line in 21st Century America*, New York, NY: Russell Sage Foundation, 2010.

28. Terry Anderson, *The Pursuit of Fairness: A History of Affirmative Action in the United States*, New York: Oxford University Press, 2005; and Beth Roy, *Bitters in the Honey: Tales of Hope and Disappointment Across Divides of Race and Time*, Fayetteville: University of Arkansas Press, 1999.

29. Thanks to Lisa S. Park and Teresa Gowan for reminding me of this point. For discussions of welfare, see Michael Brown, *Race, Money, and the Welfare State*, Ithaca, NY: Cornell University Press, 1999; Linda Gordon, *Pitied But Not Entitled: Single Mothers and the History of Welfare*, Cambridge, MA: Harvard University Press, 1998; and Gwendolyn Mink, *The Wages of Motherhood: Inequality in the Welfare State, 1917–1942*, Ithaca, NY: Cornell University Press, 1996. On the history and politics of immigrant policy in the United States, see Lisa Lowe, *Immigrant Acts: On Asian American Cultural Politics*, Durham, NC: Duke University Press, 1996; Matthew Frye Jacobson, *Whiteness of a Different Color: European Immigrants and the Alchemy of Race*, Cambridge, MA: Harvard University Press, 1999; Mai Ngai, *Impossible Subjects: Illegal Aliens and the Making of Modern America*, Princeton, NJ: Princeton University Press, 2004; Lisa Sunyee Park, *Consuming Citizenship: Children of Asian Immigrant Entrepreneurs*, Palo Alto, CA: Stanford University Press, 2005; Lisa S. Park, *Entitled to Nothing: The Struggle for Immigrant Health Care in the Age of Welfare Reform*, New York: New York University Press, 2011; and Lisa S. Park and David Pellow, *The Slums of Aspen: Immigrants vs. the Environment in America's Eden*, New York: New York University Press, 2011. For a discussion of the 1990s with respect to affirmative action and immigration reform, see David R. Roediger, "White Workers, New Democrats, and Affirmative Action," in *Colored White: Transcending the Racial Past*, Berkeley and Los Angeles: University of California Press, 2002.

30. Roderick Ferguson makes a similar argument about how the state views women of color welfare recipients. As he shows, they are often compared to "normative"

women who enact liberal notions of success through heterosexual marriage, hard work, and home ownership. In failing to live up to those ideals, welfare recipients are depicted as undeserving aberrations. See Roderick Ferguson, *Aberrations in Black: Toward a Queer of Color Critique*, Minneapolis: University of Minnesota Press, 2004.

31. Troy Duster, "Individual Fairness, Group Preferences, and the California Strategy," in Robert Post and Michael Rogin, eds., *Race and Representation: Affirmative Action*, New York: Zone Books, 1998, p. 115.

32. Anderson, *The Pursuit of Fairness*, pp. 69–70.

33. Richard Pride, *The Political Use of Racial Narratives: School Desegregation in Mobile, Alabama, 1954–1997*, Urbana and Chicago: University of Illinois Press, 2002.

34. Roopali Mukherjee makes this point about the film *A Time to Kill* in "Civil Rights, Affirmative Action, and the American South: Eyewitness to the Racial Past," *The Racial Order of Things: Cultural Imaginaries of the Post-Soul Era*, Minneapolis: University of Minnesota Press, 2006, p. 151. On *Mississippi Burning*, see George Lipsitz, "California: The Mississippi of the 1990s," in *The Possessive Investment of Whiteness: How White People Profit from Identity Politics*, Philadelphia: Temple University Press, 1998, p. 219.

35. On the "Hollywood redemption history" genre, see Mark Golub, "History Died for Our Sins: Guilt and Responsibility in Hollywood Redemption History," *Journal of American Culture*, 213 (1998): 23.

36. Lipsitz, "California: The Mississippi of the 1990s," *The Possessive Investment of Whiteness*, p. 219.

37. Dana Takagi, *The Retreat from Race: Asian American Admissions and Racial Politics*, New Brunswick, NJ: Rutgers University Press, 1992.

38. For work among literary scholars, anthropologists, and feminists, see Stanley Fish, *Is There a Text in this Class? The Authority of Interpretive Communities*, Cambridge, MA: Harvard University Press, 1980; Michael Angrosino, "The Two Lives of Rebecca Levenstone: Symbolic Interaction in the Generation of the Life History, *Journal of Anthropological Research*, 45, 3 (1989): 315–326; Geyla Frank, "Becoming the Other: Empathy and Biographical Interpretation," *Biography*, 8, 3 (1989): 189–210; and Judy Long, *Telling Women's Lives: Subject, Narrator, Reader, Text*, New York: NY: New York University Press, 1999.

Chapter 3

1. Susan Chase, *Ambiguous Empowerment: The Work Narratives of Women School Superintendents*, Amherst: University of Massachusetts Press, 1995.

2. An early version of this chapter was published as an article. See Jennifer L. Pierce, "Racing for Innocence: Whiteness, Corporate Culture, and the Backlash Against Affirmative Action," *Qualitative Sociology*, 26, 1 (2003): 53–71. Other scholars, such as Mary Louise Fellows and Sherene Razack, have used the phrase, "the race for innocence" to describe white feminist scholars' "belief that we are uninvolved in the process of subordinating others." As they argue, when confronted with their privilege, white feminists

often "retreat to subordination." See, Mary Louise Fellows and Sherene H. Razack, "Seeking Relations: Law and Feminism Roundtables," *Signs: Journal of Women in Culture and Society*, 19, 4 (1994): 1048–1083; and Sherene H. Razack, *Looking White People in the Eye: Gender, Race, and Culture in Courtrooms and Classrooms*, Toronto: University of Toronto Press, 1998, p. 14. Following Randall Kingsley's usage, I deploy the phrase to describe a *practice* among white Americans: the simultaneous disavowal and practice of racial exclusionary behavior.

3. Howard Winant, *The New Politics of Race: Globalism, Difference, Justice*, Minneapolis: University of Minnesota Press, 2004, p. xiii; Charles Gallagher, "Transforming Racial Identity Through Affirmative Action," in Rodney Coates, ed., *Race and Ethnicity: Across Time, Space and Discipline*, Boston: Brill Publishers, 2004, pp. 153–170; Eduardo Bonilla-Silva, *Racism Without Racists: Color-Blind Racism and the Persistence of Racial Inequality in the United States*, New York: Rowman and Littlefield, 2003; Peggy Pascoe, *What Comes Naturally: Miscegenation Law and the Making of Race in America*, New York: Oxford University Press, 2009; Roopali Mukherjee, *The Racial Order of Things: Cultural Imaginaries of the Post-Soul Era*, Minneapolis: University of Minnesota Press, 2006.

4. Karen Brodkin, *How the Jews Became White Folks and What This Says about Race in America*, New York: Routledge, 1999; Vincent Crapanzano, *Waiting: The Whites of South Africa*, New York: Random House, 1995; Cheryl Harris, "Whiteness as Property," *Harvard Law Review*, 106, 8: 1709–1791; Abby Ferber, *White Man Falling*, New York: Rowman & Littlefield, 1998; Michelle Fine, Lois Weiss, Judi Addleston, and Julia Marusza, "(In)secure Times: Constructing White Working-Class Masculinities in the Late Twentieth Century," *Gender & Society*, 11, 1 (February 1997): 52–68; Ruth Frankenberg, *White Women, Race Matters*, Minneapolis: University of Minnesota Press, 1990; Charles Gallagher, "White Reconstruction in the University," *Socialist Review*, 24 (1-2) (1995): 165–185; James Hartigan, *Racial Situations: Class Predicaments of Whiteness in Detroit*, Princeton, NJ: Princeton University Press, 1999; Mathew Frye Jacobson, *Whiteness of a Different Color: European Immigrants and the Alchemy of Race*, Cambridge, MA: Harvard University Press, 1999; Bonilla-Silva, *Racism Without Racists*; Ira Katznelson, *When Affirmative Action Was White: An Untold History of Racial Inequality in Twentieth-Century America*, New York: Norton, 2005; George Lipsitz, *The Possessive Investment in Whiteness: How White People Benefit from Identity Politics*, Philadelphia: Temple University Press, 1998; David Roediger, *The Wages of Whiteness: Race and the Making of the American Working Class*, New York: Verso, 1991; France Winddance Twine, *A White Side of Black Britain: Interracial Intimacy and Racial Literacy*, Durham, NC: Duke University Press, 2010; France Winddance Twine and Charles Gallagher, "The Future of Whiteness Studies: A Map of the Third Wave," *Ethnic and Racial Studies*, 31, 1 (January 2008): 4–24; Monica McDermott, *Working-Class White: The Making and Unmaking of Race Relations*, Berkeley and Los Angeles: University of California Press, 2006; Kris Paap, *Working Construction: How White Men Put Themselves and the Labor Movement in Danger*, Ithaca, NY: Cornell University Press, 2005.

5. Donald Spence, *Narrative Truth and Historical Truth: Naming and Interpretation in Psychoanalysis*, New York: Norton, 1982.

6. Mary Jo Maynes, Jennifer L. Pierce, and Barbara Laslett, *Telling Stories: The Uses of Personal Narratives in Social Science and in History*, Ithaca, NY: Cornell University Press, 2008.

7. Nancy Chodorow argues that strong feelings and emotions, such as anxiety, anger, and love, animate psychoanalytic stories about self and other. See Nancy J. Chodorow, *The Power of Feelings: Personal Meaning in Psychoanalysis, Gender, and Culture*, New Haven, CT: Yale University Press, 1999.

8. Sigmund Freud, "Screen Memories," in James Strachey (ed. and trans.), *The Standard Edition of the Complete Works Sigmund Freud, Volume III*, London: Hogarth Press, 1963 [1899], pp. 301–322.

9. For an excellent discussion of the value of personal narratives in uncovering personal memories that counter public forms of discourse, see Michelle Mouton and Helena Pohlandt-McCormick, "Boundary Crossings: Oral History of Nazi Germany and Apartheid South Africa–A Comparative Perspective," *Radical History Workshop Journal*, 48 (1999): 41–63.

10. Winant, *The New Politics of Race*, p. 58.

11. Ruth Frankenberg makes this point in *White Women, Race Matters*. Also see, Eduardo Bonilla-Silva, *Racism Without Racists*.

12. This kind of halting speech is similar to what Susan Chase refers to as "disrupted speech" and what Marjorie DeVault terms "stumbling inarticulateness." See Susan Chase, *Ambiguous Empowerment*, and *Learning to Speak, Learning to Listen: How Diversity Works on Campus*, Ithaca, NY: Cornell University Press, 2010; and Marjorie DeVault "Ethnicity and Expertise: Racial-Ethnic Knowledge in Sociological Research" in her *Liberating Method: Feminism and Social Research*, Philadelphia: Temple University Press, 1999.

13. Jerry Van Hoy, *Franchise Law Firms and the Transformation of Personal Legal Services*, Westport, CT: Quorum Books, 1997.

14. Sharon Collins, *Black Corporate Executives: The Making and Breaking of a Black Middle Class*, Philadelphia: Temple University Press, 1996; and Elizabeth Higginbotham, *Too Much to Ask: Black Women in the Era of Integration*, Chapel Hill: University of North Carolina Press, 2001.

15. Linda McGee Calvert and V. Jean Ramsey, "Speaking as Female and White: A Non-Dominant/Dominant Group Standpoint," *Organization*, 3, 4 (1996): 470.

16. Anthropologist James Scott argues that gossip functions as a form of protest against landowners by the peasants he studied in Malaysia. While Scott argues that gossip is a "weapon of the weak," here I suggest that gossip can also be a weapon of the dominant group. See James Scott, *Weapons of the Weak: Everyday Forms of Peasant Resistance*, New Haven, CT: Yale University Press, 1987.

17. Fine, Weiss, Addleston, and Julia Maruza, "(In)secure Times," pp. 52–68.

18. Avery Gordon, *Ghostly Matters: Haunting and the Sociological Imagination*, Minneapolis: University of Minnesota Press, 1997, p. 8.

19. Aida Hurtado, "The Trickster's Play: Whiteness in the Subordination and Liberation Process," in Robert Torres, Louis F. Mirón, and Jonathan Xavier Inda, eds., *Race, Identity, and Citizenship: A Reader*, Malden, MA: Blackwell, 1999, p. 226.

20. For American Studies historiography on the United States as an exceptional nation, see Leo Marx, *The Machine and the Garden*, New York: Oxford University Press, 1964; Perry Miller, *The New England Mind*, Boston: Beacon Press, 1961; and Henry Smith, *Virgin Land: The American West as Symbol and Myth*, Cambridge, MA: Harvard University Press, 1950. For an important critique of these scholars, see David Noble, *The End of American History: Democracy, Capitalism, and the Metaphor of Two Worlds in Anglo-American Historical Writing, 1890–1980*, Minneapolis: University of Minnesota Press, 1985, and *Death of a Nation: American Culture and the End of Exceptionalism*, Minneapolis: University of Minnesota Press, 2002.

21. Coco Fusco, *English is Broken Here: Notes on Cultural Fusion in the Americas*, New York: New Press, 1995.

22. National discourses of tolerance and benevolence are not unique to the United States. In Canada, for example, the national story of benevolence and generosity to outsiders is particularly powerful. In research on Canadian feminist activists' reflections on racism, for instance, Sarita Srivastava finds that Canada was described as place where everyone receives equitable treatment. Activists' claims of "strategic innocence" not only served to deny their racism and protect them from the anger of women of color, but also drew upon this national discourse. See Sarita Srivastava, "'Are You Calling Me a Racist?' Moral and Emotional Regulation of American Feminism," *Signs; Journal of Women in Culture and Society*, 31, 1 (2005): 29–62. For similar scholarship on the Netherlands, see Philomena Essed, *Understanding Racism in Everyday Life: An Interdisciplinary Theory*, London: Sage, 1991; on Canada, Sherene Razack, "Your Place or Mine? Transnational Feminist Collaboration," in Agnes Calliste and George Sefa Dei, eds., *Anti-Racist Feminism: Crucial Race and Gender Studies*, Halifax, NS: Fernwood, 2000, and Razack, *Looking White People in the Eye*; for South Africa, Crapanzano, *Waiting*; and for New Zealand, Margaret Wetherall and Jonathan Potter, *Mapping the Language of Racism: Discourse and the Legitimation of Exploitation*, Hemel Hempstead, UK: Harvester Wheatsheaf, 1992.

23. Chase, *Ambiguous Empowerment*, p. xi.

24. Rosabeth Moss Kanter, *Men and Women of the Corporation*, New York: Basic Books, 1977. She defines tokens as a numerical minority that constitutes less than 15 percent of the population.

Chapter 4

1. Ellen Ladowsky, "That's No White Male, That's My Husband," *Wall Street Journal*, March 27, 1995, p. A20. This article was excerpted from an Independent Women's

Forum publication. See Ellen Ladowsky, "That's No White Male, That's My Husband," *Woman's Quarterly*, 1, 22 (Spring 1995). The cover of the *Women's Quarterly* issue featuring this article appeared in a *60 Minutes* profile of the Independent Women's Forum in 1996. Also see Barbara Spindel, "'Human Being First, Woman Second': Anti-Feminists and the Independent Women's Forum," Ph.D. dissertation, Department of American Studies, University of Minnesota, 2003.

2. Barriers to women in law school admissions were lifted nationally after the passage of Title IX, Education Amendment of 1972, which prohibited discrimination in graduate programs receiving federal funding. Women began to enter the legal profession in increasing numbers after 1975. In BC's Legal Department, the percentage of women lawyers in the Legal Department increased after the consent decree went into effect, from 3 percent in 1974 to 18 percent in 1989. These figures are similar to national figures; in 1972, women were only 2.2 percent of the legal profession but by 1991 they constituted 20.0 percent. See John Heinz, Robert Nelson, Rebecca Sandefur, and Ed Laumann, *Urban Lawyers: The New Social Structure of the Bar*, Chicago: University of Chicago Press, 2005, p. 22–23. Sociologist Cedric Herring shows that affirmative action benefited women in employment nationally. See Cedric Herring, "African Americans, the Public Policy Agenda, and the Paradoxes of Public Policy," in Cedric Herring, ed., *African Americans and the Public Agenda: The Paradoxes of Public Policy*, Thousand Oaks, CA: Sage, 1997, p. 8.

3. For a discussion of the FMLA in 1993 and its impact on workers in one large corporation, see Mindy Fried, *Taking Time: Parental Leave Policy and Corporate Culture*, Philadelphia: Temple University Press, 1998.

4. "Lucky's Sex Discrimination Lawsuit—Women Win Damages," *New York Times*, December 17, 1993; Marc Sandalow, "House Panel Cites Glass Ceiling at Federal Reserve Bank for Women, Minorities," *San Francisco Chronicle*, December 2, 1993, p. A8; Jane Gross, "Big Grocery Chain Reaches Landmark Sex-Bias Accord," New York Times, December 16, 1993, p. A8.

5. U.S. Federal Glass Ceiling Commission, *Good For Business: Making Full Use of Our Nation's Human Capital: A Fact Finding Report for the Federal Glass Ceiling Commission*, Washington, D.C.: GPO, 1995.

6. Peter Kilborn, "For Many in Work Force, 'Glass Ceiling' Still Exists," *New York Times*, March 15, 1995, p. A22.

7. Karen DeWitt, "Job Bias Cited for Minorities and Women," *New York Times*, November 23, 1995, p. B14.

8. Associated Press, "Reverse Discrimination Complaints Rare, Labor Study," *New York Times*, March 31, 1995, p. A23.

9. Allen R. Myerson, "As Federal Bias Cases Drop, Workers Take Up the Fight," *New York Times*, January 12, 1997, sec. 1, p. 1.

10. Kirstin Grimsely, "Panel Asks Why Women Still Earn Less," *Washington Post*, June 9, 2000, p. E3.

11. Richard Stevenson, "Texaco Is Said to Set Payment Over Sex Bias," *New York Times*, January 6, 1999, p. C1; and Lawrence Zuckerman, "Boeing Agrees to Settle Case Charging Bias in Salaries," *New York Times*, November 19, 1999, p. C2.

12. For example, in the Piscataway, New Jersey, case, Sharon Taxman sued the local school board because she was laid off when an African American woman with the same seniority was not. Newspaper articles did not mention the fact that as a white woman, Taxman also benefited from affirmative action policy. See Iver Peterson, "Justice Officials Clarify Stand in Race-Based Dismissal Case," *New York Times*, September 22, 1994, B6. For a similar pattern, see discussions of the Hopwood case in Texas where Cheryl Hopwood challenged the University of Texas for rejecting her admission to law school. Richard Bernstein "Racial Discrimination or Righting Past Wrongs?" *New York Times*, July 13, 1994, p. B8.

13. Bernstein, "Racial Discrimination or Righting Past Wrongs?"

14. Bernstein, "Racial Discrimination or Righting Past Wrongs?"

15. Ira Katznelson, *When Affirmative Action Was White: An Untold History of Racial Inequality in Twentieth-Century America*, New York: Norton, 2005.

16. On the IWF, see Spindel, "'Human Being First, Women Second.'" Also see Laura Ingraham, "Enter, Women," *New York Times*, April 19, 199; Elizabeth Larson, "Women Don't Need Extra Help," *Insight*, April 24, 1995, p. 18; Ladowsky, "That's No White Male, That's My Husband"; Anita Blair, "Shattering the Myth of the Glass Ceiling," *Los Angeles Times*, May 7, 1996, p. B7; Anita Blair and Gary Reynolds, "The Big Lie About Discrimination," *Washington Times*, November 6, 1997; Laura Ingraham, "Why Are Women Endorsing Bias?" *Florida Sun-Sentinel*, May 1, 1995, p. 9A; and Sonya Jason, ". . . That's My Son," *Wall Street Journal*, March 27, 1995, p. A20.

17. Ingraham, "Enter, Women."

18. Ladowsky, "That's No White Male, That's my Husband." Also see Spindel, "'Human Being First, Women Second,'" p. 109, and Jason, ". . . That's My Son," p. A20.

19. Larson, "Women Don't Need Extra Help," p. 18

20. For an important discussion of the history of Proposition 209, see Lydia Chávez, *The Color Bind: California' Battle to End Affirmative Action*, Berkeley and Los Angeles: University of California Press, 1998, p. 252.

21. Roopali Mukherjee, *The Racial Order of Things: Cultural Imaginaries of the Post-Soul Era*, Minneapolis; University of Minnesota Press, 2006, pp. 49–50. Also see Chávez, *The Color Bind*.

22. Chávez, *The Color Bind*, p. 99; Steven A. Holmes, "Defending Affirmative Action, Liberals Try to Place Debate's Focus on Women," *New York Times*, March 2, 1995, p. B7.

23. Chávez, *The Color Bind*, p. 205. Also see DeWitt, "New Cause Helps Feminists Appeal to Younger Women," p. A10; Teresa Moore, "Taking NOW into the Future, Patricia Ireland, President of NOW," *San Francisco Chronicle*, April 21, 1996, p. 3/Z3.

24. See Holmes, "Defending Affirmative Action"; and Moore, "Taking NOW into the Future."

25. Holmes, "Defending Affirmative Action."

26. Loyle Hairston, "What Feminism Has Done to the Workplace; Welcome to the Battle," editorial desk, *New York Times*, March 24, 1995.

27. Bob Herbert, "In America: The Wrong Target," editorial desk, *New York Times*, April 5, 1995, p. A23.

28. Susan Sward, "Generation Gap, Color Gap, Women Split on Affirmative Action," *San Francisco Chronicle*, March 31, 1995, p. A1.

29. Ramon McLeod, "Family Ties Help Explain Why Women Are Split; Many Worried about Husbands' Jobs," *San Francisco Chronicle*, March 31, 1995, p. A4. Articles in other newspapers provided more detail about this issue. See, for instance, the *Chicago Tribune*, where sociologist Carlos Moskos is quoted as saying, "The fact that white women have been the greatest beneficiaries and have created the least backlash from white males—and the survey data is quite clear on that—shows that race overrides gender as a threat to white men." Lisa Anderson, "Women Escape Affirmative Action Feud," *Chicago Tribune*, May 16, 1995, p. 1. Also see Ladowsky, "That's No White Male, That's my Husband," and Jason, ". . . That's My Son."

30. Yumi Wilson, "Perceptions: Minority Women's Views Opposite of White Men's," *San Francisco Chronicle*, May 10, 1995, p. A8.

31. Susan Yoachum, "Wording Affects Polls on Affirmative Action," *San Francisco Chronicle*, September 14, 1995, p. A17. Also see Chávez, *The Color Bind*.

32. Mukherjee, *The Racial Order of Things*, p. 50.

33. Fried, *Taking Time*.

34. By contrast, European countries have had parental leaves for quite some time. In 1974, Sweden was the first to pass such legislation, followed by other European countries in the mid-1980s. Unlike the United States, sixteen European nations and Canada provide an average of thirty-three weeks of *paid* parental leave for women and men with new infants. See Peter Moss, *Childcare in the European Community, 1985–1990*, London: Commission of the European Communities, 1990, and *Childcare and Equality of Opportunity, Consolidated Report to the European Commission*, Brussels: Commission of the European Communities, 1988; Kirsten Wever, "The Family and Medical Leave Act: Assessing Temporary Wage Replacement for Family and Medical Leave," Cambridge, MA: Radcliffe Public Policy Institute, 1996.

35. For example, in my first book, *Gender Trials*, I found that the private firm I studied did *not* have a formal maternity leave before passage of the FMLA, and resolved the issue of leaves on an ad hoc, case-by-case basis. See Jennifer L. Pierce, *Gender Trials: Emotional Lives in Contemporary Law Firms*, Berkeley and Los Angeles: University of California Press, 1995.

36. Labor historians have shown that American women in unions fought for feminist concerns, such as more flexible hours in the workplace. Dorothy Sue Cobble, for instance, argues that "labor feminists" built a union movement around *time*, while male industrial unionists built a union around *money*. While white male unionists sought

pay increases and overtime to ensure their breadwinner status at home, labor feminists fought for flexible hours because they knew they would be expected to juggle the demands of work and family. See Dorothy Sue Cobble, *The Other Women's Movement: Workplace Justice and Social Rights in Modern America*, Princeton, NJ: Princeton University Press, 2004; and Nancy MacClean, *Freedom is Not Enough: The Opening of the American Workplace*, Cambridge, MA, Harvard University Press, 2006.

37. Quoted in Pierce, *Gender Trials*, p. 113.

38. Susan is also discussed in another publication. See Jennifer L. Pierce, "'Not Qualified' or 'Not Committed': A Raced and Gendered Organizational Logic in Large Law Firms," in Reza Bankakar and Max Travers, eds., *An Introduction to Law and Social Theory*, London: Hart, 2003.

39. Quoted in Pierce, *Gender Trials*, p. 123.

40. Quoted in Pierce, *Gender Trials*, p. 123.

41. Fried, *Taking Time*.

42. For professionals such as doctors and lawyers, commitment also entails ethical obligations.

43. Fried, *Taking Time*, p. 53.

44. Quoted in Lotte Bailyn, *Breaking the Mold*, Ithaca, NY: Cornell University Press, 1993, p. 81.

45. Bailyn, *Breaking the Mold*; Arlie Hochschild, *The Time Bind: When Work Becomes Home and Home Becomes Work*, New York: Holt, 2001; Cynthia Fuchs Epstein, Carroll Seron, Bonnie Oglensky, and Robert Sauté, *The Part-Time Paradox: Time Norms, Professional Life, Family and Gender*, New York: Routledge, 1998.

46. Nalalie Sokoloff, *Between Money and Love: The Dialectics of Women's Home and Market Work*, New York: Praeger, 1980; Ivy Kennelly. "'That Single Mother Element': How White Employers Typify Black Women," *Gender & Society*, 13, 2 (April 1999): 168–192.

47. Sanctions are typically court rules for the enforcement of deposition discovery where a party has sent out interrogatories or noticed a deposition and the other side has failed to respond. Judges can also issue sanctions or fines for contempt of court and other violations of civil procedure. Issuing sanction is a matter of a judge's discretion.

48. Pierce, *Gender Trials*, p. 120.

49. Tera Hunter, *To 'Joy My Freedom: Southern Black Women's Lives and Labors After the Civil War*, Cambridge, MA: Harvard University Press, 1997; Patricia Hill Collins, *Black Feminist Thought, Knowledge, Consciousness, and the Politics of Empowerment*, Boston: Unwin Hyman, 1990; Jacqueline Jones, *Labor of Love, Labor of Sorrow*, New York: Vintage, 1986; and Judith Rollins, *Between Women: Domestics and Their Employers*, Philadelphia: Temple University Press, 1985.

50. James Blackwell, *Mainstreaming Outsiders: The Production of Black Professionals*, Rowman & Littlefield, 1981; Natalie Sokoloff, *Black Women and White Women in the Professions: Occupational Segregation by Race and Gender, 1960–1980*, New York: Routledge,

1992; Sharon Collins, *Black Corporate Executives: The Making and Breaking of a Black Middle Class*, Philadelphia: Temple University Press, 1996; and Elizabeth Higginbotham, *Too Much To Ask: Black Women in the Era of Integration*, Chapel Hill: University of North Carolina Press, 2001.

51. Brent Staples, "When a Law Firm is Like a Baseball Team," editorial desk, *New York Times*, November 27, 1998, p. A42. Also see Notes 49 and 50 and Reynolds Holding, "Gains for Minority Attorneys in SF: But They Cite Frustration of Institutional Racism . . ." *San Francisco Chronicle*, December 21, 1993, p. A18.

52. See Staples, "When a Law Firm is Like a Baseball Team," p. A42; David Wilkins and Mitu Galati, "Why Are There So Few Black Lawyers in Corporate Law Firms: An Institutional Analysis," *California Law Review*, 84 (1996); and David Wilkins, "Doing Well by Doing Good? The Role of Public Service in the Careers of Black Corporate Lawyers" *Houston Law Review*, 41 (2004): 1–91.

53. In Kris Paap's *Working Construction: How White Men Put Themselves and the Labor Movement in Danger*, Ithaca, NY: Cornell University Press, 2005, she finds that white women working in male-dominated trades are often depicted as "unqualified." Her finding points to an interesting class and racial distinction. White working-class women are considered "unqualified" when they work in the trades, but "not committed" when they work in the legal profession. African American men, however, are considered "unqualified" when they work in the legal profession, as discussed in Chapter 3.

54. George Lipsitz, *The Possessive Investment in Whiteness: How White People Benefit from Identity Politics*, Philadelphia: Temple University Press, 1998; Cheryl Harris, "Whiteness as Property," *Harvard Law Review*, 106, 8 (1993): 1709–1791; David Roediger, *The Wages of Whiteness: Race and the Making of the American Working Class*, New York: Verso, 1991.

55. Black women have long confronted other gendered, racialized stereotypes, such as the "mammy" or the "angry black woman." See Adia Harvey Wingfield, "The Modern Mammy and the Angry Black Man: African American Professionals' Experience with Gendered Racism in the Workplace, *Race, Gender & Class*, 14, 1-2 (2007): 1–21; Patricia Hill Collins, *Black Sexual Politics*, New York: Routledge, 2004, and *Black Feminist Thought*; and Elizabeth Higginbotham and Lynn Weber, "Perceptions of Workplace Discrimination Among Black and White Professional Managerial Women," in Irene Browne, ed., *Latinas and African American Women at Work*, New York: Sage, 1999.

56. Susan Chase, *Ambiguous Empowerment: The Work Narratives of Women School Superintendents*, Amherst: University of Massachusetts Press, 1995, p. 18.

57. Ingraham, "Enter, Women."

58. See Angela Dillard. *Guess Who's Coming to Dinner Now? Multicultural Conservatism in America*, New York: New York University Press, 2001, pp. 57–58.

59. In Robert Entman and Andrew Rojeki's argument, this ambivalence emerges, in part, from a paradox of racial progress. In their view, "Blacks' new political assertiveness and power after World War II, and their large-scale emigration from the South,

spread White anxiety and resentment throughout the nation, even as it rendered open proclamations of racial inferiority passé. Thus it is possible that old-fashioned racism, wrong as it was on every level, coexisted with rather positive notions among many Whites. If Blacks couldn't be expected to achieve, if they were naturally inclined to slow-wittedness and laziness, then they could be regarded with paternal fondness, so long as they showed proper deference. Growing beyond the myths of genetic racial hierarchy, the current culture rejects the most overt claims of Black inferiority–and this ironically cultivates Whites impatience and hostility." See Robert Entman and Andrew Rojeki, *The Black Image in the White Mind: Media and Race in America*, Chicago: University of Chicago Press, 2000, p. 3. Also see Eric Lott, *Love and Theft: Blackface Minstrelsy and the American Working Class*, New York: Oxford University Press, 1995; Roediger, *The Wages of Whiteness*; and Lipsitz, *The Possessive Investment in Whiteness*.

60. Pierce, *Gender Trials*, p. 133.

61. At the time, I did not ask the women whether they had political affiliations with the IWF.

62. On academics, see Arlie Hochschild, "Making It: Marginality and Obstacles to Minority Consciousness," in Ruth Kundsin, ed., *Women and Success: The Anatomy of Achievement*, New York: William Morrow, 1974; on physicians, see Frances Conley, *Walking Out on the Boys*, New York: Farrar, Straus, and Giroux, 1999; and on scientists, see Jill Bystydzienski and Sharon Bird, eds., *Removing Barriers: Women in Academic Science, Technology, Engineering, and Mathematics*, Bloomington: Indiana University Press, 2006.

63. Chase, *Ambiguous Empowerment*, p. 185.

64. For a discussion of generations among feminist academics, see Hokulani Aikau, Karla Erickson, and Jennifer L. Pierce, "Introduction: Feminist Waves, Feminist Generations," in Hokulani Aikau, Karla Erickson, and Jennifer L. Pierce, eds., *Feminist Waves, Feminist Generations*, Minneapolis: University of Minnesota Press, 2007.

65. Mary Blair-Loy, *Competing Devotions: Career and Family Among Women Executives*, Cambridge, MA: Harvard University Press, 2005.

66. Heinz, Nelson, Sandefur, and Laumann, *Urban Lawyers*, p. 22–23.

67. Chase, *Ambiguous Empowerment*, p. 10; Richard Pride, *The Political Use of Racial Narratives: School Desegregation in Mobile, Alabama, 1954–1997*, Urbana and Chicago: University of Illinois Press, 2002; and Lipsitz, *The Possessive Investment in Whiteness*.

68. As other scholars have found, autobiographies written closer to the end of one's life tend to be "backward looking and self-justifying" while journals written earlier in life tend to be "forward looking and anxious." See Mary Jo Maynes, Jennifer L. Pierce, and Barbara Laslett, *Telling Stories: The Use of Personal Narratives in the Social Sciences and History*, Ithaca, NY: Cornell University Press, 2008, pp. 79–80.

69. The term "cultural toolkit" comes from Anne Swidler in her "Culture as Action: Symbols and Strategies, *American Sociological Review*, 51, 2 (1986): 273–286.

70. Feminist scholars have written about how middle-class white women draw on other women's work to support their own career autonomy. See Barbara Ehrenreich

and Arlie Hochschild, "Introduction" in Barbara Ehrenreich and Arlie Hochschild, eds., *Global Woman: Nannies, Maids, and Sex Workers in the New Economy*, New York: Henry Holt, 2002.

71. On academics, see Hochschild, "Making It"; on physicians, see Conley, *Walking Out on the Boys*; on scientists, see Bystydzienski and Bird, *Removing Barriers*; and on managers, see Patricia Yancey Martin, "'Said and Done' vs. 'Saying and Doing': Gendering Practices, Practicing Gender at Work, *Gender & Society*, 17, 4 (2003): 342–366.

72. Chase, *Ambiguous Empowerment*.

73. See Fred Pincus, *Reverse Discrimination: Dismantling the Myth*, Boulder, CO: Lynne Rienner, 2003, pp. 26–27.

74. Faye Crosby, *Affirmative Action Is Dead, Long Live Affirmative Action*, New Haven, CT: Yale University Press, 2004, p. 5.

75. For a discussion of "disrupted talk," see Susan Chase, *Learning to Speak, Learning to Listen: How Diversity Works on Campus*, Ithaca, NY: Cornell University Press, 2010.

Chapter 5

1. I have drawn these comments from students and instructors in the fiction writing classes I have taken. For a discussion of these workshops, see Appendix A.

2. Roderick A. Ferguson, *Aberrations in Black: Toward a Queer of Color Critique*, Minneapolis: University of Minnesota Press, 2004; and Zygmunt Bauman, *Intimations of Postmodernity*, New York: Routledge, 1992.

3. See Howard Schuman, Charlotte Steeh, Lawrence Bobo, and Maria Krysan, *Racial Attitudes in America: Trends and Interpretations*, Cambridge, MA: Harvard University Press, 1997.

4. For an important theoretical account of institutional racism, see David Wellman, *Portraits of White Racism*, Cambridge, MA: Cambridge University Press, 1977.

5. It is worth noting that ambivalence is a key element to post-colonial theories of racism. (Here, I am referring to those theories which analyze the cultural legacies of colonialism and imperialism for subaltern groups.) Homi Bhabha, for instance, in his classic essay, "The Other Question," theorizes the "productive ambivalence of the object of colonial discourse—that 'otherness' which is at once an object of desire and derision" to highlight the boundaries of colonial discourse in order to transgress them. See Homi Bhabha, "The Other Question . . . Homi K. Bhabha Reconsiders the Stereotype and Colonial Discourse," *Screen* 24.6 (1983): 19. Similarly, British scholar Stuart Hall and American Studies scholar Eric Lott argue that white identity is constructed through the repulsion and desire of non-white groups. See Stuart Hall, "What Is This 'Black' in Black Popular Culture?" *Social Justice*, 20 (1993): 104–114; and Eric Lott, *Love and Theft: Blackface Minstrelsy and the American Working Class*, New York: Oxford University Press, 1995.

6. Monica McDermott, *Working-Class White: The Making and Unmaking of Race Relations*, Berkeley and Los Angeles: University of California Press, 2006.

7. Deirdre Royster, *Race and the Invisible Hand: How White Networks Exclude Black Men from Blue-Collar Jobs*, Berkeley and Los Angeles: University of California Press, 2003, p. 3.

8. Jennifer Lee, *Civility in the City: Blacks, Jews, and Koreans in Urban America*, Cambridge, MA: Harvard University Press, 2002; Michelle Lamont, ed., *The Cultural Territories of Race: Black and White Boundaries*, Chicago: University of Chicago Press, 1999.

9. As I have written elsewhere, "studying up" presents a host of problems that are distinct from studying subaltern groups. See Jennifer L. Pierce, "Reflections on Fieldwork in a Complex Organization," in Rosanna Hertz and Jonathan Imber, eds., *Studying Elites Using Qualitative Methods*, Thousand Oaks, CA: Sage Publications, 1995.

10. Katherine Walsh, *Talking About Race: Community Dialogues and the Politics of Difference*, Chicago: University of Chicago Press, 2007.

Conclusion

1. In order for ruling groups to consolidate their power, Antonio Gramsci argued that ruling groups must elaborate on and maintain a popular system of ideas—through media, education, and so on—that he termed "common sense." In his argument, it is through the production and adherence to common sense that people consent to the ways in which they are ruled. Antonio Gramsci, *Selections from Prison Notebooks*, edited and translated by Quintin Hoare and Geoffrey Nowell Smith, New York: International Publishers, 1971.

2. Ryan P. Murphy, "On Our Own: Flight Attendant Activism and the Family Values Economy," Ph.D. dissertation, Department of American Studies, University of Minnesota, 2010.

3. Murphy, "On Our Own"; Karen Ho, *Liquidated: An Ethnography of Wall Street*, Durham, NC: Duke University Press, 2009; Michael Lewis, *The Big Short: Inside the Doomsday Machine*, New York: W. W. Norton Press, 2010; Ruth Milkman, ed., *Organizing Immigrants: The Challenge for Unions in Contemporary California*, Ithaca, NY: Cornell University Press, 2000; Dan Clawson, *The Next Upsurge: Labor and New Social Movements*, Ithaca, NY: Cornell University Press, 2003; and Ruth Milkman and Kim Voss, eds., *Rebuilding Labor: Organizing and Organizers in the New Union Movement*, Ithaca, NY: Cornell University Press, 2004.

4. *Citizens United v. Federal Election Commission* 558 U.S. 08-205 (2010); and *Wal-Mart Stores Inc. v. Betty Dukes et al.* 564 U.S. 10-277 (2011).

5. Luke Green, "AIG Cites Wal-Mart Decision in Attempt to Block Class Action Certification," *Securities Litigation*, August 23, 2011, accessed on August 29, 2011, from http://blog.issgovernance.com/slw/2011/08/aig-cites-wal-mart-decision-in-attempt-to-challenge-class-cetification.html.

6. Mica Pollack, *Colormute: Race Talk Dilemmas in American Schools*, Princeton, NJ: Princeton University Press, 2005.

7. For example, Ryan P. Murphy found that after buyouts and takeovers, many of the corporate archives he needed for his research in the airline industry had literally disappeared. See Murphy, "On Our Own." Also, see anthropologist Laura Nader's classic essay, "Up the Anthropologists—Perspectives Gained from Studying Up," in Dell Hymes, ed., *Reinventing Anthropology*, New York: Random House, 1972; Susan Ostrander, *Women of the Upper Class*, Philadelphia: Temple University Press, 1984; Rosanna Hertz and Jonathan Imber, eds., *Studying Elites Using Qualitative Methods*, Thousand Oaks, CA: Sage, 1995; Jennifer L. Pierce, "Lawyers, Lethal Weapons and Ethnographic Authority," in Susan Moch and Marie Gates, eds., *Qualitative Research and the Researcher Experience*, Thousand Oaks, CA: Sage Publications, 2000; Chris Shore and Stephen Nugent, eds., *Elite Cultures: Anthropological Perspectives*, London: ASA Monographs, 2002; and Ho, *Liquidated*.

8. Roderick Ferguson, *Aberrations in Black: Toward a Queer of Color Critique*, Minneapolis: University of Minnesota Press, 2004.

9. Earl Lewis, "Why History Remains a Factor in the Search for Racial Equality," in Patricia Gurin, Jeffrey S. Lehman, and Earl Lewis, eds., *Defending Diversity: Affirmative Action at the University of Michigan*, Ann Arbor: University of Michigan Press, 2004, p. 51

10. *Gratz v. Bollinger* 539 U.S. 244 (2003).

11. *Grutter v. Bollinger* 539 U.S. 306 (2003).

12. Richard Paddock, "Affirmative Action is Over, Says Longtime Foe," *Los Angeles Times*, November 26, 2006.

13. For an important critical account of how the media framed Obama's election, see Adia Harvey Wingfield and Joe Feagin, *Yes We Can: White Racial Framing and the 2008 Presidential Campaign*, New York: Routledge, 2010.

14. Adam Nagourney, "Obama Elected President as Racial Barriers Fall," *New York Times*, November 5, 2008, op-ed; Eric Dyson, "Race, Post Race," *Los Angeles Times*, November 5, 2008, "Opinion"; and Abigal Thernstrom and Stephan Thernstrom, "Is Race Out of the Race?" *Los Angeles Times*, March 2, 2008, op-ed.

15. See Scott Jaschik, "Arizona Bans Affirmative Action," *Inside Higher Education*, November 3, 2010, accessed on July 16, 2011, from http://www.insidehighered.com/news/2010/11/03/arizona

16. "Affirmative Action No Longer Needed," *Arizona Republic*, October 26, 2010, p. A1.

17. Kevin Flynn, "Coloradans Preserve Affirmative Action," *Rocky Mountain News*, November 6, 2008.

18. For a discussion of the Texas 10 percent plan, see Lani Guinier and Gerald Torres *The Miner's Canary: Enlisting Race, Resisting Power, Transforming Democracy*, Cambridge, MA: Harvard University Press, 2002. However, a more recent Texas case, *Fischer v. The University of Texas at Austin*, suggests that affirmative action may again be under assault. In this case, two white female applicants challenged the *Grutter* decision, arguing that it disproportionately benefited Hispanic students. Adam Liptak, "College Diversity

Nears Its Last Stand," *New York Times*, October 16, 2012, and Liz Halloran, "Affirmative-Action Case Could be Campaign Issue," National Public Radio, October 5, 2011, accessed on January 13, 2012, from http://www.npr.org/2011/10/05/141052635/affirmative-action-case-could-be-campaign-issue?ft=1&f=1003

19. Guinier and Torres, *The Miner's Canary*, pp. 72–74.

20. "Diversity Project in Texas," editorial, *New York Times*, November 27, 1999; "New Law in Texas Preserves Racial Mix," *New York Times*, November 24, 1999; Scott Jaschik, "10 Percent Plan Survives in Texas, *Inside Higher Ed*, May 29, 2007, accessed on July 26, 2011, from http://www.insidehighered.com/news/2007/05/29/percent.

21. Dana Takagi, *The Retreat from Race: Asian American Admissions and Racial Politics*, New Brunswick, NJ: Rutgers University Press, 1992; *2010–2011 Academic Affirmative Action Plan*, UCLA Law School, accessed on January 24, 2012, from https://faculty.diversity.ucla.edu/affirmative-action-and-equal-employment-opportunity-1/AAAP.pdf/view

22. James Traub, "The Class of Prop. 209," *New York Times Magazine*, May 2, 1999, sec. 6 p. 44.

23. Traub, "The Class of Prop. 209"; "Minority Fresh Enrollment at UCB Up," *New York Times*, December 1, 1999; and "College by the Numbers," *New York Times*, editorial, December 24, 1990.

24. Mary Wisniewski, "Court Strikes Michigan Affirmative Action Ban," Reuters, July 1, 2011, accessed on July 17, 2011, from http://www.reuters.com/article/2011/07/01/us-affirmative-action-michigan-idUSTRE7605G920110701?feedType=RSS; "No Need to Label Court's Ruling on Affirmative Action 'Nutty,'" *Battle Creek Enquirer*, August 2, 2011, accessed on August 11, 2011, from http://www.battlecreekenquirer.com/article/20110803/OPINION01/108030301/Legitimate-issue?odyssey=mod|newswell|text|Frontpage|s

25. See Adam Liptak, "College Diversity Nears Last Stand"; and Halloran, "Affirmative Action Case Could Be Campaign Issue."

26. Jennifer Lee and Frank Bean, *The Diversity Paradox: Immigration and the Color Line in 21st Century America*, New York: Russell Sage Foundation, 2010, p. 184

27. Devah Pager, Bruce Western, and Bart Bonikowski, "Discrimination in a Low-Wage Labor Market: A Field Experiment," *American Sociological Review*, 74, 5: 777–799.

28. Elizabeth Chambliss, "Miles to Go: The Progress of Minorities in the Legal Profession," American Bar Association Report, accessed on October 10, 2010, from http://www.law.harvard.edu/programs/plp/pdf/Projects_MilesToGo.pdf; John Heinz, Robert Nelson, Rebecca Sandefur, and Ed Laumann, *Urban Lawyers: The New Social Structure of the Bar*, Chicago: University of Chicago Press, 2005; Mary Noonan, Mary Corcoran, and Paul Courant, "Is the Partnership Gap Closing for Women? Cohort Differences in the Sex Gap in Partnership Chances," *Social Science Research*, 37 (March 2008); Nancy Reichman and Joyce Sterling, "Sticky Floors, Broken Steps, and Concrete Ceilings in Legal Careers," *Texas Journal of Women and Law*, 27 (2004); Rebecca Sand-

efur, "Staying Power: The Persistence of Social Inequality in Shaping Lawyer Stratification and Lawyers' Persistence in the Profession," *Southwestern University Law Review*, 36, 3 (2007); Elizabeth Gorman and Fiona Kay, "Racial and Ethnic Minority Representation in Large U.S. Law Firms," *Studies in Law, Politics, and Society*, 52 (2010): 211–238; and Erin Kelly, Samantha Ammons, Kelly Chermack, and Phyllis Moen, "Gendered Challenge, Gendered Response: Confronting the Ideal Worker Norm in a White-Collar Organization, *Gender & Society*, 22, 6 (2008): 281–303.

29. See Lauren Edelman, "Legal Ambiguity and Symbolic Structures: Organizational Mediation of Civil Rights Law," *American Journal of Sociology*, 97 (1992): 1531–1576; and Edelman with Christopher Uggen and Howard Erlanger, "The Endogeneity of Legal Regulation: Grievance Procedures as Rational Myth," *American Journal of Sociology*, 105, 2 (1999): 406–454; and with Sharon Matusik Fuller and Sally Riggs, "Legal Readings: Employee Interpretation and Enactment of Civil Rights Law," *Academy of Management Review* (January 2000).

30. For a discussion of the many ways that Americans interpret the word "diversity," see Joyce Bell and Doug Hartmann, "Diversity in Everyday Discourse: The Cultural Ambiguities and Consequences of 'Happy Talk,'" *American Sociological Review*, 72, 6 (2007): 895–914.

31. Frank Dobbin and John Sutton, "The Strength of a Weak State: The Rights Revolution and the Rise of Human Resources Management Divisions," *American Journal of Sociology*, 104, 2 (1998): 441–476; and Nicole Raeburn, *Changing Corporate America from the Inside Out: Lesbian and Gay Workplace Rights*. Minneapolis: University of Minnesota Press, 2004.

32. Rakesh Kochhar, Richard Fry, and Paul Taylor, "Wealth Gaps Rise to Record Highs Between Whites, Blacks, and Hispanics: Twenty to One," *PEW Social And Demographic Trends*, July 26, 2011.

33. Melvin Oliver and Thomas Shapiro, *Black Wealth / White Wealth: A New Perspective on Racial Inequality*, New York: Routledge, 2006 [1996].

Appendix A

1. Marjorie Shostak, "'What the Wind Won't Take Away': The Genesis of *Nisa*— *The Life and Words of a !Kung Woman*," in Personal Narratives Group, ed., *Interpreting Women's Lives: Feminist Theory and Personal Narratives*, Bloomington: University of Indiana Press, 1989, p. 232.

2. For other examples of feminist scholars on the importance of discussing revision in creative and academic work, see Carolyn Ellis, *The Ethnographic I: A Methodological Novel About Autoethnography*, Walnut Creek, CA: Alta Mira Press, 2004, and *Revisions: Autoethnographic Reflections on Life and Work*, Walnut Creek, CA: Left Coast Press, 2008; Laurel Richardson, "Louisa May's Story of Her Life" and "Afterwords: 'Louisa May' and Me," in *Fields of Play: Constructing an Academic Life*, New Brunswick, NJ: Rutgers

University Press, 1997, and *Last Writes: A Daybook About a Dying Friend*, Walnut Creek, CA: Left Coast Press, 2007.

3. Mary Jo Maynes, Jennifer L. Pierce, and Barbara Laslett, *Telling Stories: The Use of Personal Narratives in the Social Sciences and History*, Ithaca, NY: Cornell University Press, 2008.

4. Susan Geiger, *TANU Women: Gender and Culture in the Making of Tanganyikan Nationalism, 1955–1965*, Portsmouth, NH: Heineman Press, 1997.

5. As anthropologist Lila Abu-Lughod has argued, the fact that we are always "standing on shifting ground makes it clear that every view is a view from somewhere and every act of speaking, a speaking from somewhere." See Lila Abu-Lughod, "Writing Against Culture," in Richard Fox, ed., *Recapturing Anthropology: Working in the Present*, Santa Fe, NM: School of American Research, University of Washington Press, 1991, p. 141. Rather than despairing of the possibility of making any kind of "truth" claims, many scholars have sought to develop alternatives epistemologies emphasizing "situated knowledges," arguing that knowledge is produced positionally and hence always partial. See Donna Haraway, "Situated Knowledges: The Science Question in Feminism as a Site of Discourse on the Privilege of Partial Perspective," *Feminist Studies*, 14, 3 (1988); Patricia Hill Collins, *Black Feminist Thought, Knowledge, Consciousness, and the Politics of Empowerment*, New York: Routledge, 1990; Susan Krieger, *Social Science and the Self: Personal Essays on an Art Form*, New Brunswick, NJ: Rutgers University Press, 1990; Barbara Laslett, "Unfeeling Knowledge: Emotion and Objectivity in the Sociology of Knowledge," *Sociological Forces*, 5 (1990): 413–433; Helen Longino, *Science as Social Knowledge: Values and Objectivity in Scientific Inquiry*, Princeton, NJ: Princeton University Press, 1990; and Sandra Harding, *Whose Science? Whose Knowledge?* Ithaca, NY: Cornell University Press, 1991.

6. See Jennifer L. Pierce, "Appendix 1," *Gender Trials: Emotional Lives in Contemporary Law Firms*, Berkeley and Los Angeles: University of California Press, 1995.

7. Lydia Chávez, *The Color Bind: California's Battle to End Affirmative Action*, Berkeley and Los Angeles: University of California Press, 1998.

8. For discussions of "white on black" interviewing, see Marjorie DeVault, "Ethnicity and Expertise: Racial-Ethnic Knowledge in Sociological Research," *Liberating Method: Feminism and Social Research*, Philadelphia: Temple University Press, 1999; and Mary Waters, "Appendix: Notes on Methodology," in *Black Identities: West Indian Immigrant Dreams and American Realities*, New York and Cambridge: Russell Sage Foundation and Harvard University Press, 1999. For a discussion of "black on white" interviewing, see Deirdre Royster, *Race and the Invisible Hand: How Social Networks Exclude Black Men from Blue-Collar Jobs*, Berkeley and Los Angeles: University of California Press, 2003.

9. Political elites, for example, often write memoirs to establish a public persona. See, for example, historian Blanche Cook's discussion of Eleanor Roosevelt's autobiographical writing in, *Eleanor Roosevelt, Volume 1, 1884–1933*, New York: Penguin Books, 1992.

10. R.W. Connell, *Masculinities*, Berkeley and Los Angeles: University of California Press, 1995, pp. 241–242.

11. Mary Jo Maynes, "Autobiography and Class Formation in Nineteenth-Century Europe: Methodological Considerations," *Social Science History*, 16, 3 (1992): 523.

12. For a discussion of the symbolic significance of mistakes in memory, see Maynes, Pierce, and Laslett, *Telling Stories*, pp. 150–152.

13. To read more about the Loft Literary Center in Minneapolis, see "Milestones in Loft History," accessed on March 26, 2011, from https://www.loft.org/about/history.

14. See Brenda Ueland, *If You Want to Write: A Book About Art, Independence, and Spirit*, St. Paul, MN: Gray Wolf Press, 1987 [1938].

15. Following ethnographic practices of confidentiality and anonymity, I do not use names to describe workshop participants or instructors.

16. Jessica Petocz, "Power, Struggle, and Oral History," graduate seminar on personal narratives in interdisciplinary research, Department of American Studies, University of Minnesota, Minneapolis, Spring 2010.

17. See, for example, Adia Harvey Wingfield, "The Modern Mammy and the Angry Black Man: African American Professionals' Experience with Gendered Racism in the Workplace," *Race, Gender & Class*, 14, 1–2 (2007): 1–21; and Elizabeth Higginbotham, *Too Much to Ask: Black Women in an Era of Integration*, Chapel Hill: University of North Carolina Press, 2001.

18. See Kate Rushin, "The Bridge Poem," in Cherrie Moraga and Gloria Anzúldua, eds., *This Bridge Called My Back: Writing by Radical Women of Color*, San Francisco: Kitchen Table Press, 1984; and Gloria Anzúldua, ed., *Making Face, Making Soul/Haciendo Caras: Creative and Critical Perspectives by Feminists of Color*, San Francisco: Aunt Lute Books, 1990; Ann duCille, "The Occult of True Black Womanhood: Critical Demeanor and Black Feminist Studies," *Signs: Journal of Women in Culture and Society*, 19, 3 (1994); Ruth Frankenberg, *White Women, Race Matters*, Minneapolis: University of Minnesota Press, 1990; and Sarita Srivasta, "'Are You Calling Me a Racist?'" The Moral and Emotional Regulation of Antiracism and Feminism," *Signs: Journal of Women in Culture and Society*, 31, 1 (2005): 29–62.

19. See, Jennifer L. Pierce, "Traveling From Feminism to Mainstream Sociology and Back: One Woman's Tale of Tenure and the Politics of Backlash, *Qualitative Sociology*, 26, 3 (Fall 2003): 369–396.

20. Thanks to Teresa Gowan for reminding me of this point. For examples from *The New York Times* paperback best-seller list in the trade press on American authors, see titles such as *Water for Elephants, Private, Heart of the Matter, The Art of Racing in the Rain, The Postmistress,* and *The Island* (*New York Times Book Review*, April 3, 2011, p. 29). All these best-selling novels focus on family and personal relationships. The exceptions, such as Abraham Verghese's *Cutting for Stone* and Stieg Larsson's *The Girl Who Played with Fire*, are written by novelists from other nations.

21. Jane Flax, "The End of Innocence," in *Disputed Subjects: Essays on Psychoanalysis, Politics and Philosophy*, New York: Routledge, 1993.

22. Aida Hurtado, "The Trickster's Play: Whiteness in the Subordination and Liberation Process," in Rudolfo Torres, Louis Mirón, and Jonathan Inda, eds., *Race, Identity, and Citizenship: A Reader*, Malden, MA: Blackwell, 1999, p. 226

23. For examples in American Studies, see Robert Bellah, et al., *Habits of the Heart: Individualism and Commitment in American Life*, Berkeley and Los Angeles: University of California Press, 1985; and David Noble, *Death of a Nation: American Culture and the End of Exceptionalism*, Minneapolis: University of Minnesota Press, 2002. Among sociologists, see Susan Chase, *Learning to Speak, Learning to Listen: How Diversity Works on Campus*, Ithaca, NY: Cornell University Press, 2010, and *Ambiguous Empowerment: The Work Narratives of Women School Superintendents*, Amherst: University of Massachusetts Press, 1995.

24. Haruki Murakami, *What I Think About When I Talk About Running*, New York: Vintage Books, 2008, p. 79.

25. For exceptions in scholarship in anthropology that focus on developing the personality of one individual, see Ruth Behar, *Translated Woman: Crossing the Border with Esperanza's Story*, Boston: Beacon Press, 1993; and Vincent Crapanzano, *The Hamadsha: A Study on European Ethnopsychiatry*, Berkeley; University of California Press, 1981.

26. Robert Olen Butler, *From Where You Dream: The Process of Writing Fiction*, New York: Grove Press, 2005.

27. Thanks to Teresa Gowan for facilitating my discussion of this distinction.

28. As Macarena Gómez-Barris and Herman Gray argue, alternative methods are often needed to apprehend social worlds that are not attainable through conventional disciplinary methods. See Macarena Gómez-Barris and Herman Gray "Toward a Sociology of the Trace," in Herman Gray and Macarena Gómez-Barris, eds., *Toward a Sociology of the Trace*, Minneapolis: University of Minnesota Press, 2010.

Bibliography

Abu-Lughod, Lila. "Writing Against Culture," in Richard Fox, ed., *Recapturing Anthropology: Working in the Present*, Santa Fe, NM: School of American Research, University of Washington Press, 1991.

Acker, Joan. *Class Questions, Feminist Answers*, Lanham, MD: Rowman & Littlefield, 2006.

Adarand Constructors, Inc. v. Pena 515 U.S. 200 (1995).

Adelson, Joseph. Book review of *Invisible Victims*, *Academic Questions*, 4, 1 (Winter 1990–1991): 90–93.

Adorno, Theodore. *The Authoritarian Personality*, New York: Harper, 1950.

"Affirmative Action," commentary by Tom Brokaw on *NBC Nightly News*, July 19, 1995.

"Affirmative Action Levels the Playing Field," editorial, *New York Times*, November 25, 1995.

"Affirmative Action No Longer Needed," *Arizona Republic*, October 26, 2010, A1.

"Affirmative Action Showdown: UC Regents Seem Poised to End Preferences, *San Francisco Chronicle*, July 20, 1995, A1.

Aikau, Hokulani, Karla Erickson, and Jennifer L. Pierce. "Introduction: Feminist Waves, Feminist Generations," in Hokulani Aikau, Karla Erickson, and Jennifer L. Pierce, eds., *Feminist Waves, Feminist Generations*, Minneapolis: University of Minnesota Press, 2007.

Aitken, Jonathan. *John Newton: From Disgrace to Amazing Grace*, Wheaton, IL: Crossway Books, 2007.

Anderson, Lisa. "Women Escape Affirmative Action Feud," *Chicago Tribune*, May 16, 1995, 1.

Anderson, Terry. *The Pursuit of Fairness: A History of Affirmative Action*, New York: Oxford University Press, 2005.

Angrosino, Michael. "The Two Lives of Rebecca Levenstone: Symbolic Interaction in the Generation of the Life History, *Journal of Anthropological Research*, 45, 3 (1989): 315–326.

Anzúldua, Gloria, ed. *Making Face, Making Soul/Haciendo Caras: Creative and Critical Perspectives by Feminists of Color*, San Francisco: Aunt Lute Books, 1990.

Applebome, Peter. "The Debate on Diversity in California Shifts," *New York Times*, June 4, 1995, sec. 1, A1.

Associated Press. "Affirmative Action Should Focus on Poor People, Gingrich Says," *New York Times*, June 17, 1995, sec. 1, 9.

———. "Reverse Discrimination Complaints Rare, Labor Study Reports," *New York Times*, March 31, 1995, A23.

Bailyn, Lotte. *Breaking the Mold*, Ithaca, NY: Cornell University Press, 1993.

Ball, Howard. *The Bakke Case: Race, Education and Affirmative Action*, Lawrence, KS: University of Kansas Press, 2000.

Barker, Kathleen, and Kathleen Christiansen. *Contingent Work: American Employment Relations in Transition*, Ithaca, NY: Cornell University Press, 1998.

Bauman, Zygmunt. *Intimations of Postmodernity*, New York: Routledge, 1992.

Becket, Jamie. "White Firefighters Say San Jose Rigged Examination, Suit Claims Test Favored Minorities," *San Francisco Chronicle*, July 28, 1995, A1.

Behar, Ruth. *Translated Woman: Crossing the Border with Esperanza's Story*, Boston: Beacon Press, 1993.

Beitch, Herman. "Letter to the Editor," *San Francisco Chronicle*, May 13, 1995.

Bell, Daniel. *The Coming of Post-Industrial Society*, New York: Basic Books, 1973.

Bell, Derrick. *And We Are Not Saved: The Elusive Quest for Racial Justice*, New York: Basic Books, 1987.

———. *Faces at the Bottom of the Well: The Permanence of Racism*, New York: Basic Books, 1992.

———. *Race, Racism, and the Law*, 4th edition, New York: Aspen Press, 2000.

Bell, Joyce, and Doug Hartmann. "Diversity in Everyday Discourse: The Cultural Ambiguities and Consequences of 'Happy Talk,'" *American Sociological Review*, 72, 6 (2007): 895–914.

Bellah, Robert, Richard Madsen, William Sullivan, Ann Swidler, and Steven Tipton. *Habits of the Heart: Individualism and Commitment in American Life*, Berkeley and Los Angeles: University of California Press, 1985.

Bennet, James. "Clinton, at Race Forum, Is Confronted on Affirmative Action," *New York Times*, July 9, 1998, A23.

———. "Clinton Debates 9 Conservatives on Racial Issues," *New York Times*, December 20, 1997, A1.

Bennet, W. Lance. *News: The Politics of Illusion*, New York: Longman Press, 1983.

———, and Robert Entman, eds. *Mediated Politics: Communication and the Future of Democracy*, New York: Cambridge University Press, 2001.

Bernstein, Richard. "Racial Discrimination or Righting Past Wrongs?" *New York Times*, July 13, 1994, B8.

Bhabha, Homi. "'The Other Question'... Homi K. Bhabha Reconsiders the Stereotype and Colonial Discourse," *Screen*, 24.6 (1983): 19–36.

Blackwell, James. *Mainstreaming Outsiders: The Production of Black Professionals*, Rowman & Littlefield, 1981.

Blair, Anita. "Shattering the Myth of the Glass Ceiling," *Los Angeles Times*, May 7, 1996, B7.

———, and Gary Reynolds, "The Big Lie About Discrimination," *Washington Times*, November 6, 1997.

Blair-Loy, Mary. *Competing Devotions: Career and Family Among Women Executives*, Cambridge, MA: Harvard University Press, 2005.

Blank, Renee, and Sandra Slip. "White Male: An Endangered Species?" *Management Review* (September 1994): 28–32.

Bluestone, Barry, and Bennett Harrison. *The Deindustrialization of America: Plant Closings, Community Abandonment, and the Dismantling of Basic Industry*, New York: Basic Books, 1982.

Bobo, Lawrence. "Race and Beliefs About Affirmative Action: Assessing the Effects of Interests, Group Threat, Ideology, and Racism," in David O. Sears, Jim Sidanius, and Lawrence Bobo, eds., *Racialized Politics: The Debate about Racism in America*, Chicago: University of Chicago Press, 2000, 137–164.

———. "Race, Interests, and Beliefs About Affirmative Action," *American Behavioral Scientist*, 41 (April 1998): 985–1003.

Bonilla-Silva, Eduardo. *Racism Without Racists: Color-Blind Racism and the Persistence of Racial Inequality in the United States*, New York: Rowman & Littlefield, 2003.

Boudreau, John. "Effort to Outlaw Affirmative Action Promoted in California," *Washington Post*, December 27, 1990, A3.

Bowen, William, and Derek Bok. *The Shape of the River: Long-Term Consequences of Considering Race in College and University Admissions*, Princeton, NJ: Princeton University Press, 1998.

Bragg, Rick. "Affirmative Action: One City's Experience; Fighting Bias with Bias and Leaving a Rift," *New York Times*, August 21, 1995, A1.

Brodkin, Karen. *How the Jews Became White Folks and What This Says About Race in America*, New York: Routledge, 1999.

Bronner, Ethan. "Study Strongly Supports AA in Admission to Elite Colleges," *New York Times*, September 9, 1998, B10.

Brown, Michael. *Race, Money, and the Welfare State*, Ithaca, NY: Cornell University Press, 1999.

Brown, Michael, Martin Carnoy, Elliot Curie, Troy Duster, David Oppenheimer, Marjorie Schultz, and David Wellman, eds. *White-Washing Race: The Myth of a Color-Blind Society*, Berkeley and Los Angeles: University of California Press, 2003.

Brown, Wendy. *States of Injury: Power and Freedom in Late Modernity*, Princeton, NJ: Princeton University Press, 1995.

Burawoy, Michael, Alice Burton, Ann Arnett Ferguson, and Kathryn J. Fox. *Ethnography Unbound: Power and Resistance in the Modern Metropolis*, Berkeley and Los Angeles: University of California Press, 1991.

Butler, Robert Olen. *From Where You Dream: The Process of Writing Fiction*, New York: Grove Press, 2005.

Bystydzienski, Jill, and Sharon Bird, eds. *Removing Barriers: Women in Academic Science, Technology, Engineering, and Mathematics*, Bloomington: Indiana University Press, 2006.

Calvert, Linda McGee, and V. Jean Ramsey. "Speaking as Female and White: A Non-Dominant/Dominant Group Standpoint," *Organization*, 3, 4 (1996): 468–485.

Chambliss, Elizabeth. "Miles to Go: The Progress of Minorities in the Legal Profession," American Bar Association report, accessed on October 10, 2010, from http://www.law.harvard.edu/programs/plp/pdf/Projects_MilesToGo.pdf

Chase, Susan. *Ambiguous Empowerment: The Work Narratives of Women School Superintendents*, Amherst: University of Massachusetts Press, 1995.

———. *Learning to Speak, Learning to Listen: How Diversity Works on Campus*, Ithaca, NY: Cornell University Press, 2010.

Chávez, Lydia. *The Color Bind: California's Battle to End Affirmative Action*, Berkeley and Los Angeles: University of California Press, 1998.

Chodorow, Nancy J. *The Power of Feelings: Personal Meaning in Psychoanalysis, Gender, and Culture*, New Haven, CT: Yale University Press, 1999.

Citizens United v. Federal Election Commission 558 U.S. 08-205 (2010).

City of Richmond v. J. A. Croson Co. 488 U.S. 469 (1988).

Cobble, Dorothy Sue. *The Other Women's Movement: Workplace Justice and Social Rights in Modern America*, Princeton, NJ: Princeton University Press, 2004.

"College by the Numbers," editorial, *New York Times*, December 24, 1990.

Collins, Patricia Hill. *Black Feminist Thought, Knowledge, Consciousness, and the Politics of Empowerment*, New York: Routledge, 1990.

———. *Black Sexual Politics*, New York: Routledge, 2004.

Collins, Sharon. *Black Corporate Executives: The Making and Breaking of a Black Middle Class*, Philadelphia: Temple University Press, 1996.

Comacho, Lisa Marie. "The People of California Are Suffering: The Ideology of White Injury in Discourses of Immigration," *Cultural Values*, 4,4 (October 2000): 389–413.

Conley, Frances. *Walking Out on the Boys*, New York: Farrar, Straus, and Giroux, 1999.

Connell, R. W. *Masculinities*. Berkeley: University of California Press, 1995.

Cook, Blanche Wiesen. *Eleanor Roosevelt, Volume 1, 1884–1933*, New York: Penguin Books, 1992.

Cowie, Jefferson. *Stayin' Alive: The 1970s and the Last Days of the Working Class*, New York: The New Press, 2010.

Crapanzano, Vincent. *The Hamadsha: A Study on European Ethnopsychiatry*, Berkeley: University of California Press, 1981.

———. *Waiting: The Whites of South Africa*, New York: Random House, 1985.

Crosby, Faye. *Affirmative Action Is Dead, Long Live Affirmative Action*, New Haven, CT: Yale University Press, 2004.

———, and Diana Cordova. "Words of Wisdom: Toward an Understanding of Affirmative Action," in Faye Crosby and Cheryl VanDeVeer, eds., *Sex, Race, and Merit: Debating Affirmative Action in Education and Employment*, Ann Arbor: University of Michigan Press, 2000.

Curiel, Barbara Brinson. "My Border Stories: Life Narratives, Interdisciplinarity, and Post-Nationalism in Ethnic Studies," in John Carlos Rowe, ed., *Postnationalist American Studies*, Berkeley: University of California Press, 2000.

"Daily Cal Backs Vote by Regents, Race-Based Criteria Unfair, Students Say," *San Francisco Chronicle*, September 23, 1995.

Dan Clawson. *The Next Upsurge: Labor and New Social Movements*, Ithaca, NY: Cornell University Press, 2003.

Delgado, Gary. *The Rodrigo Chronicles: Conversations About America and Race*, New York: New York University Press, 1995.

DeVault, Marjorie. "Ethnicity and Expertise: Racial-Ethnic Knowledge in Sociological Research," *Liberating Method: Feminism and Social Research*, Philadelphia: Temple University Press, 1999.

DeWitt, Karen. "Job Bias Cited for Minorities and Women," *New York Times*, November 23, 1995, B14.

Dillard, Angela. *Guess Who's Coming to Dinner Now? Multicultural Conservatism in America*, New York: New York University Press, 2001.

"Diversity Project in Texas," editorial, *New York Times*, November 27, 1999.

Dobbin, Frank, and John Sutton. "The Strength of a Weak State: The Rights Revolution and the Rise of Human Resources Management Divisions," *American Journal of Sociology*, 104, 2 (1998): 441–476.

"Don't Forget About White Males," letter to the editor, *San Francisco Chronicle*, November 23, 1994.

Dovidio, John F., John Mann, and Sam L. Gaertner. "Resistance to Affirmative Action: The Implications of Aversive Racism," in Fletcher A. Blanchard and Faye J. Crosby, eds., *Affirmative Action in Perspective*, New York: Springer-Verlag, 1989, 83–97.

Drake, William Avon, and Robert Hosworth. *Affirmative Action and the Stalled Quest for Black Progress*, Urbana: University of Illinois, 1996.

duCille, Ann. "The Occult of True Black Womanhood: Critical Demeanor and Black Feminist Studies," *Signs: Journal of Women in Culture and Society*, 19, 3 (1994).

Duggan, Lisa. *Twilight of Equality: Neoliberalism, Cultural Politics, and the Attack on Democracy*, Boston: Beacon Press, 2003.

Duster, Troy. "Individual Fairness, Group Preferences, and the California Strategy," in Robert Post and Michael Rogin, eds., *Race and Representation: Affirmative Action*, New York: Zone Books, 1998.

Dyson, Eric. "Race, Post Race," opinion, *Los Angeles Times*, November 5, 2008.

Ebert, Roger. "Rocky," *Chicago Sun-Times*, January 1, 1976.

———. Film review of *A Time to Kill*, *Chicago Sun-Times*, July 26, 1996, accessed on November 29, 2011, from http://rogerebert.suntimes.com/apps/pbcs.dll/article?AID=/19960726/REVIEWS/607260302/1023.

Edelman, Laurel. "Legal Ambiguity and Symbolic Structures: Organizational Mediation of Civil Rights Law," *American Journal of Sociology*, 97, 6 (1992): 1531–1576.

———, Christopher Uggen, and Howard S. Erlanger. "The Endogeneity of Legal Regulation: Grievance Procedures as Rational Myth," *American Journal of Sociology*, 105, 2 (1999): 406–454.

———, Sally Riggs Fuller, and Sharon F. Matusik. "Legal Readings: Employee Interpretation and Enactment of Civil Rights Law," *Academy of Management Review*, 25, 1 (January 2000): 200–216.

Edley, Christopher. *Not All Black and White: Affirmative Action and American Values*, New York: Hill and Wang, 1998.

Edsall, Thomas, and Mary Edsall. *Chain Reaction: The Impact of Race, Rights, and Taxes on American Politics*, New York: Norton, 1992.

Ehrenreich, Barbara, and Arlie R. Hochschild. "Introduction" in Barbara Ehrenreich and Arlie R. Hochschild, eds., *Global Woman: Nannies, Maids, and Sex Workers in the New Economy*, New York: Henry Holt, 2002.

Ellis, Carolyn. *The Ethnographic I: A Methodological Novel About Autoethnography*, Walnut Creek, CA: Altamira Press, 2006.

———. *Revisions: Autoethnographic Reflections on Life and Work*, Walnut Creek, CA: Left Coast Press, 2008.

Entman, Robert, and Andrew Rojeki. *The Black Image in the White Mind: Media and Race in America*, Chicago: University of Chicago Press, 2000.

Epstein, Cynthia Fuchs, Carroll Seron, Bonnie Oglensky, and Robert Sauté. *The Part-Time Paradox: Time Norms, Professional Life, Family and Gender*, New York: Routledge, 1998.

Epstein, Edward, and Henry Lee. "UC Students Rally for Affirmative Action, Thousands Skip Classes, Some Clash with Police," *San Francisco Chronicle*, October 13, 1995, A1.

Epstein, Edward, and Susan Yoacham. "Affirmative Action Showdown: UC Regents Seem Poised to End Preferences," *San Francisco Chronicle*, July 20, 1995, A1.

Essed, Philomena. *Understanding Racism in Everyday Life: An Interdisciplinary Theory*, London: Sage, 1991.

Faludi, Susan. *Stiffed: The Betrayal of American Men*, New York: Morrow, 1999.

Feagin, Joe, and Eileen O'Brien. *White Men on Race: Power, Privilege, and the Shaping of Cultural Consciousness*, Boston: Beacon, 2004.

Fellows, Mary Louise, and Sherene H. Razack. "Seeking Relations: Law and Feminism Roundtables," *Signs: Journal of Women in Culture and Society*, 19, 4 (1994): 1048–1083.

Ferber, Abby. *White Man Falling*, New York: Rowman & Littlefield, 1998.

Ferguson, Roderick A. *Aberrations in Black: Toward a Queer of Color Critique*, Minneapolis: University of Minnesota Press, 2004.

Fine, Michelle, Lois Weiss, Judi Addleston, and Julia Marusza. "(In)secure Times: Constructing White Working-Class Masculinities in the Late Twentieth Century," *Gender & Society*, 11, 1 (February 1997): 52–68.

Fish, Stanley. *Is There a Text in This Class? The Authority of Interpretive Communities*, Cambridge, MA: Harvard University Press, 1980.

Fix, Michael, and Margery Turner. *A National Report Card on Discrimination in America*, Washington, DC: Urban Institute, 1998.

Flax, Jane. "The End of Innocence," in *Disputed Subjects: Essays on Psychoanalysis, Politics and Philosophy*, New York: Routledge, 1993.

Flynn, Kevin. "Coloradans Preserve Affirmative Action," *Rocky Mountain News*, November 6, 2008.

Ford, Gerald. "Inclusive America, Under Attack," editorial, *New York Times*, August 8, 1999, sec. 4, 15.

Frank, Geyla. "Becoming the Other: Empathy and Biographical Interpretation," *Biography*, 8, 3 (1989): 189–210.

Frank, Thomas. *What's the Matter with Kansas? How Conservatives Won the Heart of America*, New York: Metropolitan Books, 2004.

Frankenberg, Ruth. *White Women, Race Matters*, Minneapolis: University of Minnesota Press, 1990.

Freud, Sigmund. "Screen Memories," in James Strachey, ed. and trans., *The Standard Edition of the Complete Works of Sigmund Freud, Volume 3*, London: Hogarth Press, 1963 [1899], 301–322.

Fried, Mindy. *Taking Time: Parental Leave Policy and Corporate Culture*, Philadelphia: Temple University Press, 1998.

Friedman, Susan Stanford. "Beyond White and Other: Relationality and Narratives of Race in Feminist Discourse," *Signs: Journal of Women in Culture and Society*, 21, 1 (1995).

Fusco, Coco. *English Is Broken Here: Notes on Cultural Fusion in the Americas*, New York: New Press, 1995.

Gabriel, Teshome. "Third Cinema as Guardian of Popular Memory: Towards a Third Aesthetics," in Jim Pines and Paul Wellemen, eds., *Questions of Third Cinema*, London: British Film Institute, 1989, 53–64.

Gallagher, Charles. "Transforming Racial Identity Through Affirmative Action," in Rodney Coates, ed., *Race and Ethnicity: Across Time, Space and Discipline*, Boston: Brill Publishers, 2004.

———. "White Reconstruction in the University," *Socialist Review*, 24, 1-2 (1995): 165–185.

Gamson, William A. *Talking Politics*, Boston: Cambridge University Press, 1992.

Geiger, Susan. *TANU Women: Gender and Culture in the Making of Tanganyikan Nationalism, 1955–1965*, Portsmouth, NH: Heineman Press, 1997.

Golub, Mark. "History Died for Our Sins: Guilt and Responsibility in Hollywood Redemption History," *Journal of American Culture*, 213 (1998): 23.

Goméz-Barris, Macarena, and Herman Gray. "Toward a Sociology of the Trace," in Herman Gray and Macarena Goméz-Barris, eds., *Toward a Sociology of the Trace*, Minneapolis: University of Minnesota Press, 2010.

Gordon, Avery. *Ghostly Matters: Haunting and the Sociological Imagination*, Minneapolis: University of Minnesota Press, 1998.

Gordon, Linda. *Pitied But Not Entitled: Single Mothers and the History of Welfare*, Cambridge, MA: Harvard University Press, 1998.

Gorman, Elizabeth, and Fiona Kay. "Racial and Ethnic Minority Representation in Large U.S. Law Firms," *Studies in Law, Politics, and Society*, 52 (2010): 211–238.

Gramsci, Antonio. *Selections from the Prison Notebooks*, ed. and trans. by Quintin Hoare and Geoffrey Nowell Smith, New York: International Publishers, 1971.

Gratz v. Bollinger 539 U.S. 244 (2003).

Green, Luke. "AIG Cites Wal-Mart Decision in Attempt to Block Class Action Certification," *Securities Litigation*, August 23, 2011, accessed on August 29, 2011, from http://blog.issgovernance.com/slw/2011/08/aig-cites-wal-mart-decision-in-attempt-to-challenge-class-cetification.html

Greenhouse, Linda. "In Step with Racial Policy," *New York Times*, June 14, 1995, A1.

Grimsely, Kirstin. "Panel Asks Why Women Still Earn Less," *Washington Post*, June 9, 2000, E3.

Gross, Jane. "Big Grocery Store Chain Reaches Landmark Sex-Bias Accord," *New York Times*, December 17, 1993, A8.

Grutter v. Bollinger 539 U.S. 306 (2003).

Guinier, Lani. *Lift Every Voice: Turning Civil Rights Setbacks into a New Vision*, New York: Simon & Schuster, 2003.

———, and Gerald Torres. *The Miner's Canary: Enlisting Race, Resisting Power, Transforming Democracy*, Cambridge, MA: Harvard University Press, 2002.

Gurin, Patricia, Jeffrey Lehman, and Earl Lewis. *Defending Diversity: Affirmative Action at the University of Michigan*, Ann Arbor: University of Michigan Press, 2004.

Hairston, Loyle. "What Feminism Has Done to the Workplace; Welcome to the Battle," editorial desk, *New York Times*, March 24, 1995.

Hall, Stuart. "What is This 'Black' in Black Popular Culture?" *Social Justice*, 20 (1993): 104–114.

Halloran, Liz. "Affirmative-Action Case Could be Campaign Issue," National Public Radio, October 5, 2011, accessed on January 13, 2012, from http://www.npr .org/2011/10/05/141052635/affirmative-action-case-could-be-campaign-issue?ft=1&f=1003.

Haraway, Donna. "Situated Knowledges: The Science Question in Feminism as a Site of Discourse on the Privilege of Partial Perspective," *Feminist Studies*, 14, 3 (1988).

Harding, Sandra. *Whose Science? Whose Knowledge?* Ithaca, NY: Cornell University Press, 1991.

"Harmful Split Between UC Regents and Faculty," editorial, *San Francisco Chronicle*, December 9, 1995, A20.

Harris, Cheryl. "Whiteness as Property," *Harvard Law Review*, 106, 8: 1709–1791.

Hart, Gillian. *Disabling Globalization: Places of Power in Post-Apartheid South Africa*, Berkeley and Los Angeles: University of California Press, 2001.

Hartigan, John. *Racial Situations: Class Predicaments of Whiteness in Detroit*, Princeton, NJ: Princeton University Press, 1999.

Harvey, David. *The New Imperialism*. New York: Oxford University Press, 2003.

Hegel, G. W. F. *The Phenomenology of Spirit*, trans. by A. V. Miller. Oxford, UK: Clarendon Press, 1977 [1807].

Heinz, John, Robert Nelson, Rebecca Sandefur, and Ed Laumann. *Urban Lawyers: The New Social Structure of the Bar*, Chicago: University of Chicago Press, 2005.

Herbert, Bob. "In America: The Wrong Target," editorial desk, *New York Times*, April 5, 1995, A23.

Herring, Cedric. "African Americans, the Public Policy Agenda, and the Paradoxes of Public Policy," in Cedric Herring, ed., *African Americans and the Public Agenda: The Paradoxes of Public Policy*, Thousand Oaks, CA: Sage, 1997, 3–27.

Hertz, Rosanna, and Jonathan Imber, eds. *Studying Elites Using Qualitative Methods*, Thousand Oaks, CA: Sage, 1995.

Herzenberg, Stephen, John Alic, and Howard Wial, *New Rules for a New Economy: Employment and Opportunity in Postindustrial America*, Ithaca, NY: Cornell University Press, 1998.

Hewitt, Chris. Film review of *Ghosts of Mississippi*, accessed on April 27, 2011, from http://lubbockonline.com/news/010397/movie.htm

Higginbotham, Elizabeth. *Too Much to Ask: Black Women in the Era of Integration*, Chapel Hill: University of North Carolina Press, 2001.

————, and Lynn Weber. "Perceptions of Workplace Discrimination Among Black and White Professional Managerial Women," in Irene Browne, ed., *Latinas and African American Women at Work*, New York: Sage, 1999.

Ho, Karen. *Liquidated: An Ethnography of Wall Street*, Durham, NC: Duke University Press, 2009.

Hochschild, Arlie R. "Making It: Marginality and Obstacles to Minority Consciousness," in Ruth Kundsin, ed., *Women and Success: The Anatomy of Achievement*, New York: William Morrow, 1974.

————. *The Time Bind: When Work Becomes Home and Home Becomes Work*, New York: Holt, 2001.

Holding, Reynolds. "Gains for Minority Attorneys in SF: But They Cite Frustration of Institutional Racism . . ." *San Francisco Chronicle*, December 21, 1993, A18.

Holmes, Steven A. "Defending Affirmative Action, Liberals Try to Place Debate's Focus on Women," *New York Times*, March 2, 1995, B7.

Honan, William. "Admission Change Will Alter Elite Campuses, Experts Say," *New York Times*, July 22, 1995, 7.

————. "Regents Prepare for Storm on Affirmative Action," *New York Times*, July 19, 1995, A1.

Hopwood v. Texas 78 Fed 3d 932 (5th Cir. 1996).

Hunter, Tera. *To 'Joy My Freedom: Southern Black Women's Lives and Labors After the Civil War*, Cambridge, MA: Harvard University Press, 1997.

Hurtado, Aida. "The Trickster's Play: Whiteness in the Subordination and Liberation Process," in Rudolfo D. Torres, Louis F. Mirón, and Jonathan Xavier Inda, eds., *Race, Identity, and Citizenship: A Reader*, Malden, MA: Blackwell, 1999.

Ingraham, Laura. "Enter, Women," *New York Times*, April 19, 1995.

————. "Why Are Women Endorsing Bias?" *Florida Sun-Sentinel*, May 1, 1995, 9A.

Internet Movie Data Base, accessed on April 27, 2011 from http://www.imdb.com/

Internet Movie Database, Road to the Oscars, "Awards for Rocky," accessed on January 24, 2012, from http://www.imdb.com/title/tt0075148/awards

Jacobson, Matthew Frye. *Roots Too: White Ethnic Revival in Post-Civil Rights America*, Cambridge, MA: Harvard University Press, 2006.

————. *Whiteness of a Different Color: European Immigrants and the Alchemy of Race*, Cambridge, MA: Harvard University Press, 1999.

Jaschik, Scott. "10 Percent Plan Survives in Texas," *Inside Higher Education*, May 29, 2007, accessed on July 26, 2011, from http://www.insidehighered.com/news/2007/05/29/percent.

————. "Arizona Bans Affirmative Action," *Inside Higher Education*, November 3, 2010, accessed on July 16, 2011, from http://www.insidehighered.com/news/2010/11/03/arizona.

Jason, Sonya. ". . . That's My Son," *Wall Street Journal*, March 27, 1995, A20.

Jones, Jacqueline. *Labor of Love, Labor of Sorrow*, New York: Vintage, 1986.

Kanter, Rosabeth Moss. *Men and Women of the Corporation*, New York: Basic Books, 1977.

Karen, David. "'Achievement' and 'Ascription' in Admission to an Elite College: A Political-Organizational Analysis," *Sociological Forum*, 6 (1999).

Katznelson, Ira. *When Affirmative Action Was White: An Untold History of Racial Inequality in Twentieth-Century America*, New York: Norton, 2005.

Kelly, Erin, Samantha Ammons, Kelly Chermack, and Phyllis Moen. "Gendered Challenge, Gendered Response: Confronting the Ideal Worker Norm in a White-Collar Organization, *Gender & Society*, 22, 6 (2008): 281–303.

Kennelly, Ivy. "'That Single Mother Element': How White Employers Typify Black Women," *Gender & Society*, 13, 2 (April 1999): 168–192.

Kilborn, Peter. "For Many in Work Force, 'Glass Ceiling' Still Exists," *New York Times*, March 15, 1995, A22.

———. "A Leg Up on Ladder, But Still Far from Top," *New York Times*, June 16, 1995, A1.

Kirscheman, Joleen, and Kathryn Neckerman. "We'd Love to Hire Them, But . . . : The Meaning of Race for Employers," in Christopher Jencks and Paul Peterson, eds., *The Urban Underclass*, Washington, DC: Brookings Institution, 1991.

Kochhar, Rakesh, Richard Fry, and Paul Taylor. "Wealth Gaps Rise to Record Highs Between Whites, Blacks, and Hispanics: Twenty to One," *PEW Social and Demographic Trends*, July 26, 2011.

Krieger, Susan. *Social Science and the Self: Personal Essays on an Art Form*, New Brunswick, NJ: Rutgers University Press, 1990.

Ladowsky, Ellen. "That's No White Male, That's My Husband," *Woman's Quarterly*, 1, 22 (Spring 1995).

———. "That's No White Male, That's My Husband," *Wall Street Journal*, March 27, 1995, A20.

Lamont, Michele. *The Dignity of Working Men: Morality and the Boundaries of Race, Class and Immigration*, Cambridge, MA: Harvard University Press, 2000.

———. ed. *The Cultural Territories of Race: Black and White Boundaries*, Chicago: University of Chicago Press, 1999.

Larson, Elizabeth. "Women Don't Need Extra Help," *Insight*, April 24, 1995, 18.

Lasch-Quinn, Elizabeth. *Race Experts: How Racial Etiquette, Sensitivity Training, and New Age Therapy Hijacked the Civil Rights Movement*, New York: Norton, 2001.

Laslett, Barbara. "Unfeeling Knowledge: Emotion and Objectivity in the Sociology of Knowledge," *Sociological Forces*, 5 (1990): 413–433.

Lee, Jennifer, *Civility in the City: Blacks, Jews, and Koreans in Urban America*, Cambridge, MA: Harvard University Press, 2002.

———, and Frank Bean. *The Diversity Paradox: Immigration and the Color Line in 21st Century America*, New York: Russell Sage Foundation, 2010.

Lehmann, Nicholas. "California, Here We Come . . . ?" *TIME*, October 7, 1996.

Lempinen, Edward. "Protesters, Police Skirmish as Duke Debates CCRI," *San Francisco Chronicle*, September 26, 1996, A1.

Lewis, Earl. "Why History Remains a Factor in the Search for Racial Equality," in Patricia Gurin, Jeffrey S. Lehman, and Earl Lewis, eds., *Defending Diversity: Affirmative Action at the University of Michigan*, Ann Arbor: University of Michigan Press, 2004, 51.

Lewis, Michael. *The Big Short: Inside the Doomsday Machine*, New York: W. W. Norton, 2010.

Lipsitz, George. *The Possessive Investment in Whiteness: How White People Benefit from Identity Politics*, Philadelphia: Temple University Press, 1998.

Liptak, Adam. "College Diversity Nears Its Last Stand," *New York Times*, October 16, 2011.

Long, Judy. *Telling Women's Lives: Subject, Narrator, Reader, Text*, New York: New York University Press, 1999.

Longino, Helen. *Science as Social Knowledge: Values and Objectivity in Scientific Inquiry*, Princeton, NJ: Princeton University Press, 1990.

Lopez, Haney. *White By Law: The Legal Construction of Race*, New York: New York University Press, 2000.

Lott, Eric. *Love and Theft: Blackface Minstrelsy and the American Working Class*, New York: Oxford University Press, 1995.

Lowe, Lisa. *Immigrant Acts: On Asian American Cultural Politics*, Durham, NC: Duke University Press, 1996.

Lu, Benjamin. "Letter to the Editor," *New York Times*, September 18, 1998, A28.

"Lucky's Sex Discrimination Lawsuit—Women Win Big Damages," *New York Times*, December 17, 1993.

Lynch, Frederick. *Invisible Victims: White Males and the Crisis of Affirmative Action*, New York: Praeger, 1991 [1989].

———. "Surviving Affirmative Action (More or Less)," *Commentary* (August 1990): 44–47.

———, and William Beers, "'You Ain't The Right Color, Pal': White Resentment of Affirmative Action," *Policy Review*, 51 (Winter 1990): 64–67.

MacLean, Nancy. *Freedom is Not Enough: The Opening of the American Workplace*, Cambridge, MA: Harvard University Press, 2006.

Madson, Kelly. "Legitimation Crisis and Containment: The 'Anti-Racist-White-Hero,'" *Critical Studies in Mass Communication*, 16, 4 (1999): 399–416.

Manley, Theodoric. "Teaching Race and Ethnic Relations: Do the Right Thing," *Ethnic and Racial Studies*, 17, 1 (January 1994): 134–163.

Marshall, Jonathan. "Don't Tie Anger to Low Wages / Experts Debunk Conventional Wisdom on the 'Angry White Male' View," *San Francisco Chronicle*, May 29, 1995, D1.

Martin, Patricia Yancey. "'Said and Done' vs. 'Saying and Doing': Gendered Practices, Practicing Gender at Work," *Gender & Society*, 17, 4 (2003): 342–366.

Marx, Leo. *The Machine and the Garden*, New York: Oxford University Press, 1964.

Maslin, Janet. "A Father's Revenge for His Daughter's Rape," film review in *The New York Times*, July 24, 1996, accessed on April 28, 2011, from http://movies.nytimes .com/movie/review?res=9C03EED81639F937A15754C0A960958260.

Massey, Doug, and Julie Denton. *American Apartheid: Segregation and the Making of the Underclass*, Cambridge, MA: Harvard University Press, 1993.

Maynes, Mary Jo. "Autobiography and Class Formation in Nineteenth-Century Europe: Methodological Considerations," *Social Science History*, 16, 3 (1992): 523.

———, Jennifer L. Pierce, and Barbara Laslett. *Telling Stories: The Use of Personal Narratives in the Social Sciences and in History*, Ithaca, NY: Cornell University Press, 2008.

McCombs, Phil. "White Guys; Their Issues Are Guns and Butter. They've Had It with Democrats. Here's an Earful," *Washington Post*, November 22, 1994, D1.

McDermott, Monica. *Working-Class White: The Making and Unmaking of Race Relations*, Berkeley and Los Angeles: University of California Press, 2006.

McGirr, Lisa. *Suburban Warriors: The Origins of the New American Right*, Princeton, NJ: Princeton University Press, 2002.

McLeod, Ramon. "Family Ties Help Explain Why Women Are Split, Many Worried About Husbands' Jobs," *San Francisco Chronicle*, March 31, 1995, A4.

———. "White Men's Eroding Economic Clout Contributes to Backlash," *San Francisco Chronicle*, March 20, 1995, A7.

"Milestones in Loft History," accessed on March 26, 2011, from https://www.loft.org/ about/history.

Milkman, Ruth, ed. *Organizing Immigrants: The Challenge for Unions in Contemporary California*, Ithaca, NY: Cornell University Press, 2000.

———, and Kim Voss, eds. *Rebuilding Labor: Organizing and Organizers in the New Union Movement*, Ithaca, NY: Cornell University Press, 2004.

Miller, Perry. *The New England Mind*, Boston: Beacon Press, 1961.

Mink, Gwendolyn. *The Wages of Motherhood: Inequality in the Welfare State, 1917–1942*, Ithaca, NY: Cornell University Press, 1996.

"Minority Fresh Enrollment at UCB Up," *New York Times*, December 1, 1999.

Moody, Kim. *An Injury to All: The Decline of American Unionism*, London: Verso, 1988.

Moore, Teresa. "Black and White Youths in '2 Different Worlds,'" *San Francisco Chronicle*, January 14, 1993, B8.

———. "Taking NOW into the Future, Patricia Ireland, President of NOW," *San Francisco Chronicle*, April 21, 1996, 3/Z3.

Moore, Wendy Leo. *Reproducing Racism: White Space, Elite Law Schools, and Racial Inequality*, Lanham, MD: Rowman & Littlefield, 2008.

———, and Jennifer L. Pierce. "Still Killing Mockingbirds: Race and Innocence in Hollywood's Depiction of the White Messiah Lawyer," *Qualitative Sociology Review*, III, 2 (August 2007): 171–187.

Moreton, Bethany. *To Serve God and Wal-Mart: The Making of Christian Free Enterprise*, Cambridge, MA: Harvard University Press, 2009.

Moss, Peter. *Childcare and Equality of Opportunity, Consolidated Report of the European Childcare Network EEC*, Brussels: European Commission, 1988.

———. *Childcare in European Communities, 1985–1990*, London: Commission of the European Communities, 1990.

Mouton, Michelle, and Helena Pohlandt-McCormick. "Boundary Crossings: Oral History of Nazi Germany and Apartheid South Africa—A Comparative Perspective," *Radical History Workshop Journal*, 48 (1999): 41–63.

Mukherjee, Roopali. *The Racial Order of Things: Cultural Imaginaries of the Post-Soul Era*, Minneapolis: University of Minnesota Press, 2006.

Mulvey, Laura. *Visual and Other Pleasures,* New York: Palgrave Macmillan, 2009.

Murakami, Haruki. *What I Think About When I Talk About Running*, New York: Vintage Books, 2008, 79.

Murphy, Ryan Patrick. "The Gay Land Rush: Race, Gender, and Sexuality in Post-Welfare Minneapolis," in Twin Cities GLBT Oral History Project, eds., *Queer Twin Cities*, Minneapolis: University of Minnesota Press, 2010.

———. "On Our Own: Flight Attendant Activism and the Family Values Economy," Ph.D. dissertation, Department of American Studies, University of Minnesota, 2010.

Mydans, Seth. "A Challenge to the Concept of Disadvantaged," *New York Times*, June 18, 1995, A16.

Myerson, Allen R. "As Federal Bias Cases Drop, Workers Take Up the Fight," *New York Times*, January 12, 1997, sec. 1, 1.

Nader, Laura. "Up the Anthropologists: Perspectives Gained from Studying Up," in Dell Hymes, ed., *Reinventing Anthropology*, New York: Random House, 1972.

Nagourney, Adam. "Obama Elected President as Racial Barriers Fall," *New York Times*, November 5, 2008.

Nelson, Margaret, and Joan Smith. *Working Hard and Making Do*, Ithaca, NY: Cornell University Press, 1999.

"New Law in Texas Preserves Racial Mix," *New York Times*, November 24, 1999.

New York Times Book Review, April 3, 2011, 29.

New York Times, editorial desk, "Affirmative Action Without Fear," September 19, 1994, A16.

New York Times, letter to the editor, July 19, 1998, sec. 6, 8.

New York Times, letter to the editor, September 13, 1998, sec. 4, 20.

Ngai, Mai. *Impossible Subjects: Illegal Aliens and the Making of Modern America*, Princeton, NJ: Princeton University Press, 2004.

Nicholson, Carol. "Three Views of Philosophy and Multiculturalism: Searles, Rorty, and Taylor," *Philosophy and Education* (1998), accessed on November 30, 2010, from http://www.bu.edu/wcp/Papers/Educ/EducNich.htm.

Noble, David. *Death of a Nation: American Culture and the End of Exceptionalism*, Minneapolis: University of Minnesota Press, 2002.

———. *The End of American History: Democracy, Capitalism, and the Metaphor of Two Worlds in Anglo-American Historical Writing, 1890–1980*, Minneapolis: University of Minnesota Press, 1985.

"No Need to Label Court's Ruling on Affirmative Action 'Nutty,'" *Battle Creek Enquirer*, accessed on August 11, 2011, from http://www.battlecreekenquirer.com/article/20110803/OPINION01/108030301/Legitimate-issue?odyssey=mod | new swell | text | Frontpage | s.

Noonan, Mary C., Mary E. Corcoran, and Paul N. Courant. "Is the Partnership Gap Closing for Women? Cohort Differences in the Sex Gap in Partnership Chances," *Social Science Research*, 37 (March 2008).

Norton, Eleanor Holmes. "Affirmative Action in the Workplace," in G. E. Curry, ed., *The Affirmative Action Debate*, Reading, MA: Addison-Wesley, 1996, 39–48.

O'Brien, Ruth. *Telling Stories Out of Court: Narratives about Women and Workplace Discrimination*, Ithaca, NY: Cornell University Press, 2009.

Oliver, Melvin, and Thomas Shapiro. *Black Wealth / White Wealth: A Perspective on Racial Inequality*, New York: Routledge, 2006 [1996].

Ostrander, Susan. *Women of the Upper Class*, Philadelphia: Temple University Press, 1984.

Paap, Kris. *Working Construction: How White Men Put Themselves and the Labor Movement in Danger*, Ithaca, NY: Cornell University Press, 2005.

Paddock, Richard. "Affirmative Action is Over, Says Longtime Foe," *Los Angeles Times*, November 26, 2006.

Pager, Devah, Bruce Western, and Bart Bonikowski. "Discrimination in a Low-Wage Labor Market: A Field Experiment," *American Sociological Review*, 74, 5 (October 2009): 777–799.

Park, Lisa Sunyee. *Consuming Citizenship: Children of Asian Immigrant Entrepreneurs*, Palo Alto, CA: Stanford University Press, 2005.

Pascoe, Peggy. *What Comes Naturally: Miscegenation Law and the Making of Race in America*, New York: Oxford University Press, 2009.

Perry, Pamela. *Shades of White: White Kids and Racial Identities in High School*, Durham, NC: Duke University Press, 2002.

Peterson, Iver. "Justice Officials Clarify Stand in Race-Based Dismissal Case," *New York Times*, September 22, 1994, B6.

Petocz, Jessica. "Power, Struggle, and Oral History," graduate seminar on personal narratives in interdisciplinary research, Department of American Studies, University of Minnesota, Minneapolis, Spring 2010.

Pierce, Jennifer L. *Gender Trials: Emotional Lives in Contemporary Law Firms*, Berkeley and Los Angeles: University of California Press, 1995.

———. "Lawyers, Lethal Weapons, and Ethnographic Authority," in Susan Moch and Marie Gates, eds., *Qualitative Research and the Researcher Experience*, Thousand Oaks, CA: Sage Publications, 2000.

———. "'Not Qualified' or 'Not Committed': A Raced and Gendered Organizational Logic in Large Law Firms," in Reza Bankakar and Max Travers, eds., *An Introduction to Law and Social Theory*, London: Hart, 2003.

———. "'Racing for Innocence': Whiteness, Corporate Culture, and the Backlash Against Affirmative Action," *Qualitative Sociology*, 26, 1 (2003): 53–71.

———. "Reflections on Fieldwork in a Complex Organization," in Rosanna Hertz and Jonathan Imber, eds., *Studying Elites Using Qualitative Methods*, Thousand Oaks, CA: Sage Publications, 1996.

———. "Traveling from Feminism to Mainstream Sociology and Back: One Woman's Tale of Tenure and the Politics of Backlash," *Qualitative Sociology*, 26, 3 (Fall 2003): 369–396.

Pincus, Fred. *Reverse Discrimination: Dismantling the Myth*, Boulder, CO: Lynne Rienner, 2003.

Pollack, Mica. *Colormute: Race Talk Dilemmas in American Schools*, Princeton, NJ: Princeton University Press, 2005.

Post, Robert. "On the Popular Image of Lawyers: Reflections in a Dark Glass," *California Law Review*, 75, 1 (January 1987): 379–389.

Pride, Richard. *The Political Use of Racial Narratives: School Desegregation in Mobile, Alabama, 1954–1997*, Urbana and Chicago: University of Illinois Press, 2002.

Prose, Francine. *Reading Like a Writer: A Guide for People Who Love Books and for Those Who Want to Write Them*, New York: Harper Perennial, 2006.

Raeburn, Nicole. *Changing Corporate America from the Inside Out: Lesbian and Gay Workplace Rights*, Minneapolis: University of Minnesota Press, 2004.

Rasmussen, Birgit Brander, Eric Klineberg, Irene Nexica, and Matt Wray, eds. *The Making and Unmaking of Whiteness*, Durham, NC: Duke University Press, 2001.

Razack, Sherene. *Looking White People in the Eye: Gender, Race, and Culture in Courtrooms and Classrooms*, Toronto: University of Toronto Press, 1998.

———. "Your Place or Mine? Transnational Feminist Collaboration," in Agnes Calliste and George Sefa Dei, eds., *Anti-Racist Feminism: Crucial Race and Gender Studies*, Halifax, NS: Fernwood, 2000.

The Regents of the University of California v. Bakke 438 U.S. 265 (1978).

Reich, Robert B. *The Work of Nations: Preparing Ourselves for 21st Century Capitalism*, New York: Vintage Books, 1991.

Reichman, Nancy, and Joyce Sterling. "Sticky Floors, Broken Steps, and Concrete Ceilings in Legal Careers," *Texas Journal of Women and the Law*, 14, 27 (2004).

Reskin, Barbara F. *The Realities of Affirmative Action in Employment*, Washington, DC: American Sociological Association, 1998.

Richardson, Laurel. "Afterwords: 'Louisa May' and Me," *Fields of Play: Constructing an Academic Life*, New Brunswick, NJ: Rutgers University Press, 1997.

———. *Last Writes: A Daybook About a Dying Friend*, Walnut Creek, CA: Left Coast Press, 2007.

———. "Louisa May's Story of Her Life," *Fields of Play: Constructing an Academic Life*, New Brunswick, NJ: Rutgers University Press, 1997.

Roediger, David. *Colored White: Transcending the Racial Past*, Berkeley and Los Angeles: University of California Press, 2002.

———. *The Wages of Whiteness: Race and the Making of the American Working Class*, New York: Verso, 1991.

Rogers, Jacki. *Temps: The Many Faces of the Changing Workplace*, Ithaca, NY: Cornell University Press, 2000.

Rollins, Judith. *Between Women: Domestics and Their Employers*, Philadelphia: Temple University Press, 1985.

Rosenbaum, David. "White House Revises Policy on Contracts for Minorities," *New York Times*, June 25, 1998, A1.

Ross, Thomas. "The Rhetorical Tapestry of Race: White Innocence and Black Abstraction," *William & Mary Law Review*, 32, 1 (1990).

Roy, Beth. *Bitters in the Honey: Tales of Hope and Disappointment Across Divides of Race and Time*, Fayetteville: University of Arkansas Press, 1999.

Royster, Deirdre. *Race and the Invisible Hand: How Social Networks Exclude Black Men from Blue-Collar Jobs*, Berkeley and Los Angeles: University of California Press, 2003.

Kate Rushin. "The Bridge Poem," in Cherrie Moraga and Gloria Anzúldua, eds., *This Bridge Called My Back: Writings by Radical Women of Color*, San Francisco: Kitchen Table Press, 1984.

Sandefur, Rebecca. "Staying Power: The Persistence of Social Inequality in Shaping Lawyer Stratification and Lawyers' Persistence in the Profession," *Southwestern University Law Review*, 36, 3 (2007).

Sandalow, Marc. "House Panel Cites Glass Ceiling at Fed for Women, Minorities," *San Francisco Chronicle*, December 2, 1993, A8.

Schuman, Howard, Charlotte Steeh, Lawrence Bobo, and Maria Krysan. *Racial Attitudes in America: Trends and Interpretations*, Cambridge, MA: Harvard University Press, 1997, revised edition.

Schwartz, Bernard. *Behind Bakke: Affirmative Action and the Supreme Court*, New York: New York University Press, 1988.

Scott, James. *Weapons of the Weak: Everyday Forms of Peasant Resistance*, New Haven, CT: Yale University Press, 1987.

Searle, John. "The Storm over the University," in Paul Berman, ed., *Debating P.C.: The Controversy over Political Correctness on College Campuses*, New York: Dell, 1992.

Shore, Chris, and Stephen Nugent, eds. *Elite Cultures: Anthropological Perspectives*, London: ASA Monographs, 2002.

Shostak, Marjorie. "What the Wind Won't Take Away: The Genesis of Nisa—The Life and Words of a !Kung Woman," in Personal Narratives Group, ed., *Interpreting Women's Lives: Feminist Theory and Personal Narratives*, Bloomington: University of Indiana Press, 1989.

Sidanius, Jim, Pam Singh, John Hetts, and Chris Feerico. "'It's Not Affirmative Action: It's the Blacks': The Continuing Relevance of Race in American Politics," in David Sears, Jim Sidanius, and Lawrence Bobo, eds., *Racialized Politics: The Debate About Racism in America*, Chicago: University of Chicago Press, 2000.

Siskel, Gene. Film review of *A Time to Kill*, accessed on April 29, 2011, from http://www.youtube.com/watch?gl=US&hl=iw&v=VfMv3DLn73s.

Skrentny, John David. *The Ironies of Affirmative Action: Politics, Culture, and Justice in America*, Chicago: University of Chicago Press, 1996.

Smith, Henry Nash. *Virgin Land: The American West as Symbol and Myth*, Cambridge, MA: Harvard University Press, 1950.

Smith, Vicki. *Across the Great Divide*, Ithaca, NY: Cornell University Press, 2001.

Sniderman, Paul, and Thomas Piazza. *The Scar of Race*, Cambridge, MA: Belknap Press, 1993.

Sokoloff, Natalie. *Between Money and Love: The Dialectics of Women's Home and Market Work*, New York: Praeger, 1980.

———. *Black Women and White Women in the Professions: Occupational Segregation by Race and Gender, 1960–1980*, New York: Routledge, 1992.

Spence, Donald. *Narrative Truth and Historical Truth: Naming and Interpretation in Psychoanalysis*, New York: Norton, 1982.

Spindel, Barbara. "'Human Being First, Woman Second': Anti-Feminists and the Independent Women's Forum," Ph.D. dissertation, Department of American Studies, University of Minnesota, 2003.

Srivastava, Sarita. "'Are You Calling Me a Racist?' Moral and Emotional Regulation of American Feminism," *Signs: Journal of Women in Culture and Society*, 31, 1 (2005): 29–62.

Stacey, Jackie. *Star Gazing: Hollywood Cinema and Female Spectatorship*, New York: Routledge, 1994.

Staples, Brent. "When a Law Firm is Like a Baseball Team," editorial desk, *New York Times*, November 27, 1998, A42.

Steeh, Charlotte, and Maria Krysan. "The Polls: Trends: Affirmative Action and the Public, 1970–1995," *Public Opinion Quarterly*, 60, 1 (1996): 128–158.

Steele, Shelby. *The Content of Our Character: A New Vision of Race in America*, New York: Harper, 1991.

———. "A Negative Vote on Affirmative Action," *New York Times Magazine*, May 13, 1990, 46.

Stevenson, Richard. "Texaco Is Said to Set Payment Over Sex Bias," *New York Times*, January 6, 1999, C1.

Stoller, Paul. "The Griot's Many Burdens—Fiction's Many Truths," in Arthur Boechner and Carolyn Ellis, eds., *Ethnographically Speaking: Autoethnography, Literature, and Aesthetics*, Walnut Creek, CA: Altamira Press, 2002.

———. *Jaguar: A Story of Africans in America*, Chicago: University of Chicago Press, 1999.

Stryker, Robyn, Martha Scarpellion, and Mellisa Holtzman. "Political Culture Wars 1990s Style: The Drum Beat of Quotas in the Media Framing on the Civil Rights Act of 1991," *Research in Social Stratification and Mobility*, 17 (1999): 33–106.

Sturken, Marita. *Tangled Memories: The Vietnam War, the AIDS Epidemic, and the Politics of Remembering*, Berkeley and Los Angeles: University of California Press, 1997.

Sugrue, Thomas. *The Origins of the Urban Crisis: Race and Inequality in Postwar Detroit*, Princeton, NJ: Princeton University Press, 2005 [1996].

Sullivan, Andrew. "Let Affirmative Action Die," *New York Times*, July 23, 1995, 15.

Sward, Susan. "Generation Gap, Color Gap, Women Split on Affirmative Action," *San Francisco Chronicle*, March 31, 1995, A1.

Swidler, Anne. "Culture as Action: Symbols and Strategies," *American Sociological Review*, 51, 2 (1986): 273–286.

Takagi, Dana. *The Retreat from Race: Asian American Admissions and Racial Politics*, New Brunswick, NJ: Rutgers University Press, 1992.

Thernstrom, Abigail, and Stephan Thernstrom. "Is Race Out of the Race?" *Los Angeles Times*, March 2, 2008.

Traub, James. "The Class of Prop. 209," *New York Times Magazine*, May 2, 1999, sec. 6, 44.

Tuchman, Gay. *Making News: A Study in the Social Construction of Reality*, New York: Free Press, 1980.

Tuller, David. "True Colors: Racial Diversity May Get Lip Service in Workplace, But . . ." *San Francisco Chronicle*, March 3, 1996.

Twine, France Winddance. *A White Side of Black Britain: Interracial Intimacy and Racial Literacy*, Durham, NC: Duke University Press, 2010.

———, and Charles Gallagher. "The Future of Whiteness: A Map of the Third Wave," *Ethnic and Racial Studies*, 31, 1 (January 2008): 4–24.

Ueland, Brenda. *If You Want to Write: A Book About Art, Independence, and Spirit*, St. Paul, MN: Gray Wolf Press, 1987 [1938].

U.S. Glass Ceiling Commission, *Good for Business: Making Full Use of the Nation's Human Capital: A Fact Finding Report for the Federal Glass Ceiling Commission*, Washington DC: GPO, 1995.

Van Hoy, Jerry. *Franchise Law Firms and the Transformation of Personal Legal Services*, Westport, CT: Quorum Books, 1997.

Vera, Hernán, and Andrew Gordon. *Screen Saviors: Hollywood Fictions of Whiteness*, Boston: Rowman & Littlefield, 2000.

Wal-Mart Stores Inc. v. Betty Dukes et al. 564 U.S. 10-277 (2011).

Walsh, Katherine. *Talking About Race: Community Dialogues and the Politics of Difference,* Chicago: University of Chicago Press, 2007.

Waters, Mary. "Appendix: Notes on Methodology," in *Black Identities: West Indian Immigrant Dreams and American Realities,* New York and Cambridge, MA: Russell Sage Foundation and Harvard University Press, 1999.

Wellman, David. *Portraits of White Racism,* Cambridge, MA: Cambridge University Press, 1977.

Wetherall, Margaret, and Jonathan Potter. *Mapping the Language of Racism: Discourse and the Legitimation of Exploitation,* Hemel Hempstead, UK: Harvester Wheatsheaf, 1992.

Wever, Kirsten S. "The Family and Medical Leave Act: Assessing Temporary Wage Replacement for Family and Medical Leave," Cambridge, MA: Radcliffe Public Policy Institute, 1996.

"White Guy's Revenge," letter to the editor, *San Francisco Chronicle,* November 23, 1994.

Wildavsky, Ben. "UC Campus Debates Affirmative Action, Some Say Success in Diversifying Berkeley Student Body Back," *San Francisco Chronicle,* May 16, 1995, A1.

Wilkins, David. "Doing Well by Doing Good? The Role of Public Service in the Careers of Black Corporate Lawyers," *Houston Law Review,* 41 (2004): 1–91.

————, and Mitu Galati, "Why Are There So Few Black Lawyers in Corporate Law Firms? An Institutional Analysis," *California Law Review,* 84 (1996).

Williams, Lena. "Companies Capitalizing on Worker Diversity," *New York Times,* December 15, 1992, A1.

Williams, Patricia. *Alchemy of Race and Rights,* Cambridge, MA: Harvard University Press, 1991.

Wilson, William Julius. *When Work Disappears,* Chicago: University of Chicago Press, 1997.

Wilson, Yumi. "Men: Many Whites Say They Feel Cheated," *San Francisco Chronicle,* May 10, 1995, A8.

————. "Perceptions: Minority Women's Views Opposite of White Men's," *San Francisco Chronicle,* May 10, 1995.

Winant, Howard. *The New Politics of Race: Globalism, Difference, Justice,* Minneapolis: University of Minnesota Press, 2004.

Wingfield, Adia Harvey. "The Modern Mammy and the Angry Black Man: African American Professionals' Experience with Gendered Racism in the Workplace," *Race, Gender & Class,* 14, 1-2 (2007): 1–21.

————, and Joe Feagin. *Yes We Can: White Racial Framing and the 2008 Presidential Campaign,* New York: Routledge, 2010.

Wisniewski, Mary. "Court Strikes Michigan Affirmative Action Ban," Reuters, July 1, 2011, accessed July 17, 2011, from http://www.reuters.com/article/2011/07/01/us-affirmative-action-michigan-idUSTRE7605G920110701?feedType=RSS.

Wolf, Margery. *A Thrice-Told Tale: Feminism, Postmodernism, and Ethnographic Responsibility*, Stanford, CA: Stanford University Press, 1992.

Yoachum, Susan. "Affirmative Action Facing Hard Times, Whites Take Initiative Against Preferential Hiring," *San Francisco Chronicle*, March 20, 1995, A1.

———. "Surprises in Affirmative Action Poll, Wide Support for Cutting Programs," *San Francisco Chronicle*, March 7, 1995, A1.

———. "Wording Affects Polls on Affirmative Action," *San Francisco Chronicle*, September 14, 1995, A17.

Zuckerman, Lawrence. "Boeing Agrees to Settle Case Charging Bias in Salaries," *New York Times*, November 19, 1999, C2.

2010–2011 Academic Affirmative Action Plan, UCLA Law School, accessed on January 24, 2012, from https://faculty.diversity.ucla.edu/affirmative-action-and-equal-employment-opportunity-1/AAAP.pdf/view.

Index

1965 Executive Order 11246. *See* Great Society programs

1973 economic downturn, 21

2008 stock market crash, 148

Adelson, Joseph, 24

affirmative action: and athletics, 29, 31–33, 49; BC's program, 1–3; Bill Clinton's views of, 27, 32–34; critics of, 6, 140–141; definition of, 4–5; Derek Bok's and William Bowen's comprehensive study of, 26, 28, 33, 40; and federal contract compliance, 4–5; federally mandated programs, 5, 12; and gender, 7, 31, 84–117, 139; and gender ambivalence, 103–107, 116; in higher education, 26–28, 36, 131, 147, 161; as hurting white men, 23–40, 135, 137; as injury, 3, 7, 11, 21–41, 47–48, 50, 84, 88, 114, 139; as innocence, 3–4, 7, 9, 16, 20–21, 23–29, 41, 42; at the intersection of race and gender, 10–11, 99–103, 105–106; legislation on, 4–5, 6, 27, 145–147, 155, 161; media slant on, 34–41; perceptions by black lawyers of, 75–80; perceptions by white male lawyers of, 64–75, 80–81, 135, 140, 144–145, 155; perceptions by women lawyers of, 84, 92–117, 139, 156, 161; and pollster wording, 38, 91; representations in news media of, 12, 15, 20–23, 27–35, 70, 80, 85–92, 116, 138, 140, 146; representations in popular culture of, 12, 42–63, 81, 138, 140; and sexuality, 148; and the "unqualified" argument; 2, 25, 28, 39, 58, 70, 73, 75, 77, 80–81, 194n53; value of diversity argument, 33–34; and white middle class, 6. *See also* backlash against affirmative action; black advantage; cultural memory; quotas

Affirmative Action Is Dead, Long Live Affirmative Action, 115

227

African American: at BC Legal
    Department, 1–3, 12, 14, 72; and
    colorblind language, 143; at corpora-
    tions, 26; in film, 45–62, 167–168;
    and foreclosure, 148; and Fortune 500
    companies, 148; labor market, 25; at
    law schools, 27; lawyers, 14, 66, 82,
    140, 156, 160; in news media, 24, 39,
    138; in predominantly white fields,
    100–102; University of California
    system, 37. See also black advantage;
    blackness; Jones, Yolanda; Kingsley,
    Randall; Lewis, Tyrone
"Amazing Grace," 42, 45, 57
ambivalent racism, 11, 131–135, 196n5.
    See also affirmative action
American Bar Association, 11, 31, 71, 124,
    148
American History X, 47–48, 55, 57, 167
American Me, 61, 167
Amistad, 47–48, 51, 55, 58, 167
anti-affirmative action. See affirmative
    action
anti-discrimination lawsuits, 35, 147. See
    also individual court decisions
Arizona Proposition 107, 146
Asian American: at BC Legal
    Department, 1–2; in film, 168; and
    Fortune 500 companies, 148; as vic-
    tims of affirmative action, 28–29, 37
athletic admissions, 29, 31–33, 49
Avildsen, John, 22

backlash against affirmative action, 3, 7, 9,
    137, 145, 192n29; and Democrats, 21;
    in Michigan, 145–146; and neolib-
    eralism, 25; opposition to, 146–147;
    and personal memory, 141; and white
    working-class men, 38
Bakke, Allan. See Regents of the University
    of California vs. Bakke, The
Bauman, Zygmunt, 133–134

BC Legal Department, 12; gender demo-
    graphics, 14, 83, 112; HR, 1–2; lawsuit
    against, 1–2; racial demographics at,
    1–3, 14, 72. See also affirmative action
Bean, Frank, 147–148
Behar, Ruth, 14
Berkowitz, Peggy, 96, 104–105, 112
black advantage, 39; in print media, 28–
    29, 34, 39, 53, 146; in Rocky, 23; and
    welfare, 58–59. See also reverse dis-
    crimination; white innocence
Black Image in the White Mind, 31
blackness, 20, 22
Blair-Loy, Mary, 111–112, 116
Boeing Company sex discrimination
    case, 87
Bok, Derek, 26, 33, 40
Brigance, Jake, 42–43, 53–54. See also
    Time to Kill, A
Broadbent, Allen, 99
Brown, Mary, 84, 93–95, 103–104, 112
Bullworth, 47, 55
Burawoy, Michael, 15
Bush, George H.W., 23, 25, 155
Businessweek, 27

California Business Roundtable, 34
California Civil Rights Initiative, 5, 89.
    See also Proposition 209, California
Carlson, Susan, 93–95, 102–105, 107–
    108, 112, 116
Chase, Susan, 11, 69, 83
chilly climate, 31, 111
Citizens United v. Federal Election
    Commission, 142
Collins, Sharon, 26
Color Bind: California's Battle to End
    Affirmative Action, The, 89
colorblindness, 6, 43, 49, 61–69, 134; and
    costs for people of color, 75–80; era
    of, 143, 154–155, 163
Congressional Black Caucus, 89

Connerly, Ward, 145–146
Connor, Bull, 58, 60
Contract with America, 29
Cooperman, David, 72–74
Creed, Apollo, 22. *See also Rocky*
Crosby, Faye, 115
Cry Freedom, 47, 55, 167
cultural memory, 3, 6, 40, 142, 149; and
    affirmative action, 6–8, 15, 20–23,
    137; at BC Legal Department, 65,
    138; in Hollywood films, 44, 46, 49,
    56, 61–64; and personal memory,
    141; in print media, 40–41; and psy-
    choanalytic theory, 65–66

Dances with Wolves, 46–48, 51, 55, 167
Dangerous Minds, 47–48, 55, 168
De La Beckwith, Byron, 50
DeLaughter, Bobby, 50–56, 58
Dillard, Angela, 25
dispossession, 10
diversity. *See* value of diversity argument
Diversity Paradox, The, 148
Driving Miss Daisy, 61, 168
Dry White Season, 47, 48, 55, 167
duCille, Ann, 45, 61

Ebert, Roger, 22, 43
El Movimiento Estudiantil Chicano de
    Aztlán (MEChA), 89
Entman, Robert, 31
epistemology, 16–18, 134–136, 144–145,
    165, 176n10
Equal Employment Opportunity
    Commission, 38, 86
ethnography, 12–14, 17–18, 74–75,
    79–80, 132–136, 153–166, 174n41
Evers, Medgar, 49–50, 55, 58
Evers, Myrlie, 50, 54–56

Family and Medical Leave Act (FMLA),
    86, 92, 110, 115, 192n34

feminism, 45, 75, 89, 112, 139, 160,
    163–164, 202n36. *See also* gender;
    Independent Women's Forum (IWF);
    National Organization for Women
    (NOW)
Feminist Majority, 89
Ferguson, Roderick, 133–134
Finch, Atticus, 47–51, 59–60, 62
Fischer, Bill, 78
Frank, Thomas, 10
free market, 8, 25, 30, 34, 115
Freud, Sigmund, 65
Fried, Mindy, 97–98
Fusco, Coco, 82

Galaskiewitz, Jonathan, 68–70
Gamson, William, 23
gender, 3, 10–11, 91, 99, 102, 141, 149,
    194n55; and affirmative action in the
    media, 87; in film, 16; in law firms,
    11, 15, 98, 102, 117, 131, 140; and
    methodology, 63, 164; in the work-
    place, 11, 66, 86, 90–103, 140–141,
    149. *See also* affirmative action;
    ambivalent racism; Boeing Company
    sex discrimination; chilly climate;
    Family and Medical Leave Act
    (FMLA); feminism; glass ceiling; Glass
    Ceiling Commission; maternity leave;
    parental leave; Publix sex discrimi-
    nation case; racism; stand by your
    man; Texaco sex discrimination case;
    welfare
gendering, 82, 102, 164
*Gender Trials: Emotional Lives in
    Contemporary Law Firms*, 14, 154
Ghosts of Mississippi, 43, 51–58, 168
Gingrich, Newt, 29–30
glass ceiling, 11, 31, 40, 86, 88, 102, 110–
    111, 112, 139
Glass Ceiling Commission, 40, 86
Glory, 47, 50–51, 55, 168

good faith effort, 5, 114
good-old-boy network, 11, 139
GOP. *See* Republican
Gordon, Avery, 82
Gratz, Jennifer, 145
Gratz v. Bollinger, 145
Great Society programs, 4, 19, 25, 107,
    116
Grisham, John, 42–43, 51
Grutter, Barbara, 145
Grutter v. Bollinger, 145

Hailey, Carl Lee, 42–43, 52, 54, 56. *See
    also Time to Kill, A*
Hamacher, Patrick, 145
Harvard, 26, 101
hate crimes, 42, 50, 52
Healy, Robin, 11, 118–137, 140
Hegel, George, 57
Heritage Foundation, 24
historical memory, 58
historical truth, 66
Hochschild, Arlie, 98
Hollywood: and the "anti-racist white
    hero," 46–61, 138; and black politi-
    cians, 56, 61, 81; and genre or "white
    racial progress," 3, 7, 138, 142. *See also*
    cultural memory
Home Depot sex discrimination case,
    86–87
Hopwood decision, 87–88, 146
hostile environment, 31, 86
Hurricane, The, 61, 168
Hurtado, Aida, 82

Independent Women's Forum (IWF), 11,
    83–102, 110–117, 139
injury. *See* white injury
innocence. *See* white innocence
innocent white male. *See* white inno-
    cence

*Inside Out: Lesbian and Gay Workplace
    Rights*, 148
Invisible Man, The, 134
*Invisible Victims: White Males and the Crisis
    of Affirmative Action*, 23–24. *See also*
    white innocence
Ireland, Patricia, 89

Jackson, Jesse, 89
Jackson, Samuel L., 42–43, 52
Jacobson, Matthew Frye, 22
Jim Crow, 10, 36, 116
Johnson, Gail, 96–97, 105, 112, 116
Johnson, Lyndon, 4, 19, 116
Jones, Yolanda, 99–103, 106, 112, 116

Kennedy, John F., 50
King, Martin Luther, Jr., 49, 60
Kingsley, Randall, 9, 64–65, 70, 75–76,
    100, 156, 158
Kirp, David, 36, 39
Krysan, Maria, 38
Ku Klux Klan, 42, 52, 58

Ladowsky, Ellen, 84
Latino: at BC Legal Department, 1, 2, 72;
    and defensiveness about affirmative
    action, 70–75; demographics of, 14;
    denial of gender as an issue, 108–115;
    discrimination against, 36, 57, 148; in
    film, 167–168; and foreclosure, 148;
    and Fortune 500 companies, 26; law-
    yers, 14; neoliberal rhetoric, 72–73;
    perceptions of affirmative action for
    women, 103–107; perceptions of
    family politics, 92–103; perceptions
    of race, 67–70; in popular culture,
    183n17; success as a double-edged
    sword, 100; and Texas 10 percent
    plan, 146–147. *See also* affirmative
    action; BC Legal Department

Lee, Jennifer, 147–148
legacy status, 26, 32
legislation. *See* 1965 Executive Order 11246; Michigan Civil Rights Initiative; Proposition 209, California
Lewis, Tyrone, 75, 100
liberal individualism, 9, 22, 59, 82, 103, 112
Lipsitz, George, 9, 63
Long Walk, The, 46–47, 55, 61, 168
Losing Isaiah, 47, 55, 168
Lu, Benjamin, 28
Lydia, Chávez, 89
Lynch, Frederick, 23–24. *See also* white innocence

Malcolm X, 49
Marini, Isabella, 109–110, 112, 113–114, 116–117
Maslin, Janet, 43, 54
maternity leave, 92. *See also* Family and Medical Leave Act (FMLA)
McConaughey, Matthew, 42–43, 46, 48, 52
McCormick, Richard, 34
McDermott, Monica, 135
McGirr, Lisa, 10
memory, 157. *See also* cultural memory; historical memory; personal memory
meritocracy, 28, 37, 64, 83
methodology, 12–18, 132, 140, 153–166. *See also* ethnography
Mexican American Legal Defense and Education Fund (MALDEF), 89
Michigan Civil Rights Initiative, 146–147
Mississippi Burning, 47–51, 55, 58, 61–63, 168
Mortimer, Kathryn, 108–112, 114–117
Mukherjee, Roopali, 8, 91, 117
multicultural conservatism, 25

NAACP, 53, 56, 61
narrative truth, 66, 136, 153, 158
National Organization for Women (NOW), 11, 88, 139
Native American, 2, 46
NBC Nightly News, 27
Nelson, Sam, 70–72
neoconservative, 8–9, 10, 21, 23, 30, 41, 61, 106, 138, 149, 154; as the "white racial project," 25, 59, 68, 75. *See also* Independent Women's Forum (IWF)
neoliberal anti-racism, 56
neoliberalism, 23, 30, 41, 61, 149; and affirmative action, 25, 75, 138; and lawyers, 72, 75; and race, 8–9, 21, 30, 34, 53, 65
neoliberal reforms, 3, 141
New York Times, 27–29, 31–35, 39–40, 43, 80, 83–84, 88–89

Obama, Barack, 142, 146
O'Connor, Sandra Day, 145
Office of Federal Contract Compliance, 5
Oliver, Melvin, 148–149
Origins of the Urban Crisis, The, 10
overtime work culture, 97–98

Pager, Devah, 148
Panther, 61, 168
parental leave, 92. *See also* Family and Medical Leave Act (FMLA)
Park, Robert, 134
Parks, Rosa, 58
personal memory, 5–8, 15; and cultural memory, 141
personal narrative, 171n17, 188n9
personal responsibility. *See* neoliberalism
PEW study, 148–149
post-civil-rights-era racism, 8, 49, 65
Powell, Lewis, 20
Princeton, 26, 35, 86

Proposition 2. *See* Michigan Civil Rights Initiative

Proposition 209, California, 3, 5, 27; and higher education, 41, 147; and President Clinton, 32; support for/against based on gender, 89–90, 103–104; support for/against based on race, 38

Publix sex discrimination case, 86–87

quotas, 2, 5, 19, 89, 114, 116. *See also* *Regents of the University of California vs. Bakke, The*

racial innocence. *See* white innocence

racing for innocence: and backlash, 139; and corporate practice, 83; definition of, 9, 65, 75, 80; and lawyers, 80–83; and liberal individualism, 82

racism: institutional forms, 8–9, 32, 49, 59–60, 83, 133, 138; as racial prejudice, 9, 24–25, 55–56, 62, 133, 135; as segregation, 10, 60, 135. *See also* ambivalent racism; post-civil-rights-era racism; slavery; white innocence

Raeburn, Nicole, 148

Reagan, Ronald, 3, 23, 25, 154

Realities of Affirmative Action, The, 4

Regents of the University of California vs. Bakke, The, 5, 19–22

Republican, 29, 38, 89, 107, 116

reverse discrimination: actual cases of, 86–87; perceptions of, 7, 19, 21, 23, 27, 34–40, 58, 84, 114, 116, 137, 154

Robinson, Tom, 49, 59–60

Rocky, 22–23, 46

Rojeki, Andrew, 31

Rosewood, 61, 168

Ross, Thomas, 20

Royster, Deidre, 136

San Francisco Chronicle, 27–28, 31, 34–38, 40, 87

School of Medicine at the University of California, Davis. *See Regents of the University of California vs. Bakke, The*

Schuette, Bill, 147

screen memories, 66, 81

Searle, John, 36–39

secondary revision, 66

Shape of the River: Long-Term Consequences of Considering Race in College and University Admission, The, 26, 33, 40

Shapiro, Thomas, 148–149

Siskel, Gene, 43

slavery, 29, 45–46, 57–59, 101

Smeal, Eleanor, 89

Smith, Adam, 8

Stallone, Sylvester, 22

Stand and Deliver, 47, 55, 168

stand by your man, 84–85

Stanford, 26, 90, 102

Staples, Brent, 101

Steeh, Charlotte, 38

Steele, Shelby, 24. *See also* white innocence

Sturken, Marita, 6, 21, 40, 44. *See also* cultural memory

Suburban Warriors, 10

Sugrue, Thomas, 9

Supreme Court of the United States of America, 26, 145. *See also Citizens United v. Federal Election Commission*; *Gratz v. Bollinger*; *Grutter v. Bollinger*; *Regents of the University of California vs. Bakke, The*; *Wal-Mart Inc. v. Dukes*

Texaco sex discrimination case, 87

Texas 10 percent plan, 146–147

Thrice Told Tale, A, 17

Thunderheart, 47–48, 55, 168

TIME, 27, 31

Time Bind, The, 98

Time to Kill, A, 42–43, 46–49, 51, 54–58, 61

Title IX, 14

To Kill a Mockingbird, 49–50, 55, 59–60, 62

Tonya, 43, 52, 54, 58

Translated Women, 14

Tuchman, Gay, 39

University of California at Berkeley, 14, 26, 29, 33, 36–37, 103–104, 114, 118, 124–125, 147

University of Michigan. *See Gratz v. Bollinger; Grutter v. Bollinger*

U.S. Constitution, equal protection clause of, 19

value of diversity argument, 27, 29, 33–34, 36

Voedisch, Lisa, 107–108, 112, 116

Walk in the Clouds, A, 47, 55, 167

Wall Street Journal, 85, 88

Wal-Mart Inc. v. Dukes, 142, 147

Walsh, Katherine, 136

Washington Post, 31

welfare, 21, 25, 29, 38

What's the Matter with Kansas?, 10

white disadvantage. *See* black advantage; reverse discrimination

white injury, 3, 11, 84, 114, 139; representations in news media, 7, 21–41;

representations in popular culture, 7, 44–50

white innocence, 3–4, 9, 40; in the law, 20; representations in news media, 7, 23–28; representations in popular culture, 7, 16, 21–23; representations in scholarship, 23–24. *See also* Hollywood, and the "anti-racist white hero"; white redemption

whiteness, 9–11, 15, 20, 22, 65, 79–82, 140–142; and gender, 92, 101–103, 117; in Hollywood, 45–47. *See also* Hollywood, and the "anti-racist white hero"; white injury; white innocence

white redemption, 45, 56, 189n22. *See also* Hollywood, and the "anti-racist white hero"

White Wealth/Black Wealth, 148–149

white working-class: conditions of, 26; and construction as victims of affirmative action, 2–3, 21–23, 38, 81; in film, 46–48, 51, 57–59, 62; and racism, 134–135, 137, 141

Wideman, Jason, 67–68

Wilkins, David, 101

William, Bowen, 26, 33, 40

Wilson, Pete, 28

Winant, Howard, 8, 25, 68

Wolf, Marjorie, 17

women, 11, 88, 90

Wood, Tom, 30–31, 38

X, Malcolm, 49